Illusions of Reality

Illusions of Reality

A History of Deception in Social Psychology

James H. Korn

State University of New York Press

Published by
State University of New York Press, Albany

© 1997 State University of New York

For information, address State University of New York Press,
State University Plaza, Albany, NY 12246

Production by Cynthia Tenace Lassonde
Marketing by Theresa Abad Swierzowski

Library of Congress Cataloging-in-Publication Data

Korn, James H., 1938–
    Illusions of reality : a history of deception in social psychology
    James H. Korn
        p.   cm.
    Includes bibliographical references and index.
        ISBN 0-7914-3307-2 (hc : alk. paper). — ISBN 0-7914-3308-0 (pbk.
: alk. paper)
        1. Social psychology—Research—History.   2. Research ethics.
    3. Deception.   I. Title.
    HM251.K552   1997
    302'.072—dc20   96–25688
                                                                  CIP

10 9 8 7 6 5 4 3 2 1

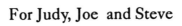
For Judy, Joe and Steve

Contents

Preface

Social psychology may be the only area of research in which the research methods sometimes are more interesting than the results. The most impressive experiments in this field produce their impact by creating situations that lead research subjects to believe that they are taking part in something other than the true experiment, or situations in which subjects are not even aware that an experiment is being conducted. These illusions of reality are created by using various forms of deception, such as giving a false statement about the purpose of an experiment, providing false information to people about how they perform on tests, or by using actors who play roles.

But psychologists did not always do this. When laboratory research in psychology began in the late nineteenth century, it was noted more for the tedious nature of the tasks that were used such as memorizing many lists of meaningless words, or repeatedly judging whether one sound was louder than another. Then some time in the 1920s reports began to appear of experiments that might sound interesting to people who were not psychologists, because the experimental situations seemed realistic and had significance for normal human experience. In this book I try to explain how it happened that social psychologists began to create these illusions, and how the use of deception in research grew to become a common practice: In the 1970s more than half the published experiments in the major journal of social psychology used deception.

My interest in this topic grew out of my teaching. In 1982 my class of senior psychology majors asked some questions about an interesting study that had been published by a famous social psychologist. We thought some aspects of this research might be unethical, depending on details of the study that had not been published. Our questions went unanswered after an exchange of correspondence over a period of several months, so I requested an investigation by the ethics committee of the American Psychological Association (APA). The psychologist in question wrote a long statement about his research to the APA, and he was judged not to have violated the ethical standards of the Association. These proceedings are confidential, which is why I have not identified this psychologist.

This case got me interested in general issues of the ethics of research with humans, and I conducted studies on judgments of the acceptability of deception, and on students' willingness to participate in research. I also began to teach a course on the history of psychology and found that, although nothing had been written specifically about deception in research, there did seem to be interesting connections to the development of experimental methods in psychology. This drew me into the earliest volumes of American psychology journals, and a search for the first use of deception.

It was my conversations with friends who were not in psychology that convinced me that it would be worth writing a book on this topic. I would describe Stanley Milgram's famous obedience experiments or the simulation of a Watergate situation or studies of staged emergencies with fake blood, and these stories would intrigue engineers, English professors, salesmen, and secretaries. Some thought the studies were clever and taught important lessons about human nature. Others wondered how psychologists could get away with these things. Because of those reactions I wanted to write a book that was not just for psychologists, but for anyone who might be interested in how social psychologists developed their dramatic methods. I have tried to avoid the use of jargon, I describe well-known experiments at length, and I explain some ideas that are familiar to psychologists.

I also hope that psychologists and their students will read this book to gain a different perspective on what has been, at least since the 1960s, a controversial topic. Some psychologists think it almost always is wrong to deceive research subjects, while others think the use of deception is essential if significant human problems are to receive scientific study. The title of this book reflects this issue. Stanley Milgram used the term *technical illusions* because he thought the word *deception* had a negative moral bias. Illusion also suggests the theatrical nature of many social psychology experiments.

Writing this book required the assistance, support, understanding, and kind criticism of many people. Were it not for Jim Anker, I might not have begun this project. He was organizing his own publishing company, and thought that people would be interested in what I had to say. He took a chance on someone who had never written a book, and I appreciated his support while I struggled with my first chapters. Barbara Nodine convinced me that this book would be interesting, and people might actually buy it and read it. Ben Kleinmuntz, my friend and former teacher, also encouraged me during the early stages of this project.

In 1933 Saul Rosenzweig published the first article on the psychology experiment as a social situation, an article that is of major significance for the topic of this book. For the past few years I have had the pleasure of attending regular seminars organized by Saul, and have benefitted from his knowledge and insights on a wide range of topics. He has provided me with a model for scholarly inquiry.

Sandra Nicks, Annette Christy McGaha, and several other student assistants worked with me on the quantitative studies that showed the growth of the use of deception in social psychology and changes in interest in the ethics of research with humans. The faculty and administrative staff in my department never complained that their chairperson spent most Fridays and many other mornings working at home. Saint Louis University, through the Beaumont Faculty Development Fund, provided the financial support that enabled me to conduct some essential interviews.

My friend and colleague, Marjorie Richey, read the entire first draft of my manuscript and gave me her perspective from many years of teaching social psychology. Another friend, Helen Mandeville, who is a retired English professor, also read that first draft. She corrected grammatical errors and some bad prose, but most importantly, she said that she liked it. Miriam Joseph, Saint Louis University reference librarian, responded to my many requests for background sources.

My greatest support comes from my family. On those mornings when I sit in front of this computer, I watch Judy drive off to work and realize how much she means to me and what a good life we have together. Her support was essential. In writing this book, I especially wanted to create something worthwhile for my sons, Joe and Steve, so that my message to "do your best" might have greater meaning.

I acknowledge the permission of Cambridge University Press and Elliott Aronson to quote from, "Leon Festinger and the art of audacity," *Psychological Science*, 2, 1991, p. 216, copyright American Psychological Society; and the permission of Scientific American, Inc. to quote from Solomon E. Asch, "Opinions and social pressure," *Scientific American, Inc.*, 193 (5), pp. 31–35. Offprint No. 450, pp. 4, 6.

—1—

Varieties of Deception

> If one makes use of elaborate arrangements or even creates situations with strong forces, as theoretical requirements also demand shall be the case, then only a very small percentage of experimental subjects will act as though they feel themselves to be experimental subjects. Others very soon get involved in the situation and accordingly become free and natural. (Kurt Lewin, 1929, quoted by MacKinnon & Dukes, 1962)

> [T]he goal is to fully convince the subject that you are in a terrible jam and feeling deeply uncomfortable about it. You sweat, you cringe, you wring your hands; you convey to the subject that you are in real trouble here—that the next participant is waiting and the God-damn stooge hasn't shown up yet. You then appeal to her to do you a favor: to play the role of the stooge and mislead the next participant. (Eliot Aronson, 1991)

Psychological science, like other sciences, finds its facts and tests its theories in the laboratory and in the real world. Throughout its history psychology has emulated other sciences in valuing objective, empirical observation under carefully controlled conditions followed by sophisticated quantitative analysis of the results. Although rigorous as research, this rigor often leads to tedious reports that make dull reading. Research in social psychology, however, contains many exciting exceptions because of the use of methods and research situations that often are creative and dramatic. Some of these studies have been like theater performances with directors, actors, and rehearsal.

Social psychologists always have shared the value placed on experimental control by their parent discipline, but as this field developed in the middle of the twentieth century, certain people and events moved much of the research toward realistic staged experiments. The key feature in this research was the use of deception to mislead research participants so they were unaware of the true purpose of an experiment, or that they even were part of an experiment. From 1965 to 1985, about half of all social psychology articles published in the United States used some form of deception. Some of this research involved moderate to extreme physical or psychological stress or invasions of privacy, and the methods used led to serious ethical questions.

This book presents the story of how the practice of deception grew in social psychology and describes the historical and cultural factors that supported this practice. There will be some discussion of the ethical controversy concerning deception, but the focus will be on how the research of social psychologists was influenced by the times and places in which they worked.

Deception in Strange Places

There are varieties of deception. There is the outright lie, but we may also mislead, delude, and beguile. All of these forms of deception have been used in psychological research. Before presenting a definition of deception, it may be helpful to consider three examples of deceptive research to illustrate the kinds of situations that make this a fascinating topic.

How Would You Like a Shot in the Arm?

Imagine yourself as one of many thousands of American college students taking your first psychology course. One day at the beginning of your class your professor introduces a graduate student who wants your help with his research. The research is described as follows:

> This is an experiment on memory. It concerns the effects of various drugs on a person's short-term memory. Your drug will be given by injection under the skin of your upper right arm. You may experience these symptoms: dryness of the throat, slight headache, and coolness in the toes and fingers.

Would you agree to volunteer for this experiment in which you would be injected with this drug? Very few people want to be injected with anything, even for good medical reasons, and most people would be concerned about the effects of the drug (Korn & Hogan, 1992).

This example is based on a study that was done at Stanford University by Gary Marshall and Philip Zimbardo (1979). Students were contacted by telephone and asked to participate in a study "being conducted by a member of the ophthalmology department concerning the influences of an injection of a vitamin supplement on visual acuity." This was a lie. The experiment was being conducted by psychologists and concerned the physiological basis of emotion.

When students came to the laboratory they were again told that this was a study of vision being done by the ophthalmology department. They also were told that a physician would administer the vitamin injection, which was described as having no major side effects, but that there would be some minor effects: dryness of the throat, slight headache, coolness in toes and fingers. This also was a lie. In fact students were injected with epinephrine (adrenalin), which produces other symptoms including increased heart rate and sweating.

Next these students were told to wait in a room with another student who was taking part in the experiment. This other student was really a confederate of the experimenter (an assistant) who was playing a role—another lie. The confederate was trained to act silly and the real purpose of the experiment was to see if the students would describe themselves as feeling euphoric or happy. The theory is that we use the cues in the situation to interpret physiological symptoms. Given the symptoms produced by adrenalin we may experience happiness or anger or some other emotion, depending on the situation.

May I Watch You Urinate?

One of the strangest examples of psychological research is the study of "personal space invasions in the lavatory" (Middlemist, Knowles, & Matter, 1976). The hypothesis was that crowding increases physiological arousal as measured by the latency and duration of urination in a men's lavatory. The prediction was that it would take a man longer to start to urinate and he would finish faster if someone were standing in the urinal next to him rather than in one that was two places away. Men were observed, while they urinated, by a person using a periscope to peek under a toilet stall that was adjacent to the urinal. The observer used two stopwatches to measure the beginning and length of time that each man urinated. The hypothesis was confirmed.

The major ethical issue here is invasion of privacy (Koocher, 1977), but deception also was involved. To force subjects to use the urinal adjacent to the toilet stall, a sign was placed on one of the urinals not occupied by the confederate. The sign said, "Don't use. Washing urinal." The other use of deception was based on the subjects' assumption that the confederate was a stranger who was in the lavatory for an obvious purpose. In most psychological research participants are debriefed, that is they are told about the purpose of the experiment and the reasons for using deception. However, in this study subjects were not informed that they had been in an experiment.

Would You Help a Bloody Stranger?

This study was done outside the research laboratory in a natural setting, a subway train in Philadelphia (Piliavin & Piliavin, 1972). One member of the research team pretended to have a seizure; sometimes he had a capsule in his mouth that he could bite to make it appear that he was bleeding. Another researcher seated on the train recorded whether and how quickly other riders came to the aid of the pretend victim. The method used in this study is a good example of the elaborate staging used in much of the research in social psychology during the 1960s and 1970s.

> Each [research] team consisted of a victim, a 'programmed by-stander,' and two observers. Two variables were manipulated: presence or absence of apparent blood coming from the mouth of the victim as he fell and presence or absence of an authoritative bystander. . . . This bystander was dressed either as an intern in a white coat, as a priest, or in ordinary street clothes. (p. 355)

The team took their assigned places on the train and the play began.

> As the train started, the victim, who had entered last at the center door, began to walk, using a cane, toward the end of the car in which the bystander was sitting. In the 'no blood' condition, he collapsed quietly directly in front of the programmed bystander. In the 'blood' condition, he did exactly the same, but in addition he released a trickle of thick red fluid from the corner of his mouth as he fell. . . . If no one had come to the aid of the victim on that trial, the by-stander assisted the victim off the train. All team members got off at the stop and transferred to a train going in the other direction for the next trial. (p. 356)

Defining Deception

The dictionary says that to deceive means to cause to accept as true what is false or to give a false impression. This happened in each of the examples that I presented in the previous section. Deception is the larger category. Its forms are beguile, mislead, delude, and lie. To beguile involves the use of charm and persuasion in deceiving, and is used by all researchers seeking to convince people to participate in their laboratory studies. To mislead refers to a leading astray that may or may not be intentional. A false eye examination led participants astray intentionally in the first example presented. To delude is to deceive so thoroughly as to obscure the truth, and to lie is to make an explicit misstatement of fact. Bok (1979) defined a lie as "any intentionally deceptive message which is *stated*" (p. 14, italics in original).

In the context of psychological research, deception is a complex concept, which Joan Sieber (1982, 1983) has described in great detail. She developed a taxonomy in which the major categories were: the means of deceiving (including seven kinds of deception), the nature of the research (e.g., naturally occurring or induced behavior), and the upset caused by the deception (Sieber, 1983). Deception research was defined as

> research in which subjects are purposely allowed to or caused to have false beliefs or assumptions or to accept as false that which is true, and in which the researcher studies their reactions; the reactions and the study of those reactions are made possible by the incorrect beliefs or assumptions of the subject. (p. 2)

At various places in this book I will refer to some examples of deception as mild and others as extreme. As these adjectives suggest, there are degrees of deception. It is easy to differentiate the extent of the deception in the examples previoulsy described from milder forms used in some other studies; for example, an experimenter may falsely identify the author of an essay as either Thomas Jefferson or Adolf Hitler. This distinction between degrees of deception is important because, over the past fifty years, there have been changes in both the quantity and the quality of misinformation given to research participants.

Sieber's (1983) taxonomy shows, however, that it is difficult to measure the intensity of deception in research because of the many dimensions of this practice. One category of her taxonomy includes weak and strong forms of deception by a researcher. In weak forms, participants may consent to being deceived. In strong forms informed consent is not obtained. Sieber notes,

> however, that even the very strongest form of deception, and the form that violates the largest number of ordinary moral obligations to persons, can be used in utterly harmless and delightful ways as well as in potentially dangerous and objectionable ways, depending on the means of deception and the nature of the research. (p. 4)

As an example of a "delightful" use of strong deception, Sieber (1982, p. 4) refers to a study in which students who had received cookies were more willing to help other people who dropped some books.

The category that is most clearly related to judgments of the intensity of deception concerns discomfort or harm caused by the deception. Sieber (1983, p. 4) discusses sources that may upset both participants and researchers. Many research treatments can upset participants: for example, pressure to deliver allegedly harmful electric shocks, receiving an injection, and falsifying test scores to lower self-esteem have all been used in psychological research.

Deceptive research may also upset those involved in perpetrating the deception.

The confederate role, in particular, which must be reenacted perhaps hundreds of times, can be extremely upsetting. Often the confederates are graduate students being socialized for a research career. One may question the appropriateness of training that is either repellent or deadening to moral sensitivities. (Sieber, 1983, p. 4; also see Oliansky, 1991)

All forms of deception will be considered in this book using this general definition of deception: to cause to accept as true that which is false. Although deception is a normal and necessary part of daily life (Nyberg, 1993), it is not a morally neutral word so its use must be justified. At several places in the following chapters, particularly in chapter 10, I will summarize the reasons that psychologists give for using deception. One social psychologist has argued that we should not use that word at all because it biases the issue. Stanley Milgram, whose studies of obedience may be the best known research in all of psychology, preferred to use a neutral term like *technical illusions* (Milgram, 1977/1992, p. 181). The title of this book is a reference to this idea.

The Significance of Deception in Research

When I was developing my plan for this book, someone told me that deception in research is not an important issue anymore because deception is less frequent, it is not as extreme now as it used to be, and the ethical issues have been resolved. In fact a large proportion of the studies in social psychology continue to involve the use of deception, dramatic methods still are used occasionally, and there is continuing discussion of the ethics of deception. Nevertheless, the general question of the importance of this topic should be considered. These are six reasons that studying the use of deception in psychological research is important:

1. It is interesting.
2. Much of the research concerns questions that are socially significant.
3. It is a topic that has been overlooked in the history of psychology.
4. Important ethical questions are involved.
5. The public image of psychology may be affected by the use of deception.
6. Deception is a general problem in our culture.

Intrinsic Interest

I do not mean to be pejorative when I refer to this area of research as psychology's theater. A theater is a place where productions are staged that concern issues of social significance as well as those of everyday life. When the productions are successful it is because of the creativity of the authors, directors, and actors. In the following chapters I will present many examples of creative research, and the analogy with stage productions will be clear. Reading excerpts from these research reports is often like reading scenes from a play.

Social Significance of the Research

Most of the research that I will discuss also is important, and interesting, because it deals with questions of obvious social significance: When do people help others who are in trouble? What makes people aggressive? What forces make us obedient to authority, and what are those that help us become independent? A concern with important social issues is closely tied to the growth of the use of deception in research. The key person at the beginning of this story is Kurt Lewin, a German-Jewish psychologist who came to the United States in 1933 after the Nazis had taken over his homeland. Not only did he inspire new approaches to laboratory research, but he also was a force in the founding of the Society for the Psychological Study of Social Issues, an organization that has been called the conscience of psychology. Lewin's legacy is the use of realistic experiments to contribute to our understanding of significant human problems.

Some of the research that I will describe, however, is not of great social significance, but concerns simple events in everyday life such as why we like some people more than others. These are not unimportant issues, but psychologists have been criticized for studying what seem to be trivial matters. In the 1970s William Proxmire, a U. S. Senator from Wisconsin, sought publicity by presenting "Golden Fleece Awards" to government-funded projects that he thought were wasteful. It seemed silly to spend thousands of dollars to find out why people fall in love. The fact is that finding a romantic partner is a difficult problem for many people, and they might find this research to be of value, whether deception is used or not. Senator Proxmire himself apparently was somewhat concerned about the importance of physical attractiveness because he underwent hair implants to eliminate his baldness.

An Overlooked Topic in History

The history of psychology has become a lively area of research, which has gone beyond traditional histories that described the march through time of great people and their ideas. Newer histories are concerned with the cultural context in which psychologists work to create their theories and methods. Elizabeth Scarborough and Laurel Furumoto (1987), for example, presented accounts of the first generation of women psychologists in America, a group of scholars who had been overlooked in previous histories. It was important to draw attention to the contributions of these women, but more significantly, Scarborough and Furumoto discovered five historical themes that explained the oversight. My purpose here is similar to theirs. Historians of psychology have not examined the origins of the use of deception in research, or the growth of that practice. I hope to provide both a description, and an explanation in terms of culture and history.

Ethical Questions

Although the use of deception in psychological research began during the 1920s, it was more than twenty-five years before psychologists began to consider the ethical issues related to this practice, and not until the 1970s that the ethics of deception became a frequent topic in the literature of psychology. In chapter 10 I will discuss the reasons for this delay. At this point it is important to recognize the ethical principles that must be considered when evaluating deceptive research. These include freedom to choose (autonomy), possible harm to individuals, and abuse of power by researchers (justice).

In addition to demonstrating the creativity of psychologists, the studies that I will describe sometimes are upsetting because the potential for harm is clear. The best-known example is Stanley Milgram's (1963) study of obedience, in which he vividly describes the emotional break down of one of his subjects. This study set off a debate about research ethics that continues to be presented in undergraduate textbooks. Research review boards now prohibit psychologists from using many of the deceptive methods that were used in the past, but an examination of how psychologists began to use deception should enlighten the ethical debate.

The Image of Psychology

However extreme or mild deception might now be or has been in the past, it has had effects beyond the discipline of psychology that makes it worthy of study. These are effects on public trust, especially on research participants themselves. Herbert Kelman (1967) concluded that "there is something disturbing about the idea of relying on massive deception as the basis for developing a field of inquiry" (p. 7). Among the effects of deception that Kelman saw was that it "establishes the reputation of psychologists as people who cannot be believed" (p. 7). He thought that this made it difficult to find naive subjects in the college student population that provides most research participants.

Consider this example of the impact of deceptive research on the university community. MacCoun and Kerr (1987) reported that they were conducting a study in which six male students were acting as a mock jury and deliberating a case. Apparently no deception was involved in this study. Suddenly, one of the students had a grand mal epileptic seizure and fell to the floor. The other students came to his aid and called paramedics for help. The experimental session was ended and the victim recovered.

While discussing this event, the experimenters wondered if any of the students thought that the seizure was faked as part of the experiment. When those students were interviewed, three of the five "spontaneously reported that they had questioned the authenticity of the attack" (MacCoun & Kerr, 1987, p. 199). Furthermore,

> Several of the bystanders also reported that the first reaction of their friends upon hearing about the seizure were expressions of suspicion. There were indications that prior knowledge of psychological research—derived primarily from coursework—was related to suspicion. For example, the most suspicious subject (who was still suspicious even after the paramedics arrived) had begun to study psychology in high school. (p. 199)

Two other bystanders said that they even looked for hidden cameras *after* the paramedics arrived.

Deception Is a Characteristic of American Culture

While I was working on this book, an article appeared in my daily newspaper with the headline, "Coach Quits after Faking Shooting at Team Rally" ("Coach Quits," 1993). "During a pep talk to players, [the coach] interceded in a fake fight he had orchestrated between two youths. Shots rang out, and [the coach] fell to the ground as phony blood spread across his shirt" (p. D1). Even the coach's son thought his father had been shot. Here was an example of life imitating psychological art.

Deception is everywhere in American culture and has a long history. In some areas, such as political advertising, everyone assumes that information will be distorted and this has led to public distrust of the groups who control these forms of communication. In this context, social psychologists do not see their deception as serious, but as comparable to the typical experiences of everyday life, which are what they seek to understand. The little lies told by psychologists are part of the same culture that includes big lies told by presidents.

Thousands of college students have taken part in studies that use deception. For any one student that deception is only one among the many encountered every day. This sometimes is used as a justification for the use of deception; it is no worse than anything that often happens to any of us. Yet that is precisely why it is an important issue. Deception in research adds to the deception that permeates our culture, but it takes place in an institution, the university, which is dedicated to the search for truth.

Deception in Other Social Sciences

Although deception is a characteristic of many areas of society, no other social science uses deception to the extent and in the way that it is used in social psychology. This is because other social sciences are not experimental; that is, they do not make extensive use of laboratory methods in research. Economists and political scientists rely heavily on data in pubic records (e.g., tax receipts, voting records). Anthropologists and sociologists generally use field research methods in which they observe people in natural situations.

If, however, one uses a definition of deception that includes studies in which participants are not aware that they are being studied, then some research in sociology would involve deception. Most sociologists believe that it is better to let people know they are part of a study, but admit that this may not be possible if the group does not want to be studied. Two sociologists whom I interviewed were hard pressed to think of any studies in their field that use explicit lies.[1] There are two important exceptions. The first was a famous study of homosexual men by Laud Humphreys (1970), who lied about who he was and about the purpose of his study when he interviewed men in their homes. When this study was published it resulted in a storm of controversy in the field of sociology, including fist fights in Humphreys's own department.

The other exception to the use of explicit deception by sociologists involves research techniques that would not typically appear in published research reports. Some sociologists advocate the use of deceptive tactics to gain access to groups that do not want to be observed. In the early to middle 1970s the principal advocate of this approach was Jack Douglas, who presented a number of "ploys" that researchers could use to gain acceptance (Douglas, 1976). These included the "boob ploy" of pretending to be submissive and spineless, the "hair-brained academic ploy" whereby one's research is made to seem highly abstract and of little interest to nonacademics, and the tactic of "revealing guilty facts about oneself, even when not true" (p. 173). Douglas believes that "it takes years to learn to be dishonest effectively" (p. 185). Most sociologists, however, reject this approach.

With these exceptions, it is social psychologists who have used deception in research, and have raised these techniques to an art form. In no other area of psychology is deception used so extensively, and when it is used in other areas it almost always is a form of social psychology. For example, in developmental psychology there are studies of the conditions under which children help others, but that is really social psychology using children as subjects. My primary concern then is with the field of social psychology. This is not a narrow specialty, but involves a large number of psychologists who have published hundreds of research articles. For many years, a large proportion of these articles reported the use of deception.

A Sense of History

This sense refers both to our ability to take the perspective of other people at another time, and to our awareness of continuity with past generations. At some point we feel the excitement of Kurt Lewin's research seminar where he and his students developed creative situations to test new ideas. We see this group of working class, white, young men (very few women at this time) being inspired by a Jewish refugee during a time of severe economic depression and threat of war.

One of the students working with Lewin was Leon Festinger, who we come to know as a master of experimental design, a demanding academic mentor, and the creator of the most dominant social psychology theory of the 1950s and 1960s. We join him as he and his colleagues infiltrate a religious cult that awaits the end of the world. We also take the place of a subject in one of Festinger's dissonance experiments, in which a boring experience is made to seem exciting.

Festinger influenced hundreds of social psychologists who accepted his views on well controlled experimental research that also was realistic for the participants. They took these values into the turbulent 1960s and applied them to the social issues that seemed to explode in this country. In the 1970s, after the Watergate burglary led to the resignation of President Richard Nixon, social psychologists even were able to create an experimental study in which subjects had a chance to become felons.

The specific topic of this book is how social psychologists came to use deception in their research, and how deception came to be used frequently and often creatively. More generally, it is about the research endeavor, the excitement that experimenters feel as they become involved in creative design, the impact that their productions have on the participants, and how these things are affected by their time in history and the values of our culture. The next chapter will describe the pattern of the development and growth of the use of deception.

—2—

The Growth of Deception

Psychologists did not always use deception in research. Before the turn of the century in the early years of this science, experimenters and research subjects often exchanged places, taking turns being the person who presented a stimulus or the person who responded. At that time experimenters were called observers, and a well-trained, experienced observer often had higher status than the experimenter because of the long hours of practice required to be able to make accurate observations. Of course, deception was not possible under these circumstances.

In this chapter I will present a quantitative picture of the growth of deception over more than a century, from 1887 to 1989, and will begin by presenting examples of the first deceptions that were published in American psychology journals. Most of the information that I will present will concentrate on deception in social psychology and personality research because surveys of journal articles have found that relatively little deception occurs in other areas of psychology. Beginning with the first issue of the *Journal of Abnormal and Social Psychology* in 1921 and continuing through the 1980s, the picture that will emerge is one of slowly increasing use of deception until about 1950, then a rapidly growing increase, especially during the 1960s, with an apparent decrease after 1980.

The First Deceptions

Finding the first article that reported the use of deception involved going back to the first journals published in the United States and looking at every article until an example of deception was discovered. The journals searched were the *American Journal of Psychology* (*AJP*), founded in 1887, the *Psychological Review*, founded in 1894, and the *Archives of Psychology*, which began publication in 1906.

Our search for the first deception covered the period from 1887 to 1910. In the journals during that time we found several examples of what appeared to be deception, but that was not always clear because of the narrative style. The authors used a style in which theory, methods, results, and conclusions sometimes were mixed in the account of the research. Although stimulus conditions were described precisely, the instructions to participants were presented briefly, if at all. Because there was no clearly separated method section, the entire article had to be read to find out whether participants had been deceived. The task was made easier, however, because the early journals mixed studies that reported the results of experiments with essays and book reviews; a large proportion of the articles were not empirical.

The first article that we found that might involve deception illustrates the problems we encountered in doing this search. Leon Solomons (1897) was interested in the process by which people learn to discriminate between a touch produced by two points on the skin and that produced by one. "At the suggestion of Professor [William] James [he] undertook an experimental investigation of this problem" (p. 246). The second paragraph of his article described a preliminary experiment with two subjects, one of whom was told the results of his attempts to discriminate two points of touch, while the other was not. After a few weeks' practice the performance of the former had improved, but that of the other had not. No data were presented.

To explore this process further,

> the first thing tried was expectant attention. The subject was told beforehand what the stimulus would be, but requested to make judgment entirely independently of this knowledge, so that the effect of suggestion upon the actual feeling might be judged. . . . The judgment was fully twice as delicate when aided in this way. (p. 248)

Solomons then varied his procedure. In evaluating this study our problem was to distinguish between suggestion and deception. Was there an explicit misstatement of fact or attempt to mislead?

> Then the subject was told that he might be deceived—that when told that the stimulus would be two, it might really be one. He was to put himself in the condition of expectation for the stimulus as it was told him it would be, but to take care he was not deceived when it came to judging. The result was always as in the previous experiment. That is, the influence of the expectation predominated, so that when touched by one point he would perceive two if he had been led to expect two; and when touched by two, set farther apart than was necessary for perceiving them as two ordinarily, he would perceive them as one if told to expect one. (p. 248)

There was a misstatement of fact: Sometimes the experimenter said he would touch the subject with one point when, in fact, he used two. However, the subject had been warned that this deception might occur. Solomons was manipulating expectancies and the subject could choose to ignore statements concerning the number of points of touch.

We found similar subtle distinctions in several other studies. A colleague of Solomons referred to work they had done together on motor automatism in which "the only subjects we had were ourselves" (Stein, 1898, p. 295). She reported her own study of this phenomenon using a larger number of subjects. The instrument she used was a board that was suspended from a ceiling and was "just large enough to support the forearm, the hand hanging over and holding a pencil. . . . [It] could be readily adjusted, and allowed the operator to move it, and guide the subject without his knowledge." The experimenter was able to control this device: "By lightly resting my hand on the board after starting a movement I could deceive the subject, who sat with closed eyes, as to whether he or I was making the movement, and I could judge also how readily he yielded to a newly suggested movement, or if he resisted it strongly." She would direct the subject, "to keep his mind off the experiment and off his arm. Sometimes I would talk to him, sometimes get him to talk to me, or to think of a definite object, or to lose himself in a day-dream" (pp. 295–296).

Gertrude Stein was the author who described this relatively flexible method of interacting with research subjects. She did her research under the direction of William James, and later developed her narrative style in the novels and poetry that made her famous. ("A rose is a rose is a rose.") Her 1898 report concerns deceptive suggestions conveyed in movements, not words. These suggestions led subjects to make certain rhythmic movements. We do not know whether they were misled by statements from Ms. Stein because the specific instructions to subjects were not given in the article.

We expected that a review of "the psychology of conjuring deceptions" (Triplett, 1900) would contain many useful examples. Norman Triplett was, however, interested in magic tricks and illusions. Among the studies described in this fascinating article, is one by Carl Seashore (1895, cited by Triplett, 1900).

His manner of procedure was to make a genuine experiment several times, then, when the association has been formed by repetition, a pretended experiment is made and the subject by reason of the suggestion responds as before. In illusions of heat produced by first sending an electric current through a silver wire held between the fingers of the subject, and finally pretending to do so, of 420 trials there were only five cases where the subject felt nothing. (p. 491)

Triplett (1900) noted that a similar method had been used by Alfred Binet with children in France and concluded that Seashore's "experiments, made upon university students, seem to prove them not less easily duped than the children of the primary school mentioned by Binet" (p. 491). American psychologists did not take full advantage of this insight for another fifty years.

We found another example that was difficult to identify as deception because there was not an exact statement of what subjects were told. Henry Sheldon (1898) was interested in the social activities of childhood, especially the educational value of games. He used this approach to get 2,906 grade school children to write about their activities:

> The test given was short and simple in character. The children were directed to write a composition or language exercise on some society or club. The only qualifying condition was that the club should be one which they had organized themselves without adult assistance. The teachers were enjoined from assisting, suggesting or in any manner influencing the pupils. The test was given in all of the grades of the school at the same time, and to prevent communi-cation between the pupils concerning the exercise, it was given unexpectedly. The children were led to believe that the work was for their teachers and had no clue to its true purpose. (p. 426)

The work was for Sheldon's research, not for the teachers, but it is not clear whether children were "led to believe" (a phrase that today is a clear indi-cator of deception) by verbal instructions or by the context of the classroom. This would qualify as deception if a false purpose for writing the exercise was either explicit or implied.

The distinction between deception and suggestion is an issue in the hallucination demonstrations reported by E. E. Slosson (1899).

> [I] had prepared a bottle filled with distilled water carefully wrapped in cotton and packed in a box. . . . I stated that I wished to see how rapidly an odor would be diffused through the air, and requested that as soon as anyone perceived the odor he should raise his hand. I then unpacked the bottle in the front of the hall, poured the water over the cotton, holding my head away during the operation and started a stop-watch. . . . I expressed the hope that, while they might find the odor strong and peculiar, it would not be too disagreeable to anyone. (p. 407)

The first hand went up in 15 seconds; eventually three-fourths of the audience claimed to perceive the smell. Slosson also described creating hallucinations of temperature and pain using bogus magnets. His instructions for producing smell hallucinations included suggestions, but there was no explicit deception.

Another classroom demonstration that has been repeated many times is an example of an early, and perhaps the first, use of confederates in psychology. *Confederate* is the term psychologists use for an assistant to the experimenter who plays some role designed to deceive the research subject. Hugo Münsterberg (1908) described an "experiment" (p. 51) that had been done six years earlier "in Berlin, in the University Seminary of Professor von Liszt, the famous criminologist" (p. 49).[1] During a class period, two students begin shouting at each other during a lecture. One draws a revolver and the other student charges toward him.

> The Professor steps between them and, as he grasps the man's arm, the revolver goes off. General uproar. In that moment Professor Liszt secures order and asks a part of the students to write an exact account of all that has happened. The whole has been a comedy, carefully planned and rehearsed by the three actors for the purpose of studying the exactitude of observation and recollection. (p. 50)

Münsterberg considered the

> most essential condition to be the complete naivete of the witnesses, as the slightest suspicion on their part would destroy the value of the experiment. It seems desirable even that the writing of the protocol should still be done in a state of belief. (p. 51)

Here there clearly was an intent to deceive.

My final two examples again concern studies of the effects of suggestion on cutaneous sensitivity. Haywood Pearce (1902) would touch a subject on the arm, the subject would try to touch himself in the same place, and the difference would be measured. Pearce presented a second stimulus, in a different location on the arm, after the first to see if he could influence ("suggest") the subject's response. Four of six subjects did not know that the purpose of the experiment was to determine the "suggestibility" of the second stimulus. They were told that its purpose "was to test the effect of distraction, to see if they could localize as well without a second stimulus" (p. 333). This is a small distinction, but it is deception.

Margaret Floy Washburn (1909) used a standard test of the two-point-difference threshold: two rubber-tipped points touch the skin of the wrist 15 mm. apart; then, after about two seconds the two points again touch the skin at a slightly different location and the subject must report whether the second set of points is farther apart or closer together than the first set. Washburn's subjects had been told that the second set would be farther apart or nearer together but, "[a]s a matter of fact, the same separation of the points was used throughout" (p. 448). That is deception.

Except for Münsterberg's staged confrontation, all these studies used mild forms of deception. Solomons's (1897) study was the first possible deception that we found, and Washburn's (1909) report was the clearest example of a misstatement of fact. It is reasonable to conclude that during the early years of American psychology deception was rare and essentially was subtle suggestion.

The *Journal of Abnormal and Social Psychology*: 1921 to 1947

Before 1920 psychology was dominated by studies of sensation and perception and by mental testing, fields in which deception was not and never would become a major research technique. The unique status of social psychology early in this century can be seen in the title of the first American journal devoted to this topic where it was associated with abnormal psychology. The *Journal of Abnormal and Social Psychology* (*JASP*) began publication in 1921 as an extension of the *Journal of Abnormal Psychology*. Research on personality also was included in this journal, although the word *personality* was not in the title.

Tracking the early growth of the use of deception in social psychology involved reading the method section of each empirical study that reported using human subjects in all issues of *JASP* from 1921 through 1947. In the first year of publication (1921), none of the six empirical studies used deception. The first use of deception reported in this journal was by Hulsey Cason (1925) in his article, "Influence of Suggestion on Imagery in a Group Situation."

> The writer gave the above list of stimuli [words or phrases that previously had been scaled so that all were equally effective] orally to the 50 members of his class in abnormal psychology with the suggestion that the first 6 stimuli in each group would not call out very vivid images, but that stimuli 7 to 12 were much more favorable for calling out clear images. An attempt was of course made to deceive the subjects. (p. 296)

We did not find another study using deception until eight years later when T. H. Howells (1933) reported that he told each participant in his study, "that he was competing for rank with the other people taking the test and that the results might have as much significance for him as his intelligence test score" (p. 15). In fact, Howells was interested in persistence, not quality of performance. "The endeavor was to arrange the circumstances of the tests in such a way that mere tenacity in voluntarily 'hanging on' would enable the subjects to achieve a high score, rather than any special ability or skill" (pp. 14–15). Misinforming subjects about the purpose of a test would become one of the most common forms of deception.

After 1933 the use of deception increased in frequency, although the pattern was irregular; the number of studies reporting deception ranged from 0 to 4 per year through 1947.[2] Of the 31 deceptive studies published in *JASP* from 1933 to 1948, 52% gave incorrect information to participants, and 42% used false cover stories. Only 7% used confederates. The deception reported in *JASP* from 1921 to 1947 was relatively modest compared to the elaborately staged experiments that began to appear later. The following examples are typical of the kind of deception that was used during this period:

> Muzafer Sherif (1935) conducted "an experimental study of stereo-types" in which ". . . subjects were presented sixteen mimeographed slips each containing a short passage of three or four lines and, so far as the judges could determine, of about the same literary value. Under each passage was placed the name of one of the sixteen authors ascribed to a different author, but in reality all passages were taken from one author, namely, Robert Louis Stevenson" (p. 372).

> Carl Smith (1936) studied "the interaction of individual opinion and group opinion." He told subjects that he would announce the opinion of the majority of the group before reading statements to which subjects would respond. "The majority opinion in each case was fictitious" (p. 142).

> John French (1941) studied "the disruption and cohesion of groups." He concealed the purpose of the experiment by telling subjects that it was about group problem-solving. "They were led, in fact, to believe that all the problems were solvable within the forty-five minutes time limit allotted" (p. 362).

> Leon Festinger (1942) gave his subjects "the average estimate of a fictitious group of 50 subjects" (p. 185) in his study of factors influencing level of aspiration.

> To determine "signs of incipient fascism," Allen Edwards (1944) told subjects that "the investigation was attempting to check upon certain opinion poll results" (p. 304).

I have referred to these as "mild" deceptions. Remember that deception is a complex concept and that, although many categories of research deception have been identified (Sieber, 1982), no one has developed a scale for the intensity or extent of deception. Mild deceptions are those that involve minimal efforts on the part of the experimenter (e.g., falsely identifying the author of an essay) and are unlikely to upset the research participant. Serious deceptions are those that are likely to upset some subjects or involve elaborate staging, as in the helping study with the bleeding victim presented in the previous chapter.

Surveys of Deception: 1948–1989

There was a rapid rise in the use of deception in the 1960s and at the same time the kinds of deception used became more dramatic and ethically controversial. That is one reason that social psychologists began to have a "crisis of confidence" in their discipline (Elms, 1975). They worried about the relevance of the problems they studied and the validity of their methods, as well as questioning the ethics of deception.

Worrying and criticizing might suffice for philosophers, but psychologists who saw themselves as empirical scientists needed data to support their concerns, and some began to survey the research literature to document the increasing use of deception. The first such survey was published in 1967 (Stricker, 1967). Lawrence Stricker was concerned with the effectiveness of deception, so most of his data were related to the use of checks for suspiciousness of subjects. He sampled 457 studies from 390 articles in four journals published in 1964, including *JASP*. Deception was used in 19.3% of the studies, but his data were not presented for each journal separately, so cannot be compared with later surveys. Stricker did conclude that in many studies the effectiveness of deception could be questioned because subjects were likely to be suspicious of the experimenter.

During the next fifteen years, several other surveys were published that examined the frequency of the use of deception in various journals. It is important to realize that in these surveys and in my own research only *published* articles were counted; masters theses, doctoral dissertations, exploratory studies, and other unpublished studies were not counted, although it is probable that similar methods, including deception, were used. So the evidence presented in this chapter concerns a fraction of the research done by psychologists who used deception.

I found seven literature surveys on the frequency of deception in research that was published before 1980. All of these reviews counted the number of articles or studies using deception in selected journals in a specific time period. However, most authors used slightly different definitions of deception, which makes it difficult to make precise comparisons across these surveys.[3]

In addition to differences in definition, the surveys sampled different journals, although they all included the *Journal of Personality and Social Psychology* (*JPSP*) or the *Journal of Abnormal and Social Psychology* (*JASP*). In 1965, the field of abnormal psychology was given its own journal and *JASP* became *JPSP*, recognizing the overlap of social psychology with research on personality. This mixing of subject matter in psychology journals can be confusing to someone trying to investigate differing methodologies used in the various sub-fields of psychology. For example, even the *Journal of Personality*, which seemingly is dedicated to one restricted topic, also published articles that most experts would identify as social psychology. For that reason I often will blur the lines between subfields to provide a broader view of the extent to which deception was used. When I refer to research in social psychology, that almost always includes some kinds of personality research as well.

JASP and *JPSP* are included in most surveys because these journals are published by the American Psychological Association (APA) and represent high-quality, mainstream research in social psychology. Some reviews compared one of these journals (*JPSP* or *JASP*) with journals in other fields of psychology to demonstrate that deception is more frequent in social psychology.

Julius Seeman (1969) compared the 1948 and 1963 volumes of four journals: *JASP*, *Journal of Personality* (*JP*), *Journal of Consulting Psychology* (*JCP*), and *Journal of Experimental Psychology* (*JEP*). Frequency of deception was highest in *JP* (1948—23.8%, 1963—43.9%) and increased from 1948 to 1963 for all journals except *JEP* (*JASP*: 1948—14.3%, 1963—36.8%; *JEP*: 1948—14.6%, 1963—10.8%; *JCP*: 1948—2.9%, 1963—9.3%).

Robert Menges (1973) compared the 1961 volume of *JASP* with five journals from 1971: *JPSP*, *JEP*, *Journal of Abnormal Psychology*, *Journal of Educational Psychology*, and *Journal of Counseling Psychology*. He wanted to determine how investigators dealt with research dilemmas involving conflicts of ethics and methods and hoped to find a trend toward more "openness and honesty" in research. The phrase, "openness and honesty," had been used in the APA ethics code to describe the ideal relationship between experimenter and research participant. Menges found the opposite trend. The frequency of deception in *JASP* in 1961 was 16.3%; in *JPSP* in 1971 it was 47.2%. One must be careful when evaluating this difference because, as I mentioned, there was a change in the content of the journal; research in abnormal psychology (where the use of deception is lower) was no longer included in 1971. Menges also found that deception was much more common in *JPSP* in 1971 than in the other journals that he surveyed.

McNamarra and Woods (1977) examined 1,430 articles in four journals from 1971 to 1974, and presented their data as totals for the four-year period. The frequency of deception in *JPSP* (57%) was much higher than in *Behavior Therapy* (14%), the *Journal of Educational Psychology* (11%), and the *Journal of Applied Behavior Analysis* (1%).

The first review to consider the type as well as the frequency of deception was that of Alan Gross and India Fleming (1982). They were interested in whether published criticisms of deception led to a reduction in its use in social psychology. Their review covered the years 1959, 1965, 1969, 1972, 1975, and 1978–1979. The journals searched were *JASP* or *JPSP* for each of those years, the *Journal of Experimental Social Psychology* (*JESP*) for each year except 1959, the *Journal of Social Psychology* for 1969 and 1978–1979, and *Social Psychology* or its predecessors for 1969, and 1978–1979. A total of 1,188 articles were reviewed.

Gross and Fleming used a broader definition of deception than that used by other authors. They included studies in which participants were not aware that they were participating in research (14% of their deception studies were in this category), which resulted in higher frequencies of deception than found in other surveys (e.g., in *JPSP* they found 47% in 1965 and 69% in 1975). Of the various types of deception used, they found the most common to be the use of a false purpose or cover story (82%), incorrect information concerning stimulus materials (42%), and use of a confederate or actor (29%). These authors concluded that deception did not decrease over the period reviewed and that "there appears to be something like an implied license to deceive participants that are paid or receive credit for their work" (p. 407).

John Adair and his colleagues (Adair, Dushenko, & Lindsay, 1985) assessed the impact of ethical codes on research practice. They presented data from four previous reviews and new data from the 1979 *JPSP* in which they found that the frequency of deception was 58.5%. The authors concluded that deception had increased over three decades and that "the extremity of some deceptions does not seem to have moderated" (p. 59). This conclusion was based on finding individual cases in which the methods used in 1979 were similar to those used in earlier controversial studies. For example, some aggression studies used a procedure involving a bogus shock machine similar to that used in Stanley Milgram's obedience studies (Milgram, 1963) that I will describe in chapter 8.

In general, all of these surveys found a pattern of increasing frequency of deception in social psychology from 1948 to 1979. There was more deception in social psychology than in other research areas, although data from these other areas has not been collected as systematically. However, as noted before, researchers used different definitions of deception and different sampling methods.

To gain a more consistent picture of the growth of the use of deception, Sandra Nicks and I, with the help of several research assistants,[4] carried out our own surveys of journals in social psychology and personality (Nicks, Korn, & Mainieri, unpublished). We began by examining all articles in each volume of *JASP* for the years 1948, 1952, 1957, 1961, and 1963. In addition, separating articles in the area of abnormal psychology from those in personality and social psychology permitted more accurate comparisons with years after 1964 when the title and content of this journal were changed.

We continued our surveys with the 1968 volume of *JPSP* and added the *Journal of Personality* (*JP*) because of the extent to which social psychology also is represented in that journal. For these two journals we included the years 1973, 1979, 1983, 1987, and 1989. Finally, to get a broader view of the use of deception in the 1980s we added the *Journal of Experimental Social Psychology* (*JESP*) for the last four years that we sampled.

Our data, shown in Table 1, are consistent with other surveys and confirm the significant growth of the use of deception from 1948 through 1979. This was approximately a four-fold increase to a level where the use of deception was reported in about half of all articles in the area of social psychology.

We now bring our picture of the growth of the use of deception up to 1989. If we consider *JPSP* and *JP*, the use of deception does appear to have decreased. The picture is complicated, however, when we consider the data

TABLE 1

Percent and Number of Articles Using Deception in Various Journals
from 1948 to 1989

Year	JASP	JASP/SP[3]	JPSP	JP	JESP
1948	9.0[1](2)[2]	12.5(2)			
1952	19.4(12)	21.3(10)			
1957	25.4(36)	31.6(36)			
1961	28.2(59)	34.0(54)			
1963	30.7(57)	37.0(51)			
1968			50.7(99)	27.5(11)	
1973			51.3(102)	31.8(14)	
1979			53.2(88)	35.7(15)	64.3(27)
1983			41.3(92)	17.4(4)	67.6(21)
1987			24.1(56)	10.7(3)	42.9(12)
1989			29.9(55)	11.1(3)	65.5(19)

[1] Represents percent
[2] Represents number of articles
[3] Without abnormal psychology articles

from *JESP*, which shows the highest percentages of deception articles and about the same level in 1989 as in 1979. As the title indicates, this journal emphasizes laboratory experimentation as opposed to naturalistic studies or surveys that are more likely to appear in the other journals we examined. Both *JESP* and *JPSP* show increases from 1987 to 1989 but two years are not sufficient to conclude that this increase is part of a regular pattern or simply due to variability in the data.

The data presented in this chapter provide a picture of the rise and, possibly, the decline of the use of deception in psychological research. Deception was uncommon before 1930 and from 1930 to 1945 less than 10% of the articles in the major journal of personality and social psychology reported the use of deception. Then there was a steady increase through the 1950s, followed by more rapid growth after 1960, and a leveling off at about 50% during the 1970s. There may have been a decrease in the use of deception in the 1980s but that has not been confirmed.[5]

There also was a change in the quality of the deception used in psychological research. Complex, staged deceptions were unusual in the published literature of psychology before 1945. When deception was used after 1950, it was much more likely to involve elaborate scenarios with confederates and complex cover stories. Social psychologists were learning to create illusions of reality in the laboratory and sometimes to manipulate reality in natural settings.

In the following chapters we will seek to understand the factors that produced this pattern of quantitative growth and qualitative change. Most of this history will be about the forty-year period from 1935 to 1975. During this period social psychology became established as a subfield of psychological science, and the major figures in this field developed their ideas. Kurt Lewin and Leon Festinger were the most important of these figures because their followers primarily were responsible for the dramatic increase in the use of deception after 1960. In the next chapter I will set the stage for the major part of my story by describing the nature of the research enterprise in psychology as it developed in the United States from 1890 to 1940.

—3—

Social Psychology Becomes Experimental

The first forty years of American psychology were years of rapid growth for this new science and a time when various approaches to doing research in psychology were tried and then modified or eliminated. Even the definition of psychology underwent a change in emphasis from William James's "science of mental life" to John B. Watson's "prediction and control of behavior." The idea that psychology is a science has dominated experimental psychology since its beginning and led to the development of methods that included deception. Social psychologists would not have become part of mainstream psychology had they not accepted the quantitative, experimental methods that had been developed to justify psychology as science.

Compared to other scientists, psychologists had unique problems because the subjects of their research were human. Kurt Danziger (1985, 1990) described three patterns of social interaction in early psychological research in which the relationship between investigator and participant varied in quality and duration. Danziger used the laboratory of Wilhelm Wundt in Germany, the methods of the early hypnotists in France, and Francis Galton's mental measurement in England as prototypes of the three patterns. Each of these patterns was transferred to the United States, and although these models were changed after being imported, the nature of the relationship between experimenter and subject remained the same.

Most experimental psychologists mark the beginning of their science with the founding of a research laboratory by Wilhelm Wundt in Leipzig, Germany, in 1879. An important feature of the Leipzig model of research was the equal or superior status of the subject. "In the Wundtian experiment, the experimental subject was the scientific observer, and the experimenter was really a kind of experimental assistant" (Danziger, 1990, p. 48). Experimenters and observers knew each other well because they worked together as professor and students in the same laboratory. They took part in each others' experiments, switching roles at different times. The most highly trained observer (subject) was the most valuable member of the research group and often would be the senior author of the published report of the research.

Wundt had many American students, but the major importer of his method to the United States was Edward Bradford Titchener, an Englishman who came to Cornell University in 1892. Titchener's systematic introspection differed from Wundt's method (Leahey, 1981) but he continued to place great value on the well-trained observer. Examination of the literature of American psychology shows what happened to this relationship. In the two major American journals that reported empirical research, about 36% of the articles from 1894 to 1896 described studies in which experimenter and observer changed roles; that was true for only about 7% of the articles in two major empirical journals from 1934 to 1936 (Danziger, 1990). The carefully trained observer-researcher had become an endangered species.

Hypnosis was the basis for the second model. This technique was developed by physicians working in Nancy and Paris, France. The relationship between experimenter (hypnotist) and subject was close and long lasting, but the experimenters clearly had higher status and exercised considerable control over their subjects, who were usually female patients. It is "here we find the first consistent use of the term 'subject' in psychology" (Danziger, 1990, p.53). The hypnotist-experimenter demonstrated various psychological phenomena (e.g., trance states, hysteria) in his subjects by manipulating their actions with direct suggestions.

The third pattern, developed by Sir Francis Galton and first used in the United States by G. Stanley Hall, was the forerunner of modern mental measurement. The investigator again had the superior status as the one in control of what is measured and because no special training was necessary to be a subject, but the relationship was brief and less intense than in the other two models. Subjects (Galton called them "applicants") came to the "laboratory," which might be a public place, and were given a series of tests. The data from a large number of people were combined and described by the mean and standard deviation, which were statistics that Galton invented.

Psychology was striving to be accepted as a science both by other academic sciences and by the nonacademic world. Experimental control and quantification would contribute to this acceptance by making results in psychology appear to be precise and objective. But there was a larger goal, the development of general laws about behavior. The physical sciences had natural laws based on the behavior of objects and psychologists wanted to have their own laws. Experiments became "a world in which individuals are stripped of their identity and their historical existence to become vehicles for the operation of totally abstract laws of behavior" (Danziger, 1990, p. 117).

One example of this attitude is that before 1900, people who provided data might actually be referred to by name (or more commonly by their initials) in published articles; after 1930 subjects were anonymous members of arbitrarily defined groups.

The first third of the twentieth century saw what Danziger (1990) called "the triumph of the aggregate." There was a shift from reporting data for individuals to reporting data for groups as Galton had done. From 1914 to 1916 the percent of articles that reported only individual data in three major journals ranged from 43% to 70%; percents of articles reporting only group data ranged from 25% to 38%. These percentages were almost reversed for the period from 1934 to 1936 when the range for reporting individual data was 28% to 31% and for group data, 55% to 61%. The preponderance of group data was even greater from 1949 to 1951, with a range in the three journals from 80% to 94% (Danziger, 1990).

In addition, a particular kind of group data came to dominate psychology, in terms of both the number of studies and the alleged superiority of the method. Groups could occur naturally (e.g., men versus women), could be defined by a distribution of test scores (e.g., average intelligence as an IQ score of 90 to 110), or could be experimental groups. In psychology, experimental came to refer to a particular method called the treatment-group approach in which individuals are assigned to one of two or more groups, one of which may be designated as the control group and the others the experimental groups. For example, fifty people might be given alcohol before a test (the experimental group) and fifty others given water (the control group). Furthermore, when random assignment to groups is used, psychologists refer to this as a "true" experiment (Campbell & Stanley, 1963), where true means that this kind of experiment is better able to rule out alternative explanations than are nonrandom group designs. Of course, randomized experiments are no more "true" than experiments in biology or chemistry that do not use separate groups, but rather make observations under controlled conditions.[1]

Research psychologists also came to rely increasingly on statistical inference to interpret the results of experiments. The abstract individual in group experiments was represented by the arithmetic mean, and scores of individuals were deviations from that mean. Inferential statistical techniques began to be used to decide whether it is likely that group means really are different or simply due to chance. By the middle of the 1930s use of the critical ratio statistic was common (Danziger, 1990), but psychology was slow to make use of the more advanced analysis of variance (Anova) statistics. This technique, which would become the workhorse of psychological statistics in the 1950s, was developed before 1925. Rucci and Tweney (1980) surveyed the use of Anova in psychology and found that before 1945 it was used in less than 5% of all articles in six major journals, with the first use occurring in

1934. Its use did not exceed 10% until 1950. Even the simpler t-test was not used commonly until after World War II.

The science of experimental psychology that had emerged by 1930 had rejected Wundt's model of the observer-researcher in favor of a combination of the other two models: One manipulated subjects in controlled situations (the French hypnotists), and the other grouped subjects for purposes of statistical analysis (Galton). Most experimental psychologists believed that this approach would lead to the development of precise, general laws of behavior. This view of psychological science fit well for the areas of learning and perception, which set the standards at that time for high-quality research. Social psychologists, however, were interested in questions that differed in an important way; their subjects had to respond to other people in social situations, rather than to lists of words or flashes of light. To become *experimental* social psychologists, they would have to find a way to control and manipulate social stimuli.

Experimental Social Psychology

Social psychology began as a collection of individual studies, having no particular identity as a specialty (Danziger, 1993). Some textbooks claim that an experiment on competition published in 1898 by Norman Triplett was the first experiment in social psychology, but many other articles published before that date that could be classified as social psychology, particularly studies of suggestion (Haines & Vaughan, 1979).

Interest in such topics as character traits and group influence was growing, however, and in 1921 the *Journal of Abnormal Psychology* became the *Journal of Abnormal and Social Psychology*. Morton Prince had founded the *Journal of Abnormal Psychology* and continued as editor of the expanded version. Then, in 1922, Prince was listed as editor "in cooperation with Floyd H. Allport" who would represent the social side of the journal. An "editorial announcement" (The Editors, 1921) gave the reasons for combining the two fields of abnormal and social psychology and outlined "the various interests now properly included under the head of social psychology." The first of these was "human traits in so far as they have importance for social life. . . . [T]he personality of the individual as one of the radiant points of social action offers a field for practical and theoretical investigation" (p. 2). Thus, from the beginning, the study of personality was closely associated with social psychology. In fact the first article in the renamed journal concerned personality traits (Allport & Allport, 1921). In 1965, this relationship would be made explicit when the journal changed its name to the *Journal of Personality and Social Psychology* and topics in abnormal psychology were again placed in a separate journal.

Other topics listed in this 1921 editorial outline included: the interaction between the individual and the group, communication, human adjustment to the social environment, and group conflict. The link with abnormal psychology was said to be a common interest in "the dynamics of human nature" and "forces underlying human conduct" (p. 2). There was also a common interest in social maladjustment. "The failure to adjust to the requirements of the social group is the ground for many departures from the normal" (p. 3). Bolshevism was given as an example of abnormal "'falling out' with the regime of society" (p. 3).

In 1924 Floyd Allport's textbook (F. Allport, 1924) launched experimental social psychology. Several sociology books on social psychology previously had been published, and one by a psychologist (McDougall, 1908), but none of these assigned the great importance to experimental research that Allport did. Hugo Münsterberg's book, *On the Witness Stand* (1908), had referred to some research, primarily demonstrations and cases, but dealt with a limited range of topics in which social psychology was applied to problems in criminal justice. Allport (1924) acknowledged Münsterberg as the one "who suggested the setting for my first experiments and who foresaw many of the possibilities which have been developed in this book" (p. vii). Allport made his purpose clear in the preface to his book: "there are two main lines of scientific achievement which I have tried to bring within the scope of this volume. They are the *behavior viewpoint* and the *experimental method*" (p. v, italics in original). Throughout the book, Allport emphasized the fundamental importance of behavior, but he did not define what he meant by "the experimental method." The research that he discussed, however, included all forms that were common at that time, observation and questionnaires, as well as laboratory manipulation. The randomized, treatment-group ("true") experiment had not yet become popular.

Allport's (1924) book included some topics not found in most contemporary social psychology textbooks, such as the physiological basis of behavior, instinct, and learning. There also were two chapters on personality. In a narrative style Allport described the state of knowledge concerning various topics and included summaries of relevant experiments where possible. For example, Triplett's (1898) study of social facilitation, which many authors cite incorrectly as the first experiment in social psychology, is included in a chapter on "response to social stimulation in the group." Allport devoted twelve pages in that chapter to a description of his own research on group influence.

The field of personality research was developing along with social psychology (Craik, 1986). Some of the research areas that became popular (e.g., motivation) cut across the two fields so that in examining the literature it is difficult to classify many articles into one or the other subfield of psychology. For example, studies of achievement motivation and level of aspiration dealt with a personality characteristic, one's need to achieve, in a competitive social situation.

The first textbooks to summarize the experimental (in the broad sense in which that term was used at this time) literature in personality appeared in 1937 (G. W. Allport, 1937; Stagner, 1937). Before 1935 single case studies and paper and pencil measures of individual traits dominated personality research. However, clinical research and theory in personality had developed primarily through the work of Freud, Jung, and other psychoanalysts. Laboratory researchers in personality were influenced by psychoanalysis and designed experiments to test hypotheses concerning concepts such as regression and repression.

During the decade of the 1920s, empirical research in personality and social psychology was dominated by the Galton model. Much of that research involved the measurement of attitudes and traits, generally through the use of questionnaires and surveys. A major project on the nature of character was an important exception to this reliance on paper-and-pencil testing and is significant in the history of the use of deception.

Studies in Deceit (Hartshorne & May, 1928) was the first volume in a project that had been initiated in 1922 by the Religious Education Association, whose members were concerned with how religion was taught to young people and with what effect. Consultation with experts led to recommendations for a formal study of "the actual experiences of children which have moral and religious significance", a study that would "apply the objective methods of the laboratory to the measurement of conduct under controlled conditions" (Fisher, in Hartshorne & May, 1928). This is an example of how psychology had convinced professional educators of the value of the "experimental" approach (Danziger, 1990).

The two principle investigators for this study were an interesting blend of backgrounds in religion, education, and psychology. Hugh Hartshorne, a Congregational clergyman, had studied at Yale Divinity School and Union Theological Seminary, but received his doctor's degree in education from Columbia University in 1913. Before joining the project he had published several articles including "Stories for Worship and How to Follow Them Up." Mark May was the psychologist, and he also had a Ph.D. from Columbia. He served as a psychological examiner during the First World War and was a research associate at Columbia when the studies on deceit were carried out.

The project involved the testing of a large sample of children in a variety of situations that would allow them an opportunity to be deceitful; i.e., to cheat. The situations included a variety of classroom examinations, social activities, and athletic contests. The investigators were quite sensitive to their own moral dilemma of using deception to study deceit:

The situations in which the children are placed are natural and wholesome situations. It is the way they handle themselves in these situations that constitutes the test of character. An examination in arithmetic or spelling, for example, is a good thing and time well spent, in addition to what one may learn from it concerning the tendency of a child to deceive in taking it. Athletic contests and parties, works of mercy and helpfulness are in themselves significant and valuable for the children over and above what the examiner may learn about their honesty or capacity for self-denial. This fact makes possible the conscientious use of these procedures in spite of the need of keeping the subject in ignorance of those aspects of the test which make it an instrument for measuring some aspect of character as well as knowledge or skill or speed. (pp. 11–12)

Later the authors repeat that

[i]n situations of this sort, which are intended to be, and are, very serious from the standpoint of the pupils, great care needs to be exercised to fulfill all promises made and to enter with entire sympathy into the program from the pupils' standpoint. (pp. 124–125)

The criteria used in selecting and designing the tests emphasized the need for control of the situation and for data that were quantifiable and reliable. In addition, "[t]he test should not put the subject and the examiner in false social relations to one another. The examiner should guard against being deceptive himself in order to test the subject" (p. 48). Nevertheless, in the "let-me-help-you test" a confederate of the experimenter offers help to a child who is working on a difficult puzzle that he or she has promised to do without help.

Initially, some of the tests were presented to students by stating a false purpose, e.g., "we are going to have some tests to-day to find out which pupils are doing the best in this class and in other classes" (p. 113). These directions later were revised to say simply, "We are going to have some tests to-day. When the papers are passed out they will be fully explained" (p. 116). The latter statement was not strictly true because only the task was explained, not the purpose.

In this research Hartshorne and May were the first to use a variety of situational tests that involved deception, including the use of confederates. The deception was mild, however, and the investigators were sensitive to the feelings of the children and to their own responsibility to be honest. The studies had theoretical significance in anticipating the person-situation controversy that emerged forty years later: A major conclusion from *Studies in*

Deceit was "that neither deceit nor its opposite, 'honesty,' are unified character traits, but rather specific functions of life situations" (p. 411).

By 1930 there had been a great increase in the amount of quantitative and laboratory research in social psychology. Much of this literature was summarized by Gardner and Lois Barclay Murphy in their 1931 book, *Experimental Social Psychology*. In 1926, they had intended "to survey the entire field [because] there were only a few hundred experimental studies . . . and a few hundred good studies in individual differences in respect to social traits" (Murphy & Murphy, 1931, p. 39). However, in only a few years the literature grew at an "amazing" and even "alarming" rate, which made it impossible for them to carry out their plan. They were forced to be selective in the topics they included and the studies they summarized.

The key word in the title of the Murphys' book is *experimental*. This was the first social psychology book to include that word in the title. The word was not defined, but the approach was discussed at length. Experimental and quantitative methods were linked closely, and one of the purposes of the book was to justify the use of these methods in social psychology, methods that would help social psychologists "find laws which are universal for the entire human family" (p. 8). The Murphys did not rule out natural observation and did not mention random assignment to groups. "The important thing is that the *significant variables should be selected and measured*. . . . The essential thing in science is to know *the conditions under which an event occurs*" (p. 23, italics in original). Their experimental social psychology was largely a study of tests, measurements, and single groups in the laboratory. Some treatment group studies were included, but the randomized experiment had not yet become dominant. However, the emphasis on quantification and the search for universal laws indicates acceptance by social psychologists of values that characterized experimental psychology in general.

A second landmark volume in the 1930s was Carl Murchison's, *A Handbook of Social Psychology* (Murchison, 1935). Murchison was a promoter of psychology who published and edited several handbooks that covered subfields of psychology. He also started a family of specialty journals including the *Journal of Social Psychology*, that began publication in 1930 with John Dewey joining Murchison as editor. The broad subject matter of that journal was indicated by its subtitle: *Political, Racial, and Differential Psychology*. That subtitle remained until 1949, and the journal continues to emphasize cross-cultural topics in psychology.

As with the Murphys' book, some of the topics in Murchison's *Handbook of Social Psychology* look much different than those included in the social psychology handbooks published after 1950. For example, the first two chapters concerned social phenomena in bacteria and plants. Chapters were devoted to insect and bird societies and to social histories of the races. Only a few chapters covered topics that might be found in contemporary textbooks. These included Gordon Allport's review of attitude research that was based mostly on questionnaires and John F. Dashiell's chapter summarizing "experimental studies of the influence of social situations on the behavior of individual human adults." Dashiell was relatively specific about what he meant by experimentation in this field: it "involves in essence *a comparison between measured achievements of the individual person when under influences from other persons physically present with the measured achievements* (in identical functions) *of the same individual when working alone*" (Dashiell, 1935, p. 1099, italics in original). He thought that "practically all worthwhile experimental work along these lines" (p. 1099) had been done within the fifteen years before he wrote his chapter, which means that he dated the beginning of experimental social psychology from about 1920. The research design that he favored, however, was not the randomized treatment group design that would become dominant later, but what we today would call a "within-group design" in which the *same* person is given both treatments and so serves as his or her own control.

Murchison himself took a dismal view of the state of the social sciences, including social psychology, in 1935.

> The social sciences at the present moment stand naked and feeble in the midst of the political uncertainty of the world. The physical sciences seem so brilliant, so clothed with power by contrast. Either something has gone all wrong in the evolution of the social sciences, or their great day in court has not yet arrived. It is with something akin to despair that one contemplates the piffling, trivial, superficial, damnably unimportant topics that some social scientists investigate with agony and sweat. And at the end of all these centuries, no one knows what is wrong with the world or what is likely to happen to the world. (p. ix)

That was a discouraging preface to a book of almost twelve hundred pages, although Murchison hoped that "serious students" would be inspired to search for the "essential components of all social behavior in all social bodies in all social situations" (p. ix). As editor he did not support one particular method, not even experimentation, but he did believe that the goal of psychology should be the discovery of fundamental laws.

The discovery of precise psychological laws required advances in methodology. New techniques for measuring social attitudes and aspects of personality were being developed between 1925 and 1935 by Louis Thurstone and Rensis Likert. The Likert scale[2] became a standard measuring tool in social psychology for studies of attitudes and opinions, and to

measure subjects' responses in social situations. Advances in the design of
these situations was a parallel development in the 1930s, and grew out of the
creative laboratory methods that had been used by Kurt Lewin and his
students in Berlin. (See chapter 4.) This work was becoming known in the
United States and Lewin's approach to research began to spread after he
came to this country in 1933. The result of these developments would be an
experimental social psychology that could test theoretical hypotheses by
placing subjects in controlled laboratory situations, taking quantitative
measures of their reactions, and using statistics to analyze these measures.

While these advances in methodology were taking place, Saul Rosenzweig, a clinical psychologist, published an original analysis of experimentation in psychology (Rosenzweig, 1933). He pointed to the fact that psychological research using humans is not the same as research in the physical
sciences involving objects, although both may use controlled situations and
quantitative measures. Research participants, who Rosenzweig called
experimentees, are people who have thoughts and feelings about the various
aspects of the experimental situation; they are not passive responders to
stimuli. For Rosenzweig, the experimental situation was itself a psychological
problem that was subject to analysis. Recognizing the human factors in the
situation would allow greater control and ultimately more valid results. He
said that the ideal relationship existed when "the subject does not even know
that an experiment is being performed on him" and then considered "ways
and means of approaching this ideal" (p. 346).

Among the types of experimental errors that Rosenzweig wanted to
control were those he classified as "errors of motivational attitude," which
included subjects' wishes to figure out the true purpose of the experiment, to
appear favorably in the situation, and to cooperate with or perhaps to outwit
the experimenter. In order to control these possibly well-intentioned, but
bothersome motives of subjects, he suggested that it may be necessary to use
deception. Rosenzweig realized that no decent person would "seriously
injure" another human being, but he thought that we could and should
deceive people in the interests of science. His article presented the first and
the clearest statement on designing experiments that control for the attitudes
that subjects bring with them and that prevent subjects from discovering the
true purpose of the research:

"(1) The use of children and unsophisticated adults is to be recommended" (p. 346). He recognized the experimenter's duty to protect naive
individuals, who make good subjects because they bring fewer biases to the
situation.

"(2) The use of stimuli or determinants which, because of their nature or
strength, arouse the subject in a normal way almost in spite of himself are
often helpful" (p. 346). Withdrawal from a pain stimulus, for example, would
be difficult to inhibit.

"(3) An expedient that is of the greatest assistance in many cases is to observe the subject from a secret outlook" (p. 347). The one-way window was not widely used at the time Rosenzweig wrote this article,[3] although now most undergraduates would be suspicious if the laboratory room had a mirror on the wall. The idea, of course, is that people are more likely to act naturally if they think they are unobserved.

"(4) The subject should be kept as far as possible in ignorance of the true object and technique of the experiment" (p. 347). Rosenzweig then gave some suggestions for using explicit deception:

(a) Mislead the subject by deliberately assigning a false object at the very outset of the experiment. . . .

It is well to give the subject some idea of what the experiment is designed to demonstrate so as to prevent him from making conjectures that will be uncontrolled. But in assigning an object for the experiment, it is well to avoid vagueness or ambiguity, for the effects of this sort of knowledge are more incalculable than are those of a definite and absolute belief. It is, therefore, better to lie outright in many cases than to prevaricate. . . .

The feelings of the [experimenter] in cases in which he employs the expedient of secretly observing the [subject] or of lying to him are not always pleasant at first. The [experimenter] must overcome certain natural inhibitions against such procedures and this is sometimes difficult. He cannot, however, allow himself to be deterred by such scruples any more than the physiologist can be deterred by the arguments of anti-vivisectionists. Provided that the [experimenter] is convinced that his procedures will in no way seriously injure the [subject], he must solace himself with the consideration that the scientific end justifies the scientific means.

(b) Keep one step ahead of the subject in sophistication as to the object of the experiment. . . .

(c) Interrogate the subject after the experiment as to the opinions he entertained during its previous course. Find out if he knew anything about the experiment before he came into the laboratory.

(d) After the experiment, initiate the subject into the 'fellowship of research' by pledging him to secrecy. (p. 348–349)

The data presented in the previous chapter showed that the use of deception began to increase after the publication of Rosenzweig's article in 1933. I have not been able, however, to find direct evidence that Rosenzweig's suggestions influenced other psychologists. His name is not listed in the index of Murchison's (1935) handbook, and it was not in the revised edition of *Experimental Social Psychology* (Murphy, Murphy, & Newcomb, 1937). Kurt Lewin and Leon Festinger, who, we will see, did more to promote the use of deception than anyone else, did not refer to Rosenzweig's paper. Mere lack of citation, however, does not necessarily mean that psychologists were unaware of or uninfluenced by Rosenzweig's suggestions.

It would not be until the 1960s that social psychologists began to use deception regularly, and when that happened they also would rediscover the human problems in their research situation. In 1962 Martin Orne published an article "on the social psychology of the psychological experiment" (Orne, 1962) and in 1964 Robert Rosenthal discussed how experimenter's expectancies influenced the results of their own experiments (Rosenthal, 1964). These articles had a significant impact on research in social psychology by drawing attention to some of the same problems that Rosenzweig had discussed in 1933, but without referring to that earlier analysis.[4]

Why was this landmark paper overlooked for more than twenty-five years? Silverman and Shulman (1970) pointed to the influence of the physical sciences model on experimental psychology. It would not be "scientific" to admit that the biases of the experimenter and the motives of the subject of the research might affect the results of experiments. "We are inevitably working with an unclean test tube, contaminated by all of the needs, anxieties, self-deceptions and intentions of someone who is aware that his behavior is being scrutinized as part of a psychological experiment" (Silverman & Shulman, 1970, p. 98). Rosenzweig essentially had said the same thing.

Suls and Rosnow (1988) also thought that in the 1930s and 1940s drawing attention to the way human biases influence psychological research might be viewed as hindering the development and status of psychology as a science. It would require that psychologists question their "faith in the impartiality of experimental research" (p. 166). They also suggested that "the phenomenon of artifacts stemming from playing a subject role pre-supposes the active influence of conscious cognitions", which "was largely inconsistent with behaviorist tenets at the time" (p. 165). Rosenzweig's article was a case of noticing that the emperor was naked.

In this chapter I have tried to show that the growth in the use of deception was closely related to social psychology becoming experimental. Perhaps the major reason that social psychologists began to use deception in their research was related to the way that psychology, in general, had developed as an experimental science; it required controlled manipulation of variables that would yield predictable responses in the subjects of the research. These subjects were humans, however, who had ideas about the experiment and at least two creative psychologists of that time, Lewin and Rosenzweig, recognized the necessity of controlling subject biases in the experimental situation. One way to do this was to create illusions of reality—deception.

The critical period in this history is 1935 to 1960 because this was the time when the two most important individuals in the history of social psychology carried out the experiments that changed the direction of this area of research. Kurt Lewin brought the real world into the psychology laboratory and provided a rich language for describing human relations. His student, Leon Festinger, created the first general theory for social psychology and he helped to make the cognitions of research subjects acceptable again. If we were to construct a genealogy of researchers who made extensive use of deception, we would find that almost all lines lead to Lewin and Festinger. Their influence will be discussed in chapters 4 and 7.

—4—

Lewin's Legacy

A German-Jewish immigrant who joined a department of home economics in 1933 radically changed the direction of American social psychology. Kurt Lewin already had a following in the United States as a result of an article published by J. F. Brown (1929) and an invited lecture at Yale University in 1929. The Yale lecture foreshadowed the nature of his impact because, although most of the audience could not understand what he said (he lectured in German), his obvious enthusiasm held the attention of his listeners (Marrow, 1969). It was not until he became a permanent resident of the United States, however, that he began to dominate our social psychology.

Lewin's most significant contributions concerned style and values, rather than theory and experiments. He developed a complex quasi-mathematical language that was not really a theory, but more a way of thinking about psychological concepts. Few people other than Lewin ever used this language, but his way of thinking inspired the design of creative situations in which real social issues could be investigated. That is the portion of Lewin's legacy that will be of most interest here because the situations created by his academic descendants often involved deception.

Lewin was charismatic, as well as creative, and that had much to do with the extent of his influence on social psychology. Edwin G. Boring (1957) described

> Lewin's able insights, his remarkable originality and zeal and his almost peerless capacity for democratic leadership. . . . We shall not understand Lewin's place in American psychology in 1933–1947 except in relation to the enthusiasm which his generous, friendly, insistent zealotry created. (pp. 723–724)

Lewin in Germany

Kurt Lewin was born September 9, 1890, in Mogilno, a town that now is part of Poland. The best account of his early years and his education is in

Alfred Marrow's biography, *The Practical Theorist*. He received his doctorate from the University of Berlin (conferred in 1916) and later obtained an academic appointment at that institution.

Lewin's early writing contained the blend of abstraction and application that would characterize his life's work. He wrote about the concept of origins in physical and biological science but also about scientific management and human relations in industry. At Berlin "during the early 1920's Lewin established a reputation as a provocative lecturer and teacher and over the years attracted many of the students at the Psychological Institute" (Marrow, 1969, p. 20). What provoked the students was his adaptation of ideas of the Gestalt psychologists. Lewin has been called a "hot" Gestaltist (Jones, 1985, p. 382) because he was interested in motivation and the dynamics of feeling and action, whereas most other Gestalt psychologists emphasized perception and thinking.

Lewin himself did not conduct laboratory experiments, but the students he attracted did carry out an impressive series of studies, primarily as doctoral research in Berlin. Most of those students were women, some of whom were foreigners who came to Germany to study something other than psychology. Their studies, "rated as among the most distinguished group of empirical inquiries in the history of psychology," (Marrow, 1969, p. 41) included the first research on level of aspiration, which later became a major topic in American social psychology, and a series of studies on uncompleted tasks. Lewin's first student chose uncompleted tasks as her topic and the results obtained by Bluma Zeigarnik were so original and impressive that the "Zeigarnik effect" for years has been described in most introductory psychology textbooks.

Marrow's summary of the thinking that led to Zeigarnik's experiment provides an example of how Lewin moved from theory to method.

> The basis for Zeigarnik's study was an effort to test Lewin's theory that the desire or intention to carry out a specific task corresponds to the building of a system of psychological 'tension' and that the need to release this tension serves to sustain goal-directed activity until the intended task is carried out. Dynamically, Lewin theorized, this means that the system created by the unfulfilled goal continues to make its influence felt in thought or action (or both) as long as the tension is not yet discharged by completion of the activity. Zeigarnik sought to discover whether the 'quasi-need' (the impulse to release the tension) functions only to accomplish the intention or whether it influences other aspects of behavior, such as memory. She designed her study so that the expression of an intention would be found in the desire to finish interrupted tasks and the effect of the quasi-

need would be seen in the tendency to remember unfinished activities more readily than completed ones. (p. 42)

The tasks included listing cities, solving riddles, stringing beads, and counting backward. Subjects (164 children and adults) were allowed to complete half of the tasks, while the other half were interrupted before completion. Later the same subjects were asked to recall the tasks. Almost twice as many uncompleted as completed tasks were recalled. This was a relatively simple situation compared to the complex social productions that would later be designed by Lewin's students in the United States, but it was a situation that provided a valid test of the tension theory.

The use of deception was unnecessary in Zeigarnik's study, but research by one of Lewin's other students in Berlin did involve deception. Tamara Dembo was interested in the causes of anger. She wondered why frustration led to anger in some circumstances but not others. "Her point of departure was Lewin's postulate that behavior is determined by the structure and state of the person in his life space and by the psychological environment at that particular moment" (Marrow, 1969, p. 45).

The situation that Dembo created was similar to one that later would be used often in psychology. Subjects were assigned a task and asked to find a solution when in fact no solution was possible.

[The] task required the subject to reach for a flower some distance away without moving his feet outside the area where he was standing. When the subject found a way to do it, he was then asked for a second solution. Most subjects were able to find both without great difficulty. They were then asked to figure out a third way, although in fact no additional way was possible. The subject's efforts to come up with one more answer were encouraged by the experimenter. Indeed, Dembo insisted on a third solution. The consequent frustration brought on a series of angry reactions, remarkable both for their intensity and for the wide range of their outward manifestation. (Marrow, 1969, p. 254)

Subjects reacted in various ways, some directing anger at the task, others at the experimenter, and others trying to get out of the situation. The experiment confirmed "Lewin's theory that behavior was a function of the total situation. It showed that the effect which a need had on the structure of the life space depended on the intensity of the need" (p. 255).

Dembo's research was conducted between 1925 and 1928 (published in 1931). Shortly after she completed her work Lewin published his view of the usefulness of deception in psychological research.

One can so arrange the experiment that the subject, during the actual course of the experiment is completely unaware of the fact that he is the subject: one pretends that another task is the experiment, then leaves the subject during the actual experiment and secretly observes him from another room. . . . [I]f one makes use of elaborate arrangements or even creates situations with strong forces, as theoretical requirements also demand shall be the case, then only a very small percentage of experimental subjects will act as though they feel themselves to be experimental subjects. Others very soon get involved in the situation and accordingly become free and natural. (Lewin, 1929, quoted in MacKinnon & Dukes, 1962, p. 677)

Lewin's analysis of the experimental situation, published in Germany in 1929, anticipated the ideas of Saul Rosenzwieg (1933) that were presented in the previous chapter.[1] In addition to suggesting the use of deception, Lewin pointed out the importance of the motives and thoughts of the experimental subject.

Behind the decision of the person 'to become an experimental subject' lie for the most part very real and often very deep life forces: the ambition to pit oneself against others; the 'idea of science'; the particular personage of the experimenter or of the instructor by whom the experiment will be conducted, etc. . . . (MacKinnon & Dukes, 1962, p. 678)

The full range of possible research deception that Lewin suggested would not be used until after he emigrated to the United States. The importance that Lewin placed on the creative design of situations is clear. Donald MacKinnon, one of Lewin's American students said, "He [Lewin] was confident that it was not necessary to re-create the same intensities in the laboratory that obtain outside it, but what *was* necessary was to set up the same dynamic system" (quoted in Marrow, p. 41). An experiment should provide an ideal situation that is well defined and well controlled but which has many elements of real situations, thus allowing the researcher to conclude that the results of the experiment could be applied outside the laboratory. This principle of "transposition" was Lewin's answer to the problem of the artificiality of psychology experiments (Danziger, 1993) and became the rationale used by social psychologists who followed him.

There are significant differences between the way Lewin and his students conducted research in Berlin during the 1920s and the methods favored by American psychologists at that time (Danziger, 1990, pp. 173–175).

The people who were the subjects of psychology experiments in this country had become abstract objects. The intent was to make them as isolated as possible from specific characteristics of the experimental situation, including the person in the role of experimenter. Dembo's research on anger is an excellent example of the contrast. In her work the experimenter herself and her interaction with the participants is part of the stimulus for the behavior of interest. Lewin expressed this idea in the form of an equation, $B = f(P, E)$, meaning that a person's behavior is a function of the interaction of the characteristics of the person and of the environment. This general common-sense notion shows how closely related are the areas of social psychology and personality.

One of the interesting aspects of Lewin's Berlin group was that it was

> more often than not female, Jewish, and eastern European. This was a rather cosmopolitan group whose spontaneous sensitivity to and awareness of social psychological questions were obviously far greater than tends to be the case in more homogeneous and more locally rooted groups. It is not surprising that their approach to the study of personality was marked by an intense sense of the embeddedness of the personality in social situations (Danziger, 1990, pp. 173 174)

It also is not surprising that this small group of east European women were attracted to a young, charismatic German male, who was Jewish as they were. The German male students would work with the senior members of the Gestalt psychology group who were closer to the Berlin mainstream in psychology. Lewin would get the outsiders.

Lewin in America

Kurt Lewin visited the United States for the fist time in 1929 when he attended the International Congress of Psychology at Yale. The *Psychological Review* had published J. F. Brown's (1929) article describing Lewin's work, so most of the audience that was present at Yale knew about his ideas. Although he spoke in German, which most of his audience may not have understood, his presentation was stimulating. It included a film in which a child was "trying to sit on a block while keeping eye contact with it. The child solved the problem amusingly and effectively by putting his head between his legs and backing up to the block" (Ash, 1992, p. 200). Along with this creative form of presentation, Lewin's personality captured the audience: "if you just took the man and his behavior—the way in which he was acting—it was quite clear that he was an original—an exciting psychologist and a dynamic person to work with" (Donald MacKinnon, quoted by Marrow, 1969, p. 51).

Lewin's next journey to America was in 1932 when he spent six months as a visiting professor at Stanford University. In January of 1933, while returning home through Russia, he heard the news that Adolf Hitler had become Chancellor of Germany. Lewin knew what was in store for Jews in Germany and immediately contacted friends in the United States asking them to help him find a position. The position he found was in the School of Home Economics at Cornell University beginning in August 1933.

Home economics seems a strange setting for an experimental psychologist with an international reputation, but these were years of severe economic depression and all jobs were scarce. For most Europeans displaced by Nazi oppression, when positions were found they were likely to be temporary and peripheral. Furthermore, "the German psychologists and, in particular, the Gestalt group, were seen as intruders, alien to the prevailing psychological atmosphere" (Mandler & Mandler, 1969, p. 375). The American establishment in psychology apparently enjoyed Lewin as a curiosity, but not as a colleague. Lewin would remain an outsider and develop his own enthusiastic group of followers.

On the positive side, both at Cornell and later at Iowa, Lewin's work was generously funded by the Laura Spelman Rockefeller Memorial Foundation. His friend, Lawrence K. Frank, helped him obtain his positions and funding, which gave Lewin better "access to facilities such as laboratory schools, and support from doctoral students and co-workers than he might have had at many university departments" (Ash, 1992, p. 200).

Lewin's sensitivity to the threat of Hitler and the Nazis also was not shared by everyone. "There is little evidence that psychological organizations, either in Germany or the United States, took immediate cognizance of the threat to academic and scientific freedom or of the threat to the individual live-lihoods and lives of psychologists" (Mandler & Mandler, 1969, p. 380). The elite in psychology were relatively secure and may have shared the desire for isolation that prevailed in this country up to the beginning of World War II (Ketchum, 1989). It must have been difficult for Lewin, a foreigner with unu-sual ideas and a Jew in a country that cared little about the fate of his people.

Lewin cared deeply about this problem. While at Cornell he spent much of his time planning a psychological institute for the Hebrew University in Palestine. The institute would be concerned with the problems faced by Jews coming to Palestine from European countries. Lewin made several trips to New York City to try to raise funds for the institute and made one visit to Palestine. His friends, however, thought his talents would be developed better in the United States, and convinced Lewin to take another position in this country.

In 1935 Lewin again moved to a place that was outside the mainstream of psychology, the Child Welfare Research Station at the University of Iowa.

Here he would gather a group of dedicated students, some of whom would remain with him through the remainder of his life. He did not require loyalty, but he received it, and at Iowa Lewin built "warmer relationships with his students than had most other eminent men in American psychology" (Marrow, 1969, p. 90). The reminiscences of Lewin's students (Marrow, 1969; Patnoe, 1988) repeat similar praises of the man and his style. Tamara Dembo's feelings were typical: "Iowa was exciting . . ., a constant feeling of something fresh and very worthwhile. For some of us it was a very deep experience" (quoted by Marrow pp. 86–87).

In addition to creating this unique social climate, Lewin attracted a special type of student:

> Many students who joined Lewin, at least after 1938, came with a practical interest in the social uses of psychological research. They found that in an era when life problems rarely received consideration from psychologists, and then only when they had reached the stage of abnormality and malfunction, Lewin's thinking was strongly life-connected. His theories were tools to attack everyday human problems. They led Lewin...to place increasing emphasis on experimental studies of the how and what-for of individual and social change—studies which later were consummated as 'action research' and 'group dynamics.' (Marrow, 1969, p. 87)

At Iowa, as at Berlin, Lewin created the environment and provided the theoretical language for students to design and conduct innovative research. The Iowa studies completed by Lewin and his students were published between 1937 and 1944 (Marrow, 1969, Appendix D). Most of the research used children as subjects because Lewin was affiliated with the Child Welfare Research Station. The topics included frustration, conflict, and competition, and often required producing negative emotions in the children, sometimes through the use of deception. In one study, for example, children two to six years of age were prevented from playing with desirable toys. The experimenter was in the same room, pretending to be involved in his own work, but actually recording the children's behavior, which included hostile actions toward objects and the experimenter (Barker, Dembo, & Lewin, 1941, reported in Marrow, 1969, pp. 120–122).

The studies of autocracy and democracy perhaps are the best known of the Iowa experiments. They are historically significant for many reasons. It was perhaps the first time that a complex real-life situation was created in a controlled laboratory setting, and the experimenters observed human interactions in groups rather than the restricted responses of one person at a time. The research had implications for significant world events at a time when the democratic nations were confronting Fascism in Europe and a militaristic regime in Japan. This research also is significant for the history of deception because of the innovative use of experimenters who played various roles, the use of confederates, and the use of hidden observers.

The studies were conducted in the attic of a building at the University of Iowa in 1938 (White & Lippitt, 1960/1972, p. vii). The first experiment was conducted by Ronald Lippitt, and the second was planned and conducted jointly by Lippitt and Ralph White. Both experiments were "under the general direction of Kurt Lewin" (White & Lippitt, 1960/1972, pp. 13, 15).

> The first experiment was comparatively simple. Two small groups of eleven-year-old children met after school to make masks and carry on other activities. The groups were similar in many ways—age, sex, etc.—but not identical. They were led by the same person (Lippitt), but with one group he played a "democratic" role and with the other he played an "autocratic" role. There were five children in each group; each met eleven times. Five observers took continuous notes on the behavior of the leader and the children in each group.

> While the groups behaved similarly at the outset, they rapidly became different, so that in the later meetings the contrast was striking. . . . In brief, there was far more quarreling and hostility in the autocratically led group, and far more friendliness and group spirit in the democratically led group. The children in the autocratic group picked on scapegoats and showed other behavior that seemed too similar to certain contemporary dictatorships to be mere coincidence. It looked as if some psychological processes of broad significance, in politics as well as in the behavior of small groups, had been isolated in test-tube form. (White & Lippitt, 1960/1972, pp. 13–14)

The second experiment was controlled better, with a design involving four groups and three different leaders. In addition to autocracy and democracy, children experienced a "laissez-faire" leader. The design was improved in other ways, but the general results were similar. "To Lewin the results of the study were a source of real satisfaction, for they substantiated his own deeply felt belief in the superiority of the democratic system" (Marrow, 1969, p. 126). Lewin (quoted by Marrow, p. 127) said,

> There have been few experiences for me as impressive as seeing the expression on children's faces during the first day under an autocratic leader. The group that had formerly been friendly, open, cooperative, and full of life, became within a short half-hour a rather apathetic-looking gathering without initiative.

The second experiment included some "special test situations" that were designed to reveal the social dynamics of the groups, for example, having the leader arrive early or late. One of the situations involved the use of someone who now would be called a confederate.

[The] 'stranger' episode . . . always took place while the leader was out. A strange graduate student, clad and functioning as a janitor or electrician, would come in to replace an electric light bulb or to sweep up. During his task he would draw the club into conversation, first in a friendly or matter-of-fact way, asking them about their leader and what the club was about. Later he would criticize the work of some of the children or of the group as a whole. (White & Lippitt, 1960/1972, p. 24)

Edward Jones (1985) discussed the significance of this research in the history of social psychology and listed the features that came to be associated with the Lewinian approach. These are elements that are present in most of the later research that used deception:

1. A complex situation is created, and its features can be manipulated systematically, with observations that provide a quantitative check on the success of the manipulation.
2. Every effort is made to keep the situation as natural as possible and to inhibit self-consciousness in the subjects. The use of actors is an important feature of this element.
3. Changes are made in follow-up experiments as a result of initial observations.
4. The detailed observation of social behavior is the dependent measure, reflecting an interest in interpersonal processes.
5. Follow-up interviews are conducted to assess each subject's perceptions of the experience (debriefing).

All these elements enhance the validity of the research. Today psychologists talk about external and ecological validity. That is, they want to create experimental situations that are like real-world situations and can be generalized from the laboratory to those situations, which lends credibility to psychological research because its relevance is obvious. Kurt Lewin made social psychology relevant.

Not all of the research that was published as the "Iowa studies" was done at Iowa. Lewin spent the spring semesters of 1938 and 1939 at Harvard where several of his students began their work with him. One of these students was John French, whose study of "organized and unorganized groups under fear and frustration" (French, 1944) provides another good example of one of the first studies in which the use of deception was an essential feature of the design.

The purpose of the research was to discover differences in how the two types of groups function in situations created to produce fear or frustration. There were sixteen groups (eight of each type, fear and frustration) with six people per group. Thirteen of the groups were composed of Harvard under-graduates. Three of the organized groups "were clubs from a neighborhood house in the Italian section of East Boston" (p. 235). The experiment began during the Spring of 1939, Lewin's second semester at Harvard.

> The general method was the same for all sixteen groups: (a) a frustration situation produced by working on insoluble problems; (b) a fear situation in which smoke poured into the locked room. The purpose of the experiment was carefully concealed from the subjects. They were told that it was an experiment in group problem solving and led to believe that all the problems were soluble. When the problem-solving session was over, the experi-menter announced that the experiment was finished, dismissed the observers from the room, but asked the subjects to stay a few minutes to fill out a questionnaire. The experimenter then left the room on a pretext, locking the door as he went out. Thus the group was alone in a locked room, in an apparently 'nonexperimental' situation, when the smoke started to come in. To the subjects, therefore, the two situations appeared quite different even though they were contiguous in time. (French, 1944, p. 236)

The ceiling of the experimental room contained one-way screens through which participants could be observed. The observation methods were modifications of those used by Lippitt in the autocracy-democracy studies. In addition, a concealed microphone led to phonograph recording apparatus. Sound effects were provided by a siren borrowed from a fire truck and located in a distant part of the attic. All of this was an extremely elaborate setup that was unusual at this time.

Although the subjects who were filling out questionnaires had been told that the experiment was over, the experiment really ended when,

> [a]t a different signal from the observer (indicating that the group had started to break out of the room or that they were not fright-ened), the experimenter entered and explained that the smoke was just something he wanted to try out for a contemplated future exper-iment. He asked them to keep it strictly secret, and then instructed

them to write a full description of just how they felt, what they did and why. (p. 240)

"The reactions of the thirteen groups subjected to the fear situation varied all the way from fairly complete skepticism to genuine panic." Only "three of the groups . . . apparently accepted the situation as a real fire without considering the possibility that it might be a hoax" (French, 1944, p. 270). Seven of the groups actually attacked the door; in one group someone tried to pick the lock.

This experiment did not "work." That is, the people in most of the groups did not interpret the situation in the way the experimenters had intended. That was not important, however, for Lewinian analysis. French was interested in what *did* happen. Thus, the extent of skepticism in the groups became part of the analysis.

The more skeptical the group, the more they expressed aggression against the experimenter. In the three groups for whom the fear situation was an unambiguous fire, there was little aggression expressed against the experimenter after the discovery of the smoke. In the groups which were convinced of a hoax, on the contrary, there was disparagement of psychologists in general or openly expressed aggression directed against the experimenter and the observers. In some groups there were even elaborate fantasies about what they would like to do to the experimenter in retribution. . . . The behavior of the individuals appeared to be more determined by the social situation existing at the moment than by the physical situation, which was the same for most groups. (p. 272)

In this study we see many of the deceptive elements that would be repeated later in social psychological research: a bogus task, misinformation from the experimenter, and hidden observers.

The Lewinian repertoire of research situations included simple tasks and measures, such as those used by Zeigarnik, and more elaborate staged situations using various deceptions. An important element common to all these situations was that the experimenter was part of the situation, a variable to be manipulated. In Lewin's language, the experimenter created tension, set up barriers, and was a vector in a force field.

The Father of Deception

The Lewinian approach dominated social psychology into the 1980s and deception was used in much of that research. How did deception come to be

an important part of Lewin's own research and that of the next two generations
of social psychologists? First, it fit with his theory, his way of thinking, and his
personal experiences. Second, Lewin created a social climate that encouraged
students to accept and promote his ideas. This took place in the context of a
culture that valued this approach, even if the establishment in psychology did
not. The attitude of the establishment may have helped to bring greater cohe-
siveness to Lewin's group.

Lewin's field theory provided a language that was partly visual for
talking about research. A person exists in a psychological field, a life space in
the mind that is not the same as the physical space in the world. Needs,
tensions, and forces operate in the psychological field in the present to
influence a person's behavior. For Lewin the present, not the past, was of
primary psychological importance. He could describe these forces in words,
but preferred to use a "Jordan curve" or oval to describe the person's psychological field.

Shelley Patnoe (1988) linked this basic idea with Lewin's style of
experimentation:

> If behavior can best be understood by understanding the forces
> operating in a given situation, then the best way to understand those
> forces, and therefore behavior, is to create that situation under con-
> trolled conditions. By carefully changing one aspect of that controlled
> situation, the dynamics operating can begin to be understood. (p. 6)

This kind of reasoning led Lewin and his students to their creative designs
of situations in which they could observe the dynamics of anger, frustration,
conflict, and cooperation in the laboratory under controlled conditions.
These forces do not appear naturally in the laboratory, however, so they must
be created and this often required the use of deception.

In reading the accounts of the research of Lewin's students, one might
be troubled by the kinds of situations that were created. Children became
the scapegoats for the hostility of other children. College students and
adolescents from East Boston were frightened by the threat of fire. However,
there was less concern for the rights of children and college students in 1940
than there is today, and the distress that was produced was temporary and not
too severe. Yet psychologists had rarely done this kind of thing before.

There is no evidence that Lewin or the students who worked with him
expressed concern for the emotional effects of their research on the participants. Lewin himself may not have given it much thought. Although he was
a "practical theorist," his thinking was highly abstract; he often turned practical, everyday issues into theoretical discourses. During a casual walk in the
winter he would draw Jordan curves in the snow to illustrate his analysis of

some topic of conversation. He was the idea person, and his students interacted with the subjects in the research.

If he did think about the feelings of research participants, he may not have been bothered by their degree of distress. He was a Jew who had been forced from his homeland by a much stronger oppressive force than any of his subjects might have experienced and he continued to see anti-Semitism in his new country. In 1944 he learned that his mother had died in an extermination camp somewhere in Poland (Marrow, 1969, p. 140). "His pursuit of the truth about the hearts and minds of men caused him to subordinate his own pain to the service of other sufferers" (Marrow, p. 228). He had suffered and would dedicate his life to the great social issues of prejudice and group conflict. Whatever distress his research subjects experienced was nothing in comparison with his own, and their relatively mild discomfort served an important purpose.

The laboratory analog of the real world began with Lewin, and the use of deception in the laboratory was a practical necessity, not a problem. The students who helped to create these situations passed the Lewinian style on to the next generation of social psychologists. Lewin and his students formed a distinct group, and the characteristics of that group help to explain how Lewin made such a profound impact on social psychology.

First, there was Lewin himself, as person and leader. Marrow's (1969) biography contains numerous statements concerning Lewin's personal style. "He was extraordinarily expressive: this was part of his charm, the reason he stirred people so much. . . . [Donald MacKinnon said] '. . . he was an original—an exciting psychologist and a dynamic person to work with'" (p. 51). Lewin interacted with his students in a highly democratic way. "'The autocratic way he insisted on democracy was a little spectacular,' [Robert] Sears has observed. 'There was nothing to criticize - but one could not help noticing the fire and the emphasis'" (p. 127). Lewin did not dominate the group, but clearly he influenced it.

> Erik Wright recollects that 'none of the group ever felt that he was on stage when he spoke. He was among his peers, sharpening his ideas on their criticisms of his experimental procedures or recruiting assistants for some phase of a project. How Lewin kept the talk moving constructively without seeming to direct it at all has stuck in the minds of many of us.' (pp. 88–89)

John French said that Lewin's "relationships with his students could be intimate without becoming crippling; they retained their independence of mind while realizing their fullest potential" (p. 90). Dorwin Cartwright said, "it is clear that Lewin was the ultimate source of all this stimulation, but his influence was exerted in large measure through the interacting social system that had grown up around him. His ideas dominated this microculture, but he was never domineering" (p. 90). "'If he had an idea and a student had a different one, Lewin would talk about his and the student could talk about his own. We felt that we were operating as equals'" (Alex Bavelas, p. 104).

Lewin not only permitted and accepted the independent views of students, he also created a climate that encouraged their free expression. That did not prevent him from forcefully stating his own views. [He] "'was so strongly involved in what he was doing that he couldn't help being evangelical'" said Roger Barker. "'He was not always objective, except that he was determined to search for truth'" (p. 102). According to Jerome Frank, "'he was intensely ambitious. Confident of the importance of his own ideas, he accepted the contributions of others but had a way of melting them into his point of view'" (p. 114). So this democratic leader also provided a distinct model for the development of strongly held, but empirically based, theoretical beliefs.

Lewin worked with groups of students at two places in the United States, one group at Iowa and the other at MIT. There was some overlap between the groups; for example, Leon Festinger went from Iowa to MIT with Lewin. In both places, however, the students were self-selected and shared some common characteristics. First, they were independent thinkers. Many could have attended established graduate programs but instead selected the Child Welfare Research Station (Iowa) or the Research Center for Group Dynamics (MIT). They were interested in Lewin's blend of theory, research, and application. Robert Krauss called them, "hard-headed idealists" (Patnoe, 1988, p. 13).

Most of Lewin's group were older and had more experience than the typical graduate student, which may have helped them to maintain their independence in the system. Almost all of the students were men (except Beatrice Wright and Marilyn Radke Yarrow), whereas the Berlin group had been mostly women. That gender imbalance was not unusual for graduate programs in the United States at that time.

The group had a common and important goal: the application of psychological research to significant social problems. There was some tension in the group concerning the relative emphasis on basic research and application (Patnoe, 1988, p. 19), but Lewin was able to manage this and move the group forward. All students learned the Lewinian language of field theory. "'It was a kind of enforced discipline that got imposed on us to think of everything in that language and to become fluent in it'" (Thibaut, in Patnoe, p. 50).

There also was a belief that the group was special because it was at the forefront of research in psychology.

In addition to the common language they learned, there was also a sense of excitement and urgency. There was a feeling of being on the cutting edge. '. . . [I]t was partly a conveying to us of the imminence of big discovery. We thought we were always on the verge of a frontier. We were the avant guard of what would be the future of social psychology and it was that kind of conviction and excitement.'" (Thibaut, quoted by Patnoe, p. 51)

This sense of being special was enhanced by being an in-group on the outside of the establishment. Lewin was at Iowa while Kenneth Spence was there as the leading representative of the Hullian behaviorism that was one of the major forces in American experimental psychology. At MIT he was in Harvard's back yard and in the neighborhood of Yale and Brown, institutions where psychologists generally were interested in other problems, primarily in the areas of learning and sensory perception.

These were the ingredients of Lewin's influence: a charismatic, democratic leader; independent, creative students; a shared belief in the importance of their purpose and special place in the field of psychology. Although social psychology has taken a different direction (Cartwright, 1978), the extent of Lewin's influence is recognized widely. For the story being presented here, the greatest influence was the invention of dynamic laboratory situations for the study of social behavior. These illusions of reality often involved deception, which was used without being questioned.

A kind of mystique has developed around the memory of Kurt Lewin (Danziger, 1993). Homage is paid to his creative genius as an experimenter without considering his philosophy, which "was either ignored or else met with total incomprehension" (Danziger, 1993, p. 27). A few of Lewin's students tried to continue his approach, but most went in a direction more consistent with mainstream American psychology. His legacy is not in the theory or method of social psychology, but in the spirit of social action that is an important part of this field.

In the 1950s Leon Festinger would become the next major figure in American social psychology and the person who may have done the most to stimulate the use of deception in the laboratory. As a student of Lewin he provides continuity to this history. Before discussing his work, however, two other contributions must be described. First, the work of psychologists in military service during World War II, and, second, the research of Solomon Asch, another psychologist who was outside the mainstream of psychology.

personality

—5—

Military Deception

War dominates a culture like nothing else. Some people are well off during an economic depression, natural disasters occur in limited areas, but all people are affected when their country is at war. Like everyone else in the United States, psychologists were deeply involved in World War II and the discipline of psychology was changed by their experiences.

> Never in its relatively short history has the field experienced such rapid growth and development. As a result of the pressures created by the war for the solution of hundreds of social problems social psychologists found themselves drawn into wartime activities that called for the sharpening of research tools recently designed and for the invention of new tools previously unimagined. (Cartwright, 1948, p. 333)

Many eminent (and those who would become eminent) psychologists of the time entered military service as officers, and others, including Kurt Lewin, consulted with the military as civilians. Those who remained in universities often were given greatly increased teaching loads. Herbert Simon, who would later become a Nobel laureate, was not accepted for military service because of his color blindness. He and his colleagues at Illinois Institute of Technology had teaching loads of fifteen to eighteen hours a week (Simon, 1991, p. 94).

Most psychologists who went to war were involved in research and selection. Research topics included influencing civilian morale (bolstering us and discouraging them), analyzing international relations, determining domestic attitudes and needs, and studying the psychological problems of a wartime economy (Cartwright, 1948). One research project, which Dorwin Cartwright (1948) considered "a milestone in the history of social psychology" because of its "excellent research design" (p. 341), evaluated the effect of strategic bombing on the will to resist in Germany and Japan.

Psychologists developed new techniques for public opinion surveys, attitude scaling, and individual testing. Among the latter was a test "developed in the War Department for the detection of incipient army criminals. . . . [A] Biographical Case History sheet indicated the likelihood of . . . becoming a moral casualty while in the service" (Cartwright, 1948, p. 342).

Cartwright's review of social psychologists' activities during World War II showed that their work produced results that directly affected government policy. For example, studies of the determinants of spending and saving were used to devise programs to combat inflation. Studies of absenteeism supported the need for improved community facilities and led to the rejection of a program that would have publicly identified malingering workers. Cartwright concluded that, "compared to the period before the war, . . . the involvement of social psychologists in practical problems of social management is now high" (p. 348).

Assessment of Men

Most psychologists conducted their studies using paper and pencil tests and surveys. There was no time to carry out controlled laboratory experiments when working for the military services. One military unit did, however, make extensive use of situational tasks for selection purposes. That was the Office of Strategic Services (OSS), which was charged with conducting espionage activities, and later would evolve into the Central Intelligence Agency (CIA). Psychologists working for the OSS played an important part in designing and using tests for the selection of men who would become spies and saboteurs. Some of these tests involved deception.

The OSS began as the Office of the Coordinator of Information before the war in July 1941. The change in name took place on June 13, 1942, and the office was placed under the Joint Chiefs of Staff. The tasks of the office were to collect and analyze strategic information, and to plan and operate special services (Lowenthal, 1978). The OSS was organized into various branches to carry out its tasks. These branches included research and analysis (R&A), secret intelligence (SI), special operations (SO), counter-intelligence (X-2), morale operations, and schools and training. The latter branch included the assessment staff, composed mainly of psychologists.

There was a status hierarchy among the sections that was related to the degree of physical risk involved in their work.

Inside the OSS R&A could not compete for prestige against SI or SO. . . . Above all, there was X-2 . . . covering counter-intelligence; these were the tough, silent jobs that made strong men quake. In an atmosphere of male bonding, SI and X-2 were the coaches, the clever men, the quarterbacks, while SO housed the rest of the jocks. R&A gave refuge to the weenies and wimps, the glassy-eyed students on the campus who came out to cheer the team on and who burrowed in the libraries. . . . (Winks, 1987, p. 61)

The Schools and Training branch also was part of the cheering section.

All the branches relied heavily on university faculty for staffing. But not just any university faculty. Most of the upperlevel staff came from the elite eastern private universities, with Yale University having more than its share of OSS leaders (Winks, 1987).[1]

[T]here [was] a need for far-ranging individualists who truly believe that solutions to problems can be found, who believe that environmental constraints help make problem solving interesting, being part of the puzzle, not simply encumbrances to be cursed. A university community is a political environment; so is an intelligence community. Neither is based on equity. No wonder that there would be in the early years of the OSS, such an affinity with the university community. . . . (Winks, p. 25)

Economics, history, and political science were the academic disciplines from which most of the OSS positions were filled. The one group dominated by psychologists was the Assessment Staff in the Schools and Training Branch. Their work is described in the book, *Assessment of Men: Selection of Personnel for the Office of Strategic Services* (The OSS Assessment Staff, hereafter, Staff, 1948). "The undertaking [was] reported because it represents the first attempt in America to design and carry out selection procedures in conformity with so-called *organismic* (Gestalt) principles" (p. 3). This indicates some link with the Lewinian perspective, and with Lewin himself, a relationship that I will discuss later.

The Assessment Staff was a diverse group that included psychiatrists and anthropologists, as well as psychologists with various interests.[2] They were able to subordinate their differences in experience and theoretical preference to concentrate on a single purpose—"to eliminate the unfit" (p. 9). There was agreement among the staff on the need for realistic selection tasks:

since most of the critical situations which were confronting the majority of OSS men in the field were both novel and stressful, we made our testing situations novel and stressful. Thus it may be said that the situational tests used at OSS assessment stations were as lifelike as circumstances permitted, incorporating some of the major components of situations that would naturally arise in the course of operations in the field. (p. 42)

The candidates for selection were treated in ways that were similar to the way research participants later came to be treated in universities. There was a cover story made up by the staff (actually a series of stories), a series of tests that often involved the use of deception, and a final debriefing in which the true purpose was explained.

The instructions to the men were designed to give them an accurate picture of the purposes of the assessment without revealing the details necessary to ensure that all tasks would appear to be real. Thus, they were told that they were "being sent to the country to attend an assessment school for three days where [they] would be asked many questions and given a number of tests by a group of psychologists and psychiatrists" (p. 62). They also were "assured that those who had preceded [them] had almost invariably enjoyed it" (p. 62). That was stretching the truth more than a little. Each man was required to make up his own false cover story. "[H]e would not be known by his own name," and "[h]e was not to talk about himself or say or do anything that would reveal his true identity" (p. 62). His ability to maintain this cover was one of the tests. Each man at the assessment station was then interacting with others who were playing roles in situations that often were not what they appeared to be.

Some of the tests were stressful; others were frustrating. The candidates were worried about how they had performed and some were afraid that they had failed. To relieve this anxiety, the assessment staff talked with the men after each test.

> It was essential in the assessment of men for overseas assignments in time of war that we see them in stressful and upsetting situations. Yet it was clear that the success of the program depended on our ability to ensure their cooperation and their best efforts in all test situations. A special effort was therefore made to dispel the disturbing effects of certain procedures. We made it a principle, after each upsetting test, to provide an opportunity for catharsis by having the candidate talk the situation over with a member of the staff, who tried to help him get over his feelings of failure and restore his self-confidence. (p. 93)

Today psychologists would call this debriefing or desensitization, and would include an instruction like this one, which was given to the OSS candidates: "You will certainly want to talk about the various procedures with each other, but we have to ask you not to do so until you have all been through them" (p. 67).

Most of the assessment tasks did not involve deception, but were openly designed and presented as tests of candidates' ability to solve problems. The "construction task," however, was an elaborate deception. "Ostensibly this was a test of the candidate's ability to direct two helpers in building with him a frame structure out of simple wooden materials" (Staff, 1948, p. 102). It seemed to be a test of leadership but was really a test of emotional stability and frustration tolerance. The two helpers were really confederates of the assessment staff who assumed the names Kippy and Buster.

> Kippy acted in a passive, sluggish manner. He did nothing at all unless specifically ordered to, but stood around, often getting in the way, either idling with his hands in his pockets or concerned with some insignificant project of his own. . . . Buster, on the other hand, played a different role. He was aggressive, forward in offering impractical suggestions, ready to express dissatisfaction, and quick to criticize what he suspected were the candidate's weakest points. (p. 103)

Kippy and Buster were referred to as "stooges" (p. 111) in the staff report.

Apparently this task was quite realistic because the OSS report states that some men hit their assistants and "were so shaken by their experience . . . that they begged to be released from the assessment program and from OSS, if work in the organization required that one remain calm and in control of himself in such circumstances" (p. 112).

The debriefing took place in a "post-construction interview" that provided "an opportunity for emotional catharsis" (p. 112). Although this interview was "intended to be therapeutic" (p. 113), assessment continued. The candidates were asked what they thought of their experience. Some sensed that the helpers were role playing and the situation was testing something other than leadership. Others, "with quivering upper lips and trembling hands, nevertheless insisted that they had not been the least upset" (p. 113) by the task. In addition, "it was possible to make some estimate of how quickly the man could recover from disturbing experiences" (p. 113). Even "lunch provided the staff with an opportunity for an intuitive grasp of the nature of some candidates" (p. 121).

The tasks used by the OSS assessment staff varied in the extent to which they simulated conditions that successful candidates would likely face as spies and saboteurs. It is unlikely that a spy would ever have to supervise disruptive workers, but the purpose of the construction task was assessment of emotional stability, more than of leadership. A different situation also was a test of emotional stability, but was related to a situation that might occur in wartime. It involved a stressful interview under bright lights. Each man had a few minutes to make up a cover story and then had to face three interviewers who tried to get him to break his story.

The situation was "sufficiently stressful to arouse in some of our subjects crippling and incapacitating attacks of anxiety" (p. 137). Even the instructions could be stressful.

> [One man,] after reading the instructions, insisted that he could not go through with the test. A little later the director . . . found the candidate in his bedroom, sitting on the edge of his cot, sobbing. Upon reading the instructions he had imagined that on reporting to the basement he would be beaten by the staff, and he was overcome with fear that under this provocation he might commit some extreme act of violence. (p. 138)

Another interview was conducted after the stress interview, apparently for the purpose of relaxing the candidate and obtaining his opinion about the situation. In fact it was another attempt to get him to break his cover story. However the only time that explicit deception was used in relation to the stress interview was at the end of the day on which that test took place. The staff member who had been the interrogator would "tell the class some amusing incidents that had occurred during pervious Stress Interviews, some of them fictitious and some exaggerated, but all having for their purpose the amusement of the group" (pp. 145–146).

The justification was clear for producing strong emotions and using deception with this large group of men. It was necessary for the efficient conduct of the war. The OSS was interested in the savings gained by eliminating those unfit for duty, but the most important reason was the amount of harm prevented.

> It consists of the friction, the impairment of efficiency and morale, the injury to reputation of an organization that results from the actions of a man who is stupid, apathetic, sullen, resentful, arrogant, or insulting in his dealings with members of his own unit or of allied units, or with customers or citizens of foreign countries. To this must be added the irreparable damage that can be done by one who blabs. Diminution in the number of men of this stamp—sloths, irritants, bad actors, and free talkers—was one of the prime objectives of the assessment program. (p. 9)

The selection procedures were in the interest of the candidates as well. A man would be exposed to great danger and should have some sense of confidence that his performance would be likely to save his life. Not all military research was so clearly in the interest of the participants.

The OSS program taught psychologists that it is possible to design controlled situations that provide intimate views of human nature, situations that are difficult or impossible for the research subject to resist. Although Kurt Lewin was not directly involved, he was a consultant to the OSS Assessment Staff and his approach to research is evident. He often traveled from Iowa to Washington and "participated in many committees of social scientists, administrators, and military personnel working on a wide range of problems" that included "the relationship between psychological warfare, target setting, field operations, and evaluative reconnaissance" (Marrow, 1969, p. 156). However, Margaret Mead, who knew Lewin well, said that the OSS was certainly "congruent with the things which Kurt said, but I don't think he was influential in this particular operation" (Lewin papers, Akron Archives). She thought the OSS "was more a Murray thread," referring to Henry A. Murray, the founder of the Harvard Psychological Clinic and the first American to develop a comprehensive personality system. He is best known as the developer of the Thematic Apperception Test (TAT), in which people express their fantasies and motives through the stories they tell about ambiguous pictures.

The Director of the OSS assessment station near Washington was Donald MacKinnon, an associate of Murray's from the Harvard Clinic who had studied with Lewin in Berlin. But it was Henry Murray's approach to assessment of personality that was most evident in the techniques used by the OSS. At the Harvard clinic Murray had developed a comprehensive system for the psychological assessment of individuals that included a broad range of tests and interviews, the results of which were discussed in staff meetings called the Diagnostic Council. According to MacKinnon, Murray's "preeminence among the senior officers [of the OSS staff] was evident almost from the start" (Robinson, 1992, p. 281), and his approach to assessment was adapted to the selection problems of the OSS. Apparently Murray was disappointed by the results of the application of his methods because near the end of the OSS Assessment Staff report he admitted that there had been mistakes in selection and little evidence that these tests were worth the price. It was said at the time that "the government uses social science the way a drunk uses a lamp post, for support rather than light" (Alexander Leighton, quoted by Mabee, 1987, p. 10).

Stress and Deception in Military Research

The OSS assessment program introduced the armed services to stressful situational tasks that could be useful in selection and training. Psychologists have continued to work for the military in peacetime, as well as during wartime, by providing clinical and other professional services, and conducting research. Much of that research was classified as secret, but some has been published. This includes research done by psychologists working at military installations, employed by institutes that conduct research under contract with the military, and in universities where their research is supported by grants from military agencies. Some of the most extreme cases of stressful research deception have been supported this way.

Many of the unusual military applications of psychological research have been described in Peter Watson's book, *War on the Mind*, which is based primarily on government reports from the 1950s and 1960s. Among the more unusual studies reported by Watson are those on the use of witchcraft in a counter-insurgency campaign in the Congo and on cultural differences in the sense of smell. The latter was an attempt to find aversive odors that could be used in combat or terrorism. Watson also described an attempt to desensitize men to the observation of pain and suffering of others, in which a man had his head clamped in a vice, his eyelids propped open, and then was shown films in which people were mutilated. The purpose was to remove emotions that might interfere with killing by men who were being trained as assassins. The Pentagon denied this story but Watson claimed to have confirming evidence (Watson, 1978, p. 250).

Research that was both deceptive and extremely stressful was conducted for the Army at the Leadership Human Research Unit in Monterey, California (Berkun, et al., 1962). The problem studied was "degradation of behavior in combat" with the goal of developing training procedures that would reduce the severity of this problem. Deception was used here, as in other studies, to help make contrived situations appear to be real. The experimenters designed five "stressor situations" that were believable for most of the research participants.

The "Ditching" Situation

Men in their first eight weeks of Army Basic Training were taken to an airport "purportedly to participate in a study of the effects of altitude on psychomotor performance. One experimenter, supposedly conducting this study, and another experimenter disguised as a steward accompanied [them]" (p. 5). Each man was given a folder containing "emergency instructions," a life preserver, and a parachute harness. After take-off, at 5,000 feet, an emergency was simulated. The aircraft lurched, one propeller stopped, and other malfunctions were described over an intercom. "As the aircraft passed within sight of the airfield, [they] could see fire trucks and ambulances on the airstrip in apparent expectation of a crash landing" (p. 5).

In the midst of apparently preparing to ditch the plane in the nearby ocean, the "steward" administered questionnaires to the men "under the pretext that this would furnish proof to insurance companies that emergency precautions had been properly followed. These papers were supposedly to be put in a waterproof container and jettisoned before the aircraft came down on the ocean" (p. 5). The report states that only five of sixty-six men were not fooled by all of this.

Additional measures, including a urine sample, were taken after a safe landing at the airport. These measures supported "the conclusion that this situation was perceived as threatening by [subjects]" (p. 7). But the effects were not strong enough, so a "study was designed to further explore the experimental arousal of fear of death or injury to self" (p. 7).

Three Threats to Life and Limb

This study included three apparently life-threatening situations that differed only in the nature of the contrived cause of the threat. In each of the three situations the subjects of the research were new army recruits not yet in basic training. Each man was taken to an isolated place and left alone with a radio for communication. Cues then were provided that were designed to convince the man that his life was in danger or that he might be injured seriously. He could be rescued by reporting his location on the radio transmitter, but that equipment was designed to fail. His ability to repair the radio was one measure of "degradation of behavior in combat."

In one of the three situations a man "hears over his radio that an accident with radioactive material has resulted in dangerous fallout over his area. He is led to believe that the accident occurred during the exercise but is definitely not an intentional part of it" (p. 7). A second situation was "the same, except that the 'accident' was a forest fire surrounding [the] outpost" and the man was "enveloped in artificial smoke generated about 300 yards away" (p. 8). The third situation was the one that produced the strongest effects on the men.

> [A] series of explosions simulates a barrage of artillery shells coming in and bursting near S. These explosions substantiate reports which S hears on his radio to the effect that some artillery shells appear to be hitting outside the designated target area. The explosions constitute the most salient of the perceptual supports used in these three situations. (p. 8)

The same procedure introduced and followed each of the three stressor situations and contained a variety of deceptions. When the men boarded a bus to be transported to the military reservation, they "were informed by an officer that they were to be used to test new concepts of atomic-age warfare and that they would be called upon to perform individually rather than as units" (p. 8). Later, "a lecture was given on the purpose of the experiment as it was intended they should perceive it." The men were visited by "representatives of the Command Post, the fictitious headquarters of the military exercise and the actual operational headquarters of the experimenters" (p. 8). The equipment also was fictitious.

> The radio set (in fact, a basically simple two-way wired intercom) was overburdened with dials, lights, and knobs intended to camouflage the performance measures. All wires were hidden, and all sounds within 50 feet of the set were heard and recorded at the Command Post regardless of the activity of S. (p. 8)

> [A] tape recording . . . contained miscellaneous simulated, but apparently real, radio transmissions dealing with the military exercise. . . . All three Experimental groups were warned in identical messages, of the necessity for imminent evacuation. (p. 9)

All situations proved to be effective in producing stronger emotional arousal than the ditching situation. Two of the men in the artillery situation tried "to run away from their posts and were called back by the experimenter by means of a speaker concealed in the radio set" (p. 14). Apparently this was not a sufficient demonstration and a fifth situation was designed.

Demolitions

In this situation stress was produced not by threat of injury to oneself, but by making someone feel responsible for an injury to someone else. A trainee who "was ostensibly part of a work detail helping the experimenters set up a tactical training problem" (p. 23) was taken to a bunker in an isolated area of the military post. He was given these instructions:

> We're wiring in some explosives down in the canyon below, but we need a remote-control circuit up here. . . . All I want you to do is match these colored wires with the colored wires that are already on the screws, red to red, blue to blue, etc. When you get all the wires hooked up, then throw this switch so we can use the circuit. I'm going down below now and work on that end of it with the rest of the men. (pp. 23–24).

The trainee also was given a "rigged" radio for communication with other positions in the exercise.

The experimenter left the man to do his wiring. When he threw the switch it "set off a 5-pound charge of TNT down in the canyon. The explosion rocked the bunker, sometimes shaking things off shelves" (p. 24). He then heard a voice over his radio:

Upstairs, can you hear me? Listen, if you can hear me, we had an explosion down here and I think someone was hurt. I want you to stay right there. Listen, if you can hear me, wait right there and don't touch anything. Listen, are you sure you did that wiring right? (p. 24)

Shortly after that he heard that a man had been badly hurt and he was to call for help. As in the other exercises the radio would not work and had to be fixed. This again was one of the performance measures.

While working on the radio, the trainee heard other prerecorded messages concerning "the difficulty of keeping the injured man alive, a reference to the fact that the Military Police will want to question the S, and a final message that someone is on the way up to question him" (p. 24). The entire test lasted 45 minutes from the time of the explosion. During that time a "senior experimenter" was hidden nearby, "monitoring all sounds from the S's post, ready to intervene in case of a severe emotional reaction," (p. 24) which never happened. "After leaving the bunker, the S spent at least an hour with a senior, clinically trained psychologist going over his complete reaction to the situation and having his questions answered candidly." In addition, "each S returned for a second interview 1 week later to establish that there was no residual effect" (p. 24). No such effects were reported.

The interviews showed the effectiveness of this situation. Trainees typically were startled by the explosion and felt they had done something wrong. They tried to reassure themselves in various ways; for example, reliance on authority ("they wouldn't have you do something that wasn't safe") or denial of responsibility ("I did just as he told me"). These defensive thoughts weakened as time went on and the men "described themselves as having felt 'scared,' 'shaking,' nervous,' 'worried,' and as having been plagued with feelings of being somehow responsible for the man's injuries" (p. 27). They also experienced confusion and feelings of inadequacy when trying to perform their repair task.

Most [subjects] reported difficulty in concentrating on and deriving meaning from the instructions. They reported having to read and reread the instructions while being bothered by thoughts of the condition of the injured man, the necessity for hurrying, fears of being unable to repair the set, concern over their personal responsibility for the accident, and the consequences of having this on their consciences or, in a few cases, the punishment that would be awaiting them. (p. 28)

The test situation ended when the experimenter entered the bunker and handed the trainee a clipboard holding a fifteen-word "subjective self-report," a list of words to describe feelings ranging from "wonderful" to "scared stiff." In spite of showing signs of extreme tension and concern for the supposedly injured man, the trainees "accepted the . . . clipboard, appeared to quickly scan the list of 15 words, circle one, and handed the clipboard back without any apparent break in their preoccupation concerning fixing the telephone and getting help" (p. 29).

At this point about one-fourth of the men realized that they were part of an experiment. Most others caught on when asked to complete a digit span test, but a few continued in the "same uncomprehending manner." This was clearly a powerful situation; the men were so convinced of its reality that even tasks that should have appeared absurd were thoughtlessly accepted.

I have described these experiments in some detail not because they were carried out by military personnel, but because they contain elements of control of research participants that are present in all psychological research that uses deception. Some of these elements are controlling factors in all research with human participants. One important factor is the position of authority of the experimenter. For example, one might question whether young Army trainees would confess to having long-term negative emotional effects from participation in this experiment. However, the authority imposed by the military is not different in principle from authority imposed by university faculty who require students to participate in research.

Military Medicine

Considerable stress and anxiety have been produced in psychological research with and without deception. One's judgment of the severity of these effects may lessen when the work of psychologists is compared with that of the medical personnel who worked for the military services. Psychology does not deal directly with issues of life and death; medicine does. That is an important distinction that underlies ethical issues in research using human participants. The stressor situations described in this chapter are about as close as psychologists have come to threatening human life.[3] Contrasting psychological stress with the stress produced in medical research adds perspective to our concerns about deception.

In a comment on the history of life-threatening medical research, David Rothman (1987) described World War II as a "turning point in human experimentation in the United States."

For the first time, clinical investigations became well-coordinated, extensive, and centrally funded team efforts; experiments were now frequently designed to benefit not the research subjects but others—namely, soldiers vulnerable to the disease in question. And this transformation occurred just when wartime conditions were undercutting a sensitivity to the need to obtain the consent of subjects or to respect their rights. (pp. 1196–1197)

The same situation held for psychology, although on a much smaller scale.

The major funding source for such experiments was the Committee on Medical Research, which provided about $25 million in research contracts. "Its chief concerns were to create antidotes to dysentery, influenza, venereal diseases, and malaria, which would require extensive trials with human subjects." It was difficult to find volunteers for this research, so "researchers with links to custodial institutions had an edge in securing grants" (p. 1197). These are three examples provided by Rothman (p. 1197) of the medical research that was conducted:

Children at the Ohio Soldiers and Sailors Orphanage were injected with varieties of dysentery bacteria. Five experiments all were unsuccessful and produced severe side effects including 105° F temperature, severe headache and backache, nausea, vomiting, and diarrhea. This research also used retarded residents of a Dixon, Illinois, institution and at the New Jersey State Colony for the Feeble-Minded.

At the Manteno Illinois State Hospital, back ward psychotic patients "were injected with malaria through blood transfusions and then given antimalarial therapies." The researchers relied more on the use of prisoners. "One floor of the prison hospital at the Statesville, Illinois, penitentiary was turned over to the University of Chicago for research on malaria, with some 500 inmates *volunteering*" (italics mine). The side effects were severe.

A team in Philadelphia tested influenza vaccines "by administering the vaccine to several hundred residents at the nearby state facility for the retarded . . . and at a correctional center for young offenders and then, three or six months later, challenging them with influenza." Control groups received the virus, but not the vaccine.

One justification for conducting this kind of research used an analogy with military service.

A wartime environment also undercut the protection of human subjects, because of the power of the example of the draft. Every day thousands of men were compelled to risk death, however limited their understanding of the aims of the war or the immediate campaign might be. By extension, researchers doing laboratory work were also engaged in a military activity, and they did not need to seek the permission of their subjects any more than the selective service or field commanders did of draftees. (p. 1198)

The research also was justified by ideas about appropriate wartime sacrifices on the home front. Everyone should be doing their part, even the retarded, the insane, and prisoners. Rothman (p. 1197) quoted *The New York Times* as an example of this attitude. "The public response was not to ask whether prisoners were able to give voluntary consent, but to congratulate 'these one-time enemies to society' for demonstrating 'to the fullest extent just how completely this is everybody's war.'"

Life-threatening medical research continued after the war. In an article that is a classic in research ethics, Henry Beecher (1966) described twenty-two cases in which patients' lives had been endangered in research without informing them of the risks or obtaining their consent. Beecher's cases had been published between 1950 and 1965 (Rothman, 1987).

The work that psychologists do for the military is similar to that which they do as civilians. Clinical psychologists help military personnel with problems such as depression and drug abuse. Educational psychologists design training manuals. Experimental psychologists work on problem-solving techniques and help to design instruments using their knowledge of sensory perception. Social psychologists are concerned with topics such as group dynamics and attitude change. At times in the past, however, military psychologists, unlike their civilian colleagues, conducted experiments that involved severe physical and psychological stress. They did this in the interest of national security, justified in ways that were similar to the reasons invoked during World War II. We may never know all that was done and then classified as secret.

—6—

A Voice of Independence

Imagine your dismay on being confronted by a group of people who all tell you something that clearly is counter to the evidence provided by your senses. Imagine as well the creativity required to design a situation that would provide a laboratory test of the ability to resist that kind of group pressure. Solomon Asch's studies of independence and conformity are among the most significant in the history of psychology. They are models of rigorous analysis of a socially relevant question based on a well-controlled research design. They also are important for the history of deception because of Asch's extensive use of confederates; in one of Asch's experiments (Asch, 1955), a single naive subject encountered fifteen actors.

In this chapter I will focus on these studies of group pressure. Most textbooks refer to this research as Asch's conformity studies. However, in his writing and in my interview with Asch, it is clear that his interest was in the ability of people to remain independent in the face of strong group pressure, and in fact his results show that most people did resist that pressure. It is important to note that Solomon Asch made important contributions in other areas of social psychology and in perception, and that his ideas constitute an enduring legacy that is insufficiently recognized (Rock, 1990). Before presenting the details of Asch's research I will provide some background on his life and thought.

Solomon Asch was born in 1907, in Warsaw, Poland, and grew up in the neighboring town of Lowicz, which he described as "a small religious environment where the relation of people to the forces around them was very near and strong. In that setting man is very important, not just to himself, he's important in the scheme of things, and this feeds an interest in human nature" (Ceraso, Gruber, & Rock, 1990, p. 3).[1] His family migrated to the United States in 1920 and he spent his adolescent years among immigrants on New York's Lower East Side.

Asch attended the City College of New York, where he majored in literature and science and encountered psychology. "Toward the end of my undergraduate days, I heard there was a science called psychology, and I assumed—wrongly—that its concerns coincided with mine. So you might almost say that I came into psychology by mistake" (Ceraso, et al., p. 4). His view of psychology came from literature and philosophers, including William James; it was not the behaviorist view that had become popular at the time. Nevertheless, he went to Columbia University for graduate school and studied with some of the leaders of American psychology, doing quantitative studies of learning. He received his doctoral degree in 1932. His first faculty appointment in 1932 was at Brooklyn College where later he began his group-pressure research in the early 1940s.

Although Asch did his graduate work in one of the leading quantitative-behavioral institutions of the day, his major intellectual influence came from Gestalt psychology in the person of Max Wertheimer. Asch had been exposed to Gestalt ideas at Columbia and must have been excited by them, because when he read that Wertheimer was coming to New York, he sought him out. "He represented to me a kind of ideal of what a psychologist should be. For the first time I was meeting a man whose range of interest and whose concern with human questions was what psychology needed" (Ceraso, et al., p. 7). Although Kurt Lewin had a closer link to the founders of Gestalt psychology (he was with them on the faculty at Berlin), his thinking took a different direction, and it was Asch who brought the Gestalt spirit to social psychology.

The heart of Gestalt thinking is the statement that the whole is different from the sum of its parts, an idea that was in conflict with the experimental practice of dividing behavior into specific variables that could be manipulated and analyzed. For Asch, "a human psychology necessarily had to be social psychology," and any "account of human experience would of necessity be cognitive" (Asch, 1952/1987, p. ix). This emphasis on thinking did not conform with the behaviorism that prevailed in the 1940s. The Gestalt approach was "to portray human beings as a whole, not as a collection of mechanisms or facts" (p. ix). In opposition to what he saw as "a drift toward the trivialization of human possibilities, indeed of human existence," Asch did not underestimate human intellectual capacity and potential, but held the belief "that under certain conditions people are capable of acting reasonably" (p. ix). These hardly seem radical views, but his place in psychology at the time is indicated by a reviewer of his 1952 textbook, *Social Psychology*, who said, "there is no doubt that Asch is a deviant" (quoted by Asch, 1952/1987, p. x). His research on group pressure grew out of his humanistic belief that people have the strength to act reasonably.

Group Pressure: Independence and Conformity

The idea for these studies came at a time when events in Europe must have challenged Asch's belief in human rationality. The research began at

Brooklyn College in the early 1940s with "informal exploratory studies done to establish whether the planned situation would be feasible."[2] The general question that concerned Asch was, how, and to what extent, do social forces constrain people's opinions and attitudes? His exploratory research led to the development of a situation that was used in an extensive series of studies (Asch, 1955):

> A group of seven to nine young men, all college students, are assembled in a classroom for a 'psychological experiment' in visual judgment. The experimenter informs them that they will be comparing the lengths of lines. He shows two large white cards. On one is a single vertical black line—the standard whose length is to be matched. On the other card are three vertical lines of various lengths. The subjects are to choose the one that is of the same length; the other two are substantially different, the difference ranging from three quarters of an inch to an inch and three quarters.
>
> The experiment opens uneventfully. The subjects announce their answers in the order in which they have been seated in the room, and on the first round every person chooses the same matching line. Then a second set of cards is exposed; again the group is unanimous. The members appear ready to endure politely another boring experiment. On the third trial there is an unexpected disturbance. One person near the end of the group disagrees with all the others in his selection of the matching line. He looks surprised, indeed incredulous, about the disagreement. On the following trial he disagrees again, while the others remain unanimous in their choice. The dissenter becomes more and more worried and hesitant as the disagreement continues in succeeding trials; he may pause before announcing his answer and speak in a low voice, or he may smile in an embarrassed way.
>
> What the dissenter does not know is that all the other members of the group were instructed by the experimenter beforehand to give incorrect answers in unanimity at certain points. The single individual who is not a party to this prearrangement is the focal subject of our experiment. He is placed in a position in which, while he is actually giving the correct answers, he finds himself unexpectedly in a minority of one, opposed by a unanimous and arbitrary majority with respect to a clear and simple fact. . . .
>
> The instructed majority occasionally reports correctly in order to reduce the possibility that the naive subject will suspect collusion

against him. (In only a few cases did the subject actually show suspicion; when this happened, the experiment was stopped and the results were not counted.) There are 18 trials in each series, and on 12 of these the majority responds erroneously. (p. 4)

Although this was the first research to use several confederates, it did not require the extensive rehearsal that was necessary in Festinger's research (see chapter 7), and perhaps in Lewin's as well.

The instructed majority consisted of male college students who had volunteered for the purpose. During a training session the general purport of the experiment and their role in it was explained. The majority was instructed to announce the judgments clearly and firmly, but not to take issue with the critical subject. They were also advised not to look directly at him and to refrain from feigning surprise at his answers. . . . [T]he situation did not call for histrionic talents or any elaborateness of action. (Asch, 1956, pp. 3–4)

The experimenter's role was that of "impartial chairman" (p. 8) who showed his awareness of disagreement, but not surprise. He presented the stimuli and recorded the answers in a matter-of-fact way, while discouraging discussion and other interruptions.

The results showed that most people resisted group pressure and responded independently. For example, in one study that is frequently cited (Asch 1956, p. 10), about 63% of responses by all subjects were correct and independent of the majority. Although most subjects went along with the majority at least once out of twelve opportunities, only 5% always conformed; on the other hand, 24% never conformed. Asch expected that most people would not conform, but he was surprised at the number who did.

I will not describe all of the many variations of this study that Asch has published, but will provide some examples to indicate the depth with which he pursued this problem. He found that increasing the number of opponents beyond three had little effect on conformity; the percent of incorrect responses was about the same (31%) when there were either 3 or 15 opponents (Asch, 1955). When one of the confederates gave a correct response, thus providing an ally for the real subject, conformity was reduced greatly (Asch 1955). In the major report on the group pressure studies (Asch, 1956), Asch presented nine experimental variations on his basic situation. Asch had made his point and had stimulated other investigators to study the finer details of the effects of group pressure.

The group pressure situation had a strong impact on most research participants. Henry Gleitman,[3] who was one of Asch's research associates, said the postexperimental interview lasted thirty to sixty minutes. "Their response was often very dramatic when you told them [that] it was a lie. . . . There was certainly some emotion, in some cases some crying."[4] All of the subjects that Gleitman remembered interviewing said the experiment was interesting and that they learned something about themselves. Asch (1956) presented many quotations to indicate how subjects thought and felt about the pressure that they experienced. These reports show Asch's phenomenological orientation; he was more concerned with the quality of the experience than the quantity of responses. This form of analysis allowed Asch to conclude:

> Our observations suggest that independence requires the capacity to accept the fact of opposition without a lowered sense of personal worth. . . . The compliant person cannot face this ordeal because he translates social opposition into a reflection of his personal worth. Because he does so the social conflict plunges him into pervasive and incapacitating doubt. (Asch, 1956, pp. 51–52)

Typically, when the majority chose the incorrect line, the "first reaction was one of puzzlement" (Asch, 1956, p. 27), followed by silent attempts by subjects to explain the situation to themselves. As disagreements continued, subjects, including most of those who remained independent, began to doubt themselves and experienced a considerable amount of tension. Some would not even look at the lines and others cleverly reinterpreted the directions by saying, for example, that they thought they were supposed to judge the *width* of the lines.[5] Many began to "fear that they were suffering from some defect" (Asch, 1956, p. 31), such as poor vision or inability to understand the instructions. Others feared the disapproval of the group and "many stressed the sense of loneliness at being separated from others" (p. 31). There were also reports of guilt related to concern that the participant had spoiled the results of the experiment. An unusual, chilling statement came from a subject who "expressed the view that 'the duty of a government is to do the will of the majority, even if you are convinced they are wrong'" (p. 46).

Even the experimenters were affected by the situation. Henry Gleitman described the embarrassment that he felt when subjects conformed under conditions where the correct answer was most obvious. "You are ashamed for them and I have the sense of embarrassment I have when I see an actor who blows his lines. I want to sink through the floor with him."[6]

Asch was quite concerned with the degree of tension that he created "but was confident that it was well within the tolerance of" the students who participated in his research.[7] He thought the tension would only be temporary because, the experimental episode arose too suddenly and lasted too briefly to arouse the sinister fear that the incomprehensible disagreement would accompany them through life. The subjects knew that they were in an experiment, and retained a healthy confidence that soon they would be back in the familiar world out of which they had been jolted. (Asch, 1956, p. 67)

It was at about this time that the ethics of research was just beginning to be discussed by psychologists. The first statement of the ethical principles of psychologists, including a section on research, was published in 1953 (American Psychological Association, 1953). Asch wrote that the group pressure experiments "can be justified on the ground of their potential scientific value provided the investigator treats the subject with respect, and succeeds in conveying to him that he is making a contribution. In such matters one can only rely on the sensitiveness and human feeling of the experimenter" (1956, p. 1). Asch's own sensitivity was expressed in his discussion of the ethics of his research, which could have served as a model for the ethical reasoning used by later social psychologists to justify their use of deception.

In addition to believing that his participants had the emotional strength to tolerate the group pressure, Asch had evidence that most of them learned something important: "[T]he greater number of subjects felt that they had taken part in an experiment with a bearing on serious human questions. . . . They found it illuminating to consider their earlier doubts, temptations, and surrenders in the light of the subsequent disclosure of the actual state of affairs" (1956, p. 52). Some who remained independent were encouraged by their ability to meet the challenge; some who yielded learned "to show more respect for the feelings of resistance and the struggle for independence." Others, however, "slurred over the significance of the situation and refused to think about it" (1956, p. 53).

Although there were indications of extreme tension for many participants, Asch said that "there were no harmful effects." This conclusion did not resolve the ethical issue for Asch:

Nevertheless the involuntary participation, the fact that the subject was, without his knowledge or consent, placed in a situation in which he revealed himself (without the other participants revealing themselves in turn) remains a problem. . . .

[These] circumstances place a special responsibility on the experimenter and obligate him to surround the procedure with proper safeguards. It has been the writer's experience that far more important than the momentary pain or discomfort of the procedure is the way in which the experimenter deals with the subject. When subjects grasp the aim, when they see that the experimenter respects their feelings and that he depends upon them for help in clarifying what has happened, they become for the time being collaborators and cease to regard the problem from an entirely personal standpoint. (p. 53)

No other psychologist had expressed such clear concern for the feelings of research participants, nor had anyone explicitly stated an ethical justification for using deception in research.

Deceptive research also is justified on the basis of benefits to society. Asch thought that his work was an important contribution to our understanding of social life, although he did not present this conclusion in the context of his discussion of ethics:

Life in society requires consensus as an indispensable condition. But consensus, to be productive, requires that each individual contribute independently out of his experience and insight. When consensus comes under the dominance of conformity, the social process is polluted and the individual at the same time surrenders the powers on which his functioning as a feeling and thinking being depends. That we have found the tendency to conformity in our society so strong that reasonable intelligent and well-meaning young people are willing to call white black is a matter of concern. It raises questions about our ways of education and about the values that guide our conduct. (Asch, 1955, p. 6)

This significant series of studies stimulated a large amount of further research on conformity and dissent. One of the first modifications in the Asch procedure was to make it more efficient, so that an experimenter would not have to hire several students to be confederates (Brown, 1986, p. 39). In this modified situation, subjects did not work face to face, but in individual booths isolated from other subjects. Lines were projected on a screen and choices were made by pressing one of three buttons to indicate the correct line. Subjects saw what they were told were the responses of other subjects, but which in fact were controlled by the experimenter, who was able to confront several people at once with a unanimous majority giving incorrect judgments. Some experimenters continued to rely on face to face situations but used only three confederates, because Asch had shown that there was not much of an increase in conformity with larger numbers of confederates.

Donald Campbell (1990) provided a new perspective on this research that is in the spirit of Asch's view of human nature and also is relevant to understanding the effectiveness of deception. Asch believed that people were rational and acted reasonably in his experiments. Campbell said, "It is reasonable and required that we believe and use the reports of others. 'Trust' is a better term for what is observed in these experiments than is 'conformity'" (p. 41).

Although he has a highly favorable opinion of Asch and his research, Campbell thinks less well of much of the subsequent work in this area.

> Conformity experiments deliberately break the normally existing rational grounds for trust and self-respect by drastic experimental artificiality. Through deception they create a setting in which trust is *locally* unjustified. . . . Most of the hundreds of existing conformity studies have been done by researchers who are themselves very conformant to the current fads in their discipline. Along with this, they have implicitly created a deprecating social distance between themselves and those fellow human beings whom they have duped into 'conforming.' (p. 41)

Why isn't Asch included with this group of cynical, manipulative researchers? Campbell does not say, but I think there are two reasons for placing Asch in a superior position. First, he initiated this line of research to test his theory of human rationality; he expected dissent and in fact most people were independent most of the time.[8] He conducted research until he gained a reasonably complete understanding of the problem. Others who continued the research manipulated details that made little difference in advancing our knowledge of this phenomenon.

The second reason for viewing Asch more favorably concerns (to use Campbell's phrase) his epistemological moral imperatives; that is, what we should and should not do to gain knowledge. Based primarily on his reading of Asch's social psychology textbook (Asch, 1952/1987), Campbell derived three moral norms related to how (not necessarily what) we learn in social situations:

> *Trust*: It is our duty to respect the reports of others and be willing to base our beliefs and actions on them.
>
> *Honesty*: It is our duty to report what we perceive honestly, so that others may use our observations in coming to valid beliefs.
>
> *Self respect*: It is our duty to respect our own perceptions and beliefs, seeking to integrate them with the reports of others without deprecating them or ourselves. (Campbell, 1990, p. 39)

It is this moral, rational view of human nature, as well as his originality, that sets Asch apart from most other researchers. He assumed that people will do both what is right and what is reasonable in their interactions with others. Of course, not everyone does this and the fact that Asch was disappointed with his results supports Campbell's analysis.

An Independent Voice

Solomon Asch holds a unique position in the history of social psychology. His fame comes from one portion of his work, which textbook authors generally misrepresent as conformity research (Friend, Rafferty, & Bramel, 1990). His significant influence on psychology, however, is the result of the enduring power of his ideas. Henry Gleitman, Asch's colleague at Swarthmore College around 1950, described Asch as "insulated" meaning that he was independent both theoretically and in terms of academic social networks.[9] He was not an academic politician. He did not like attending conventions, was not elected to offices in professional organizations, and, although he had students who became important figures in American psychology (Rock, 1990), he was not a dominant leader as Leon Festinger was. There are no stories of Asch's authority in his laboratory, and he had no regular weekly meetings to socialize his followers. He did not give a label to his theoretical position, as Festinger did with cognitive dissonance, which would have made it easier to promote and attack. The general ideas of Gestalt psychology were sufficient for Asch. He continued to be concerned with the phenomonology of human experience, and that was not in the mainstream of the dominant cognitive-behaviorist social psychology.

He also was not part of the Lewin tradition and that academic network. He knew Kurt Lewin and admired his work, but they did not meet often.[10] Gleitman doubted that Lewin had much of an effect on Asch, because Asch followed Wertheimer's Gestalt ideas and interest in thinking.[11]

A contrast between the ideas of Asch and Leon Festinger can be seen in Asch's review of Festinger's book, *A Theory of Cognitive Dissonance*.

[I]t constructs a model and operationally defined derivations ready for immediate test. There is a brisk clarity about it; it seems to shun obscurity automatically. Yet a vital ingredient is missing. It does not find a place for the description of phenomena, of what the investigator has seen with his own eyes. There is not a report in this book of what some *one* individual did or said. The empirical studies are not occasions for observation; their sole function is to speak the monosyllabic language of levels of confidence [i.e., statistics]. (Asch, 1958, p. 194)

Asch might have added that in Festinger's book there also was no indication of a concern for the ethical issue of the use of deception, an issue that did concern Asch.

Do not think that Asch was a recluse. He held positions at Rutgers and Princeton, where he did research and taught. He had close social relationships with other psychologists, including Fritz Heider (Heider, 1983), a man who had a great influence on modern theory in social psychology. These were people who shared Asch's values and interests, which did not include networking for personal or ideological advancement. But as Henry Gleitman said so well, "Asch was by himself. He never had to face the criticism of the world."[12] This image conveys the impression of Solomon Asch as a person of quiet, not strident, independence, and of one who is disappointed with the view of human nature present in much of the psychology of his time. He is honest first to himself, although aware that in the past some social psychologists either did not agree with him or ignored him. Gleitman concluded that Asch is, "now recognized as one of the best there ever was in social psychology, perhaps the best."[13] Solomon E. Asch died February 20, 1996.

Asch's studies of independence and conformity made extensive use of confederates to deceive research participants at a time when the use of deception was much less common than it would later become. It is difficult to trace the source of the research design. How did Asch get the idea for using a group of role-playing students who would lie about their responses in an attempt to influence other students?

One possible source comes from Asch's academic life. During the 1930s he was a colleague of Max Hertzman at Brooklyn College. Hertzman was interested in Lewin's ideas, an interest that he would pass on to Leon Festinger. These ideas, of course, included the design of realistic research situations that sometimes included deception by the experimenter. Some of Asch's early published research used mild forms of deception (e.g., Asch, 1940).

Asch also became interested in Muzafer Sherif's work on the psychology of social norms (Sherif, 1936/1966). Sherif studied the difference between individual and group judgments of the apparent movement of a point of light that actually was fixed in one position in a dark room (the autokinetic effect). A group of three people would develop a norm or consensus concerning the amount of apparent movement that was different from individual judgments. Asch was impressed by the use of an ambiguous situation to study group dynamics and agreed with Sherif's Gestalt interpretation. However, Sherif did not use confederates or deceive subjects in other ways.

There is no evidence that Asch's group pressure research was influenced directly by the major historical events that took place between 1940 and 1955. Asch was not part of the group of psychologists working with the Office of Strategic Services in World War II and said that he was not influenced by that group.[14] One could see the relevance of his research to the powerful pressure to take anticommunist positions during the early 1950s when Senator Joseph McCarthy was exerting his influence, but Asch never published his view of the Wisconsin Senator or the independent courage of those who refused to be intimidated by him.

It appears that in conducting the group pressure research over a period of at least ten years, Asch was not driven by a need to be relevant to contemporary social problems, but by his theoretical interests and the need to support his belief in individual rationality. He believed that people had the strength to resist unreasonable group opinions and to tolerate the embarrassment and other uncomfortable feelings produced by lone dissent. His concern was with the understanding of enduring truths about social life, not with immediate relevance, although his research had (and still has) potentially significant applications.

It makes sense that an independent thinker would study independence. And it makes sense that someone who respects people as rational beings would be sensitive to his research participants' discomfort with their irrationality. His use of deception (stating a false purpose and using many confederates) was essential for the effectiveness of his research, but he did not seem comfortable with it, and was not willing to tell me how he developed the design for the group pressure situation. The situations used by Lewin and Sheriff could have been suggestive, but Asch's creativity as a scientist is as likely a source of the design.

In the early 1950s, while Asch was concluding his research on independence, Leon Festinger had begun to develop what would become perhaps the most influential theory in the history of social psychology. It would stimulate hundreds of experiments, most of which would use deception.

Leon Festinger, The Seminal Theorist

Leon Festinger was the major figure in social psychology for almost two decades following World War II. He had been a student of Lewin's at Iowa, then joined Lewin as a colleague at MIT, and, after Lewin's death, was responsible for the most significant theoretical and methodological developments in social psychology. Some judgments of his contributions are extremely laudatory (Aronson, 1991; Zuckier, 1989). One obituary (Zajonc, 1990) compared Festinger to Dostoevski and Picasso, saying that his methods are "nothing short of a high form of art" and that, if Festinger had not been born it is "doubtful if experimental social psychology would have emerged as a discipline at all," just as the works of great artists would not exist had the artists not been born.

One of Festinger's students suggested that he played St. Paul to Lewin's Christ (John Darley, in Patnoe, 1988). That is an apt metaphor to use to describe the relationship of these two Jewish men. It indicates that Festinger was the one who carried Lewin's spirit into the laboratory and spread his version of Lewin's gospel, converting the multitudes around the country. Festinger was very much his own person, however. Even as a beginning graduate student at Iowa in 1939 at the age of 21, he showed his independence by working in the rat lab rather than on Lewin's problems. But the link with Lewin was strong and clear.

Rather than comparing Festinger to artists, saviors, and saints, it would be more appropriate to compare him to the great directors of stage or film, because of Festinger's skill in creating realistic situations in the laboratory. His research methods were inspired by Lewin, and if we think of his experiments as stage productions, then the confederates are actors reciting from a script, and the performances are intended to involve participants, not to make fools of them. That is how Festinger and his students conceived their research.

The many contributions of Leon Festinger cover an unusual range of topics that go beyond social psychology to visual perception and even beyond psychology to archeology (Schachter & Gazzaniga, 1989). This chapter begins with a discussion of the importance of Festinger's ideas, especially his theory of cognitive dissonance, which many consider to be his most influential idea. Then I will go back to Festinger's years at Iowa and MIT to describe the development of his research. His most dramatic studies were done at Minnesota and Stanford and it is from this research that we get the sense of involvement that he created for research participants, although they rarely knew what they were involved in.

The Seminal Theorist

Kurt Lewin, who thought that nothing was as practical as a good theory, did not really have a theory, but a language for talking about research. Festinger, however, did develop several important theories in his lifetime and these ideas continue to be influential. His earliest work, which he began as an undergraduate, was on the topic of level of aspiration and used Lewin's framework. Then, with Dorwin Cartwright, he formulated a quantitative theory of decision (Cartwright & Festinger, 1943), which used Lewin's research language but added a mathematical presentation of the theory that was not in Lewin's style.

At MIT and Michigan, Festinger's research on social communication and group influence led him to develop a theory of social comparison processes (Festinger, 1954). He was interested in how people form opinions and how we know what to do in various situations. His theory began with the hypothesis that people have a "drive" to evaluate their opinions and abilities. When there is no objective, nonsocial means available for this evaluation, we judge ourselves in comparison with the opinions and abilities of other people. If we are uncertain that a story was intended as a joke, we look to see if others are laughing. Students check their knowledge by asking other students if they did well on a test. Furthermore, the theory goes, we tend to compare ourselves to others who are similar in ability, so I compare my writing to that of psychology textbook authors, not to that of John Updike.

This was the first true theory developed in social psychology. It contained explicit hypotheses with corollaries and derivations, all of which could be tested experimentally. This approach to research—formulating a theory that generates hypotheses that can be specified as operations for testing in the laboratory—fit well with American psychology in the 1950s. The dominant force at that time was the neobehaviorism of Clark Hull and Kenneth Spence, who deduced elaborate equations to explain maze behavior in rats and the conditioning of the eye blink in humans. Social comparison theory had an apparent precision that made it respectable, but its relevance to everyday life put it out of the main stream of psychology in the United

States. This is not a criticism of Festinger's theory because, as he said, "Precision is highly desirable but only if one has retained the reality and essence of the question" (in Schachter & Gazzaniga, 1989).

When Festinger's theory of social comparison was published in 1954 he was at the University of Minnesota and had begun to develop the theory of cognitive dissonance. This truly was a seminal theory because it provided the seeds for hundreds of studies during the decade following its publication and eventually led to the theories that dominate social psychology today. The theory of cognitive dissonance is relatively simple and was presented clearly and at length in a book (Festinger, 1957) that reported both laboratory and field studies in support of the theory.

Festinger began with the concise statement that "the individual strives toward consistency within himself." Our attitudes and opinions generally are consistent with one another and with what we do, but this is not always the case and that is what interested Festinger. Sometimes there is an inconsistency between two beliefs or between what one believes and does, like the cigarette smoker who believes the warning on the cigarette package but continues to smoke. The mental state produced by such an inconsistency is cognitive dissonance. Festinger stated two basic hypotheses (1957, p. 3):

1. The existence of dissonance, being psychologically uncomfortable, will motivate the person to try to reduce the dissonance and achieve consonance.
2. When dissonance is present, in addition to trying to reduce it, the person will actively avoid situations and information which would likely increase the dissonance.

These basic statements led to many other hypotheses and to research that produced results that went beyond commonsense expectations. For example, if you give people a reward (money) for telling a lie, they are more likely to come to believe the lie for a small reward than for a large reward. The theory survived its critics and more than thirty years later continued to stimulate research. It has been said that, "conceptually and experimentally, dissonance theory has been social psychology's most notable achievement" (Zukier, 1989). Leon Festinger was a man of great influence. Let us look more closely at what happened in and out of his laboratory.

Predissonance Years

Only a few basic facts about Leon Festinger's personal life have been published. He did not write an autobiography, although he was asked to do so, because he considered that kind of activity "to be mere puffery" (Aronson,

1991). We know that he was born May 8, 1919, in New York City, the son of Alex Festinger, a manufacturer of embroideries, and Sara Solomon Festinger (Zajonc, 1990). Much more is known about his academic career. He attended City College in New York, where he received his B.S. degree in 1939. Like many other college students before and since, he had trouble deciding on a major. He wanted to study science, but was bored by physics and chemistry. His first course in psychology also was boring, but he thought that he was running out of time and should make a decision (Patnoe, 1988). He finally found something that excited him when one of his professors, Max Hertzman,[1] introduced him to the ideas of Kurt Lewin. This led to his first research in psychology and a publication with Hertzman on the topic of level of aspiration (Hertzman & Festinger, 1940).

He went to the University of Iowa for his graduate work because Lewin was there, and he maintained his relationship with his teacher until Lewin died in 1947. Festinger arrived in Iowa with great enthusiasm for Lewin's ideas concerning tension systems, the remembering and completion of interrupted tasks, and other ideas from the Berlin days. "Unfortunately for me," said Festinger, "by the time I arrived, the things that fascinated me were no longer on center stage" (Festinger, 1989, p. 548). Lewin had become more interested in social psychology, particularly the behavior of groups. So, "undeterred, and enjoying the tolerance of others," Festinger went ahead with more research on level of aspiration, decision making, statistics, and the appetite of laboratory rats. His "youthful penchant for rigor" made the loose methodology of social psychology seem unappealing (Festinger, 1989).

Some of Festinger's Iowa research certainly looks like social psychology and he used a relatively mild form of deception in his level-of-aspiration experiments. In these studies, subjects' scores on tests of verbal ability or information were compared with scores of fictitious groups that subjects thought were real (e.g., other undergraduates). Subjects were then asked what score they expected or intended to get on their next test to determine their level of aspiration (Hertzman & Festinger, 1940).[2]

World War II began while Festinger was at Iowa. He thought of himself as "one of the original draft dodgers" and could not imagine himself in a uniform with a gun (Patnoe, 1988, p. 253). He was kept from that fate by a series of deferments based on his academic status. Festinger contributed to the war effort, as many other psychologists did, by teaching and research. One of his jobs was to teach statistics in the Army Specialized Training Program. He moved to the University of Rochester in 1943 and was there until 1945 as senior statistician for the Committee on Selection and Training of Aircraft Pilots (Zajonc, 1990). His most direct research contribution (unpublished) concerned the question of what would make a new drinking container most acceptable, which led to the finding "that the use of a new container is more acceptable if the type of beverage it contains is also new" (Marrow, 1969, p. 156).

It took only three years for Festinger to finish his doctoral work at Iowa. After his work as a statistician at Rochester, he rejoined Lewin at the MIT Research Center for Group Dynamics. "The years at M.I.T. [were] momentous, ground breaking, the new beginning of something important" (Festinger, 1989, p. 548). After Lewin's death, Festinger, along with Dorwin Cartwright and others, moved the Center to the University of Michigan. In spite of his disdain for loose methodology, Festinger must surely be identified as a social psychologist during and after his days at MIT. Here he began to conduct more dramatic experiments using deception. For example, in a study of the role of group belongingness, two assistants pretended to be either Catholic or Jewish. An election was rigged to see if girls of the two different religious groups would vote for a person of their own religion. The Catholics did, but the Jewish girls did not (Festinger, 1947).

Dissonance and the Shaping of Social Psychology

Festinger stayed at Michigan until 1951, when he went to the University of Minnesota. Here he continued his studies of group influence and began the work that led to the theory of cognitive dissonance. Shortly after Festinger came to Minnesota, Bernard Berelson of the Ford Foundation asked him to review the research literature in the area of communication and social influence. While conducting this review he became intrigued with a study of the spread of rumors following a 1934 earthquake in India. The rumors predicted that worse disasters would happen. Festinger and his students wondered why people would spread rumors that would increase their anxiety rather than reduce it.

[P]erhaps these rumors predicting even worse disasters to come were not 'anxiety provoking' at all but were rather 'anxiety justifying.' That is, as a result of the earthquake these people were already frightened, and the rumors served the function of giving them something to be frightened about. Perhaps these rumors provided people with information that fit with the way they already felt. (Festinger, 1957, p. vii)

This insight led to many long discussions during which a theory was developed and to the design of experiments that tested the theory. Festinger's book, *A Theory of Cognitive Dissonance*, describes much of the research from his laboratory and others, as well as a variety of nonlaboratory research, in support of the theory. All the studies from Festinger's laboratory used some form of deception to create degrees of dissonance. Many of the studies involved only moderate levels of manipulation and deception. For example, some subjects heard a speech by a fictitious "authority" and others were told that a list of numbers was random when in fact it was in an order determined by the experimenter.

Other situations were more elaborate, however, such as one in which subjects were led to believe that they were taking part in marketing research. They were to select and evaluate one of eight products (e.g., toaster, desk lamp) and would be given one of them as a gift in return for their participation. This method allowed the creation of degrees of dissonance in attitudes toward the products that were and were not chosen. At the end of the experimental session, however, subjects were told that they "could not be allowed to take a valuable gift home . . . since the experimenter was only a poor graduate student at the time." They "took this in good grace" and received "credit in their introductory psychology course for their participation" (Brehm, 1956, quoted in Festinger, 1957, p. 64).

The best known of all the laboratory dissonance experiments was conducted by Festinger with James M. Carlsmith after Festinger had moved to Stanford in 1955 (Festinger & Carlsmith, 1959). Not only was it an important test of dissonance theory, it is a good example of the use of elaborate multiple deception and of research as theater. Festinger and Carlsmith wanted to know what would happen to a person's private belief if that person is forced to do or say something contrary to that belief. According to the theory, the person should realize that what he said is opposed to what he believes. A person's awareness of this difference is what Festinger called dissonance, an uncomfortable feeling that can be reduced by a change in the private belief. That is a powerful idea because it means that you can change peoples' opinions by changing their behavior. The problem was how to manipulate the behavior and measure the opinion. Festinger and Carlsmith did this by rewarding people for saying something contrary to their private opinion, a procedure they called "forced compliance." They also made a surprising prediction, "that the *larger* the reward given to the subject, the *smaller* will be the subsequent opinion change" (p. 204, italics mine). Commonsense, as well as the prevailing reinforcement theories of the 1950s, would predict that behavior change is more likely with a larger reward.

If there is any experiment that can be considered a classic in social psychology and deception, it is this study of the "cognitive consequences of forced compliance" by Festinger and Carlsmith. Not only is it important for the theory being tested, but it is a model of the careful preparation required to set up deceptive situations. The deception began weeks before the experiment itself, when an instructor in the introductory psychology course at Stanford told the students that they were required to participate in research, that the psychology department was evaluating that research (which was not true), and that they would be interviewed following their participation.

When students arrived at the laboratory to take part in a study called "measures of performance," they were reminded about the interview and then presented with their first task: "putting 12 spools onto a tray, emptying the tray, refilling it with spools, and so on" (p. 204). The subject did this for about one-half hour and then was given a new task: on "a board containing 48 square pegs [h]is task was to turn each peg a quarter turn clockwise, then another quarter turn, and so on" (p. 204). To make it appear that the task really was a measure of performance, the experimenter operated a stop watch and took notes. The hour spent working on these monotonous tasks provided an experience intended to lead to a somewhat negative opinion about the experiment.

When "the second task was over, the [experimenter] conspicuously set the stop watch back to zero, put it away, pushed his chair back, lit a cigarette," (p. 205) and proceeded to provide a false explanation of the purpose of the experiment. Note that Festinger and Carlsmith (who was the experimenter) provided exact details of what the experimenter did and long quotations of what he said. These were well-rehearsed stage directions with a memorized script.

This was the *false* explanation: The student was in a control group that was given the boring tasks with only minimal instruction. In the other group, a student had been hired to meet the next research participant and tell him about the tasks. The experimenter then showed the subject (the real research participant) a sheet of paper that was "headed 'for group B' which had written on it: It was very enjoyable, I had a lot of fun, I enjoyed myself, it was very interesting, it was intriguing, it was exciting" (p. 205). Having a student, rather than the experimenter, do this supposedly made the situation more realistic for the next (alleged) participant.

Next, the real subject underwent "forced compliance" as the experimenter continued his script:

> Now, I also have a sort of strange thing to ask you. The thing is this. [Long pause, some confusion and uncertainty in the following, with a degree of embarrassment on the part of the *E*. The manner of the *E* contrasted strongly with the preceding unhesitant and assured false explanation of the experiment. The point was to make it seem to *S* that this was the first time the *E* had done this and that he felt unsure of himself.] The fellow who normally does this for us couldn't do it today—he just phoned in, and something or other came up for him—so we've been looking around for someone that we could hire to do it for us. You see, we've got another subject

waiting [looks at watch]. . . . [P]erhaps we could take a chance on
your doing it for us. . . . (p. 205)

The script continued with the intent of convincing the subject that his
help was needed and that, if he agreed to be hired, he would be paid either
one dollar or twenty dollars for his help. That was the one variable manipulated in this experiment. For two of the experimental groups the only
difference was that in one group subjects were offered one dollar and in the
other group, twenty dollars. There also was a third group in which subjects
were not asked to help and were offered no money.

When a subject agreed to help he was told that the next subject was in
the adjacent room and that "what we want you to do is just sit down and get
into a conversation with her and try to get across the points on that sheet of
paper" (pp. 205–206). The "next subject" was a female undergraduate hired
to play that role.

[She] said little until the *S* made some positive remarks about the
experiment and then said that she was surprised because a friend of
hers had taken the experiment the week before and had told her that
it was boring and that she ought to try to get out of it. Most *S*s
responded by saying something like 'Oh, no, it's really very interesting. I'm sure you'll enjoy it.' The girl, after this listened quietly,
accepting and agreeing to everything the *S* told her. The discussion
between the S and the girl was recorded on a hidden tape recorder. (p.
206)

Then the experimenter returned, concluded this part of the experiment
with some additional false information, and introduced the subject to the
"interviewer" who supposedly was evaluating the research for the
psychology department. Actually this was another experimenter who
obtained the subject's opinions and quantitative ratings on several aspects of
his experience. At the end of the interview, the true purpose of the experiment was explained and reasons were given for all steps in the procedure.
Finally, all subjects in both the one- and twenty-dollar conditions were asked
to return the money. They all "were quite willing" to do so.

The data analysis for this elaborate experiment was relatively simple.
The most important result was that the subjects in the one-dollar condition
rated the tasks as significantly more enjoyable than did subjects in the
twenty dollar and control conditions. A one-dollar reward also made then
more willing than other subjects to say that they would participate in a
similar experiment in the future. The theory of cognitive dissonance was
supported: If you were paid twenty dollars to say that a boring task was

weird

interesting, then you did it for the money; what you said was consistent with what in fact you thought. But if you were only paid one dollar, that created a state of dissonance, and you were forced to change your opinion of the tasks because no reasonable person would do such a boring task for only a dollar.

The researchers had nothing to say about the fact that data from 11 of 71 subjects (15%) had to be discarded because those people either were suspicious (five subjects) or refused to complete both phases of the study (six subjects). This finding may lead one to wonder how many participants in other studies simply are playing along with a game that they realize is a set-up. Stricker (1967) reported that few researchers who used deception reported that they bothered to check for suspiciousness and when they did so, the procedures tended to be inadequate.

Research as Theater: I

Festinger said that his methodological approach emerged from Lewin's emphasis on the importance of the problem and "from the insistence on trying to create, in the laboratory, powerful social situations that make big differences. . . . So experiments were done with . . . a large dose of bravura and enthusiasm" (Festinger, 1989, p. 550). He said that "even though you may have to contrive an artificial or semi-barren situation, you want that situation to be real and important to the subject" (Patnoe, 1988, p. 255).

In Festinger's laboratory, and later in most of social psychology, experiments became theatrical stage productions or "little dramas" and research design required the talents of a playwright (Patnoe, 1988, p. 270). Eliot Aronson said that Festinger was "always concerned about having a scenario that would make sense for the subject and engage his interest while it was testing your hypothesis" (Patnoe, 1988, p. 224). For Aronson, who was Festinger's student, "it's controlling the experience of the subject—having the subject experience the thing you intend for the subject to experience—*that's* playwrighting. . . . *[T]hat's* the important thing" (Patnoe, 1988, 225–226). This metaphor was accepted by the next generation of social psychologists. Aronson's student, Harold Sigall, thinks he is a good experimenter because, "I can design an experiment and come up with the scenario and write the script and do all that kind of direction that I think will involve the subject" (Patnoe, 1988, p. 213).

Aronson called Festinger's approach to research an "audacious methodological stance" because Festinger thought "social psychologists could manipulate *any* variable in the laboratory." This is "little more than an idle boast unless it is coupled with great craftsmanship and . . . artistry in the lab" (Aronson, 1991, p. 216). Aronson has provided an excellent description of the theatrical skill that was required for this kind of research, using the forced compliance study as an example.

Anyone who ever worked with Leon will remember (almost certainly with a groan) the time and energy spent in fine-tuning the procedure and in rehearsing the script until we got it right. For example, in the classic Festinger-Carlsmith experiment (which I consider the single most important experiment in social psychology), you don't simply *tell* the subject that the stooge didn't show up and you'd like her³ to play the role of the stooge by informing the next subject that packing spools is an interesting and enjoyable task. You must go much further than that; the goal is to fully convince the subject that you are in a terrible jam and feeling deeply uncomfortable about it. You sweat, you cringe, you wring your hands; you convey to the subject that you are in real trouble here—that the next participant is waiting and the God-damn stooge hasn't shown up yet. You then appeal to her to do you a favor: to play the role of the stooge and mislead the next participant.

One of the most vivid memories of my years as a graduate student in Leon's lab involves the exciting and tedious hours Leon and I spent prior to that experiment, coaching and directing the performance of a very precocious Stanford undergraduate named Merrill Carlsmith until he got it right. Initially, Merrill, who even then had a brilliant research mind, persisted in delivering his lines in a very stiff and wooden way; we kept walking him through the procedure, over and over again, until he eventually became extremely convincing. In these situations, Leon was a regular Lee Strasberg and the rest of us felt ourselves to be a part of the Actor's Studio. Art and craftsmanship in the service of science. It was an exciting, exhausting process—and it almost always paid off.

. . . The kinds of hypotheses to be tested demanded a high degree of realism and we rose to the occasion. The audacity to believe that we could rise to any occasion is Leon's unique and permanent legacy to the discipline. (Aronson, 1991, p. 216)

Prophecy and Privacy

Audacity is a good word to use to describe Festinger's approach to research. The word means bold or arrogant disregard for normal restraints and Aronson uses it with admiration. One of the first tests of the theory of cognitive dissonance was a field study of a religious group that had predicted the end of the world (Festinger, Riecken, & Schachter, 1956). In this study the investigators disregarded the normal restraints on invasion of privacy when they used deception to infiltrate that group to observe what happened when their prediction of disaster was not confirmed.

Festinger knew that throughout history individuals had predicted disasters that would destroy the world and had gathered groups of believers. When the disasters did not occur, the typical result was not a change in belief, but an increase in proselytizing for the group. These fascinating events could be explained by Festinger's theory, which included a list of five "conditions under which we would expect to observe increased fervor following the disconfirmation of a belief" (Festinger, Riecken, & Schachter, 1956, p. 3; unless otherwise noted all quotations in this section are from this source):

1. The belief must be held with deep conviction and be related to the actions of the believer.
2. The believer must have shown commitment to the belief by having taken some action that is difficult to undo.
3. The belief must be stated specifically so that it can be disconfirmed by events.
4. The evidence disconfirming the belief must be recognized by the believer.
5. The believer must have support from a sympathetic group of other believers. Without that support the belief would be abandoned.

The history of doomsday groups provided support for these propositions. In Festinger's view, that was not a sufficiently valid test of his theory, because historical records had little to say about what happened after the predicted disasters failed to occur, which makes it difficult to prove or disprove dissonance theory. An article on the back page of a newspaper provided the opportunity for a more careful study.

The headline was: "PROPHECY FROM PLANET. CLARION CALL TO CITY: FLEE THAT FLOOD. IT'LL SWAMP US ON DEC. 21, OUTER SPACE TELLS SUBURBANITE." The article reported that Mrs. Marion Keech (names of people and places were all fictitious) had received messages by automatic writing sent by superior beings from another planet whose observations of the earth led them to conclude that the deluge was coming. It would happen on December 21. Festinger and his associates enthusiastically "seized the opportunity to collect direct observational data. . . ." (p. 30).

The messages instructed Mrs. Keech to tell others about the coming disaster so that she and other believers could be saved by a flying saucer that would come for them. She was able to attract a small group of followers (the Lake City group) who met to discuss the messages and prepared to be saved from the flood. One of her followers formed a group of college student believers ("The Seekers") in another town.

On December 20, the group met at Mrs. Keech's house and made their final preparations for salvation. The minutes before midnight passed in complete silence. The believers sat motionless as the clock chimed twelve, "each stroke painfully clear in the expectant hush" (p. 162).

> One might have expected some visible reaction, as the minutes passed. Midnight had come and gone, and nothing had happened. The cataclysm itself was less than seven hours away. But there was little to see in the reactions of the people in that room. There was no talking, nor sound of any sort. People sat stock still, their faces seemingly frozen and expressionless.
>
> Gradually, painfully, an atmosphere of despair and confusion settled over the group. They re-examined the prediction and the accompanying messages . . . and discarded explanation after explanation as unsatisfactory. . . . [The believers] were all visibly shaken and close to tears. It was now almost 4:30 A.M. and still no way of handling the disconfirmation had been found. (Festinger, Riecken, & Schachter, 1958, pp. 161–162)

Suddenly, at 4:45, Mrs. Keech received a message that she read to the group. They heard these words with joy: "And mighty is the word of God— and by his word have ye been saved—for from the mouth of death have ye been delivered and at no time has there been such a force loosed upon the Earth." The force of their good faith had saved the world. Soon another message instructed Mrs. Keech to tell the world what had happened. She immediately telephoned the newspaper, the first time she had ever done that. Members of the group then took turns calling newspapers, magazines, and radio stations. The proselytizing had begun and, in Festinger's terms, dissonance was being reduced.

Not all believers had been able to go to Mrs. Keech's home. Some of the college students went home for Christmas vacation where they were isolated and surrounded by nonbelievers. They did not take part in proselytizing and their beliefs were either given up or weakened. The presence of social support was one of the conditions for increased proselytizing stated by the theory.

This entire story, presented at length in the book, *When Prophecy Fails*, is based primarily on the notes made by five graduate students who were hired as participant observers. A "methodological appendix" to the book tells an equally fascinating story about how the research team infiltrated the group and took part in their activities. It was a clear invasion of privacy: "our investigation was conducted without either the knowledge or the consent of

N r W

the group members" (p. 234). The only place where sensitivity to the rights of the believers is expressed is in the forward to their book where the authors say that "by the disguises employed we have tried to protect the actual people involved in the movement from the curiosity of an unsympathetic reader." However, enough information was provided so that it would not have been difficult at that time to find the newspaper accounts of the activities of this group, which would reveal their identity.

The deceptive approach was used because the believers would not allow reporters or other outsiders in their meetings. Deception began when one of the authors telephoned Mrs. Keech, saying that "he happened to be visiting Lake City 'on business'" (p. 235) and was interested in the newspaper article. She accepted this reason and later allowed two of the investigators to interview her and another woman in her home for over three hours.[4] "Thus it was easy to make the acquaintance of these two persons and to establish a basis for future contacts" (p. 236).

But it was not that easy to infiltrate the Seekers. Resistance to admitting strangers to the group had to be overcome by hiring two graduate students who made up stories about having psychic experiences. These experiences so impressed the believers that they readily accepted the student observers. One of the hired observers made up this dream:

> I was standing on a hill: and I looked up and there was a man standing on top of the hill with a light all around him. There were torrents of water, raging water all around, and the man reached down and lifted me up, up out of the water. I felt safe. (p. 237)

This was an obvious foreshadowing of the predicted flood, and the story probably was created based on information that had been obtained by Festinger during his earlier three-hour interview with Ms. Keech.

The story was quite successful and was repeated many times to other believers. It was too successful, however, because to be accepted by the believers, "[w]e had unintentionally reinforced their beliefs that the Guardians were watching over humanity and were 'sending' chosen people for special instruction about the cataclysm and the belief system" (p. 238). Although the Festinger team was aware that they were now promoting unreasonable beliefs, they continued to create false cover stories to allow additional observers to be accepted by the believers.

> There is little doubt that the addition of four new people to a fairly small group within ten days had an effect on the state of conviction among the existing members. . . . It was an unfortunate and unavoidable set of events—we had no choice but to establish local

observers . . ., to do it quickly, and to 'push' as much as we dared to
get our people well enough received so they could begin to move
about in the groups, ask questions, and have a reasonable expectation of getting answers. (p. 240)

The investigators had made a choice; the believers' right to privacy was
subordinated to the psychologists' need to test their theory. In his review of
When Prophecy Fails, Brewster Smith (1957) was quite negative in his
judgment of the ethics of this research: "Prying by means of false pretenses
goes against the grain of most of us, and, in the present case, it goes beyond
the deceptions that have become almost conventional in some areas of
psychological experimentation—experimentation on subjects, be it noted,
who have agreed to be studied" (p. 91). And, he added, "it is hard to avoid
the conclusion that covert participant observation, as in the present study, is
ethically bad" (p. 91). In spite of these strong concerns, Smith concluded that
"it is probably fortunate that competent scientists of good will" (p. 92)
advanced our scientific knowledge by conducting this research.

Invasion of privacy is an ethical problem, and involvement in the group
process was a problem of method. Ideally, participant observers are neutral;
they should neither hinder nor enhance the activities being observed. That
ideal is impossible to attain. The observers in Festinger's team had to
respond to outsiders on behalf of the believers, took turns at leading group
meetings, and on one occasion acted as a channel for a communication from
outer space. Two female observers became residents in a believer's home and
one of them took care of the children for a day. The report of the research
documented these methodological problems, but the authors do not question
the validity of their results because, "at no time did we exercise any influence whatsoever on proselyting activity" (p. 243). The extent of that activity
was the measure that would determine how cognitive dissonance was
reduced, which was the point of the research.

Was it necessary to use this elaborate deception to test the theory? Think
of the many hours that went into planning the infiltration, the hundreds of
person-hours the observers spent with the believers, the reports of the
observations that filled about "sixty-five reels of one-hour tapes, yielding
almost one thousand pages of typescript" (p. 248), and the time spent
analyzing the data. A simpler, more honest approach could have been used
and in fact was used in a similar study of a group that predicted a nuclear
holocaust (Hardyck & Braden, 1962). Without using deception Festinger's
research team could have learned about the ideas of the believers, discovered
that they resisted contact with outsiders before the date of the predicted
disaster, and sought converts after that date.

The Festinger Family

When Prophecy Fails was written while Festinger was at the University of Minnesota. In 1955 he moved to Stanford University, where he conducted most of the laboratory research supporting the theory of cognitive dissonance. During the 1960s his interest changed to the area of visual perception. After moving to the New School for Social Research in 1968, he became interested in archeology and studied the transition from prehistoric life to modern society.

It was at Stanford that Festinger trained many of the students who carried on his version of the Lewin tradition. After Kurt Lewin died in 1947 his students moved in two different directions in their research (Danziger, 1993). Some preferred to study human behavior in natural settings while others, led by Festinger, saw laboratory experiments as the best approach. This second group admired Lewin's "dramatic, yet systematic, manipulation of complex social situations," but did not consider "what Lewin had done to be a genuine scientific experiment. . . . The mixture of awe and puzzlement with which many young American experimentalists regarded Lewin's demonstrations had something in common with the reaction of children enchanted by a magician pulling rabbits out of a hat" (Danziger, 1993, pp. 30–31).

Festinger and Lewin were similar in some important ways. They both were concerned with asking significant psychological questions and with the relationship of theory to experimental data obtained from the field as well as the laboratory. Both men were powerful charismatic leaders of their respective research groups. Lewin, however, was more of a social activist and was more permissive and tolerant with his students. At Stanford, Festinger had a reputation for being "devastating" (Patnoe, 1988, p. 220). "People who were not very clear thinkers were usually humiliated" (Mills, quoted by Patnoe, p. 242). Judson Mills expected that Festinger "would share some experiences he had had as a student and that there would be sort of a feeling of being part of a tradition that was associated with Lewin. But I don't remember anything like that. Festinger was very interested in what *he* was doing" (Patnoe, 1988, p. 243).

The evening meeting in which research was discussed was a unifying and socializing feature of both the Lewin and Festinger groups and was adopted by some of Festinger's students. People would try out ideas and designs for experiments. Eliot Aronson's memory of Festinger in these meetings is not at all of someone devastating, but rather of someone who was "very gracious, . . . always alive and always on target" (Patnoe, p. 225).

As a social system, Festinger's family was like Lewin's group: a strong, charismatic leader; bright, self-selected students; and a shared belief in the importance of their research. Commitment to the group was strengthened by the difficulty of the initiation; one had to be able to withstand Festinger's demands and criticism in order to be accepted. Festinger said that he had created a "psychotic environment" because the research was so abnormally important: "doing research is what you *do*. You become involved in it, addicted to it, and it just becomes a way of life. . . . The leadership has to create it" (Festinger in Patnoe, p. 261). He was very much involved in the day-to-day activities of his laboratory. His office was near student offices and the lab, so he could easily drop by to discuss ideas and could observe the research in progress.

After Festinger, no one has had such a dominant place in social psychology.[5] Many of the theoretical developments from 1960 to 1990 were based on or were reactions to dissonance theory and the procedures used in the laboratory were elaborations of Festinger's methods. The theater of the laboratory with its actors and illusions continued to grow significantly and after 1960 social psychology consisted largely of stage productions. This period includes the obedience research of Stanley Milgram, the most famous of the directors of the little dramas of the laboratory.

—8—

Stanley Milgram and the Illusion of Obedience

"Extraordinary."

"Devilish."

"The most important experiments in the history of psychology."

These quotations are comments on Stanley Milgram's studies of obedience (Milgram, 1974). This research is among the most important in psychology and certainly is the most controversial psychological research ever done. It was the basis for a two-hour television dramatization, *The Tenth Level*, with William Shatner of *Star Trek* fame in the leading role as the experimenter. Sixty-minutes devoted a segment to the research. Milgram's book, *Obedience to Authority*, was reviewed on the front page of the *New York Times Book Review* (Marcus, 1974) and stimulated a series of letters in response to the review. No other research in psychology has come close to getting this much public attention. The emotional reactions to the research have been extreme, both within and outside the field of psychology.

Why was this research so impressive and why does it continue to fascinate students and scholars (Miller, Collins, & Brief, 1995)? First, it deals with a significant issue that finds relevance in normal life as well as in the nightmares of history. Comparisons were made with the holocaust, the My Lai massacre in Viet Nam, and other events in which horrible crimes were committed by people who explained that they were only following orders. Second, the design is creative ("devilishly ingenious," according to one critic [Marcus, 1974]), well controlled, and carried out through a series of experiments designed to investigate various explanations. That design included a variety of deceptions. Finally, the results were surprising, not only the extent to which people would obey an order to harm another person, but also the extreme emotional discomfort experienced by the participants in the research. The use of deception and the strong negative effects on some participants led to an intense debate on the ethics of these studies and of other research in psychology. Before this time few psychologists had questioned the ethics of deception.

In this chapter I will review Milgram's first publication on this topic and some of his and other researchers' variations exploring the conditions of obedience. I will highlight the major methodological and ethical criticisms of his research. The literature commenting on Milgram's obedience research is so extensive that an entire book has been written to summarize related research and commentaries (Miller, 1986).

Milgram's pattern of data collection and publication was unusual. He conducted eighteen separate experiments, involving about 1,000 research subjects, within about a three-year period from 1960 to 1963. His first publication on this topic was sent to the *Journal of Abnormal and Social Psychology* in July of 1962 and was published about one year later (Milgram, 1963).[1] A few other variations were reported in 1965 (Milgram, 1965), but it was not until Milgram's book, *Obedience to Authority*, appeared in 1974 that all eighteen experiments were published. The reactions to this research were related to this publication pattern. Psychologists reacted to the 1963 article, some with strong comments on the ethics of the research and others by designing studies to explore various explanations for the surprising results. The intellectual world beyond psychology reacted to the 1974 book.

Psychologists and recent students of psychology are familiar with the method and results of this research. I will review the general research situation and the results of several experiments for readers who took their undergraduate psychology courses some years ago or who may never have had these courses. Milgram and other investigators completed a large number of experiments using a design similar to the one used by Milgram in the first study on this topic that he published in 1963 (Milgram, 1963). Another reason to review this study carefully is that, as Arthur Miller (1986) pointed out, "Though it constituted but one piece of a complex and much larger puzzle, it was the 1963 publication that became fixed in the mind of the academic community (and other audiences as well) as *the* Milgram experiment" (p. 3).

Behavioral Study of Obedience

In response to a newspaper advertisement or a letter, forty men, aged 20 to 50 and representing a wide range of occupations, came to the "elegant interaction laboratory" (p. 372)[2] at Yale University to take part in what they believed would be a study of memory and learning. They were paid $4.50 for their participation. When they arrived at the laboratory each participant met two other men. One was the experimenter who was not Milgram, but a 31-

year-old biology teacher who was playing the role of the experimenter, while Milgram observed the situation through a one-way mirror. The other person was introduced as another subject, but would in fact become "the victim," played by a 47-year-old accountant, "whom most observers found mild-mannered and likeable" (p. 373).

As a pretext for administering shock, subjects were told that the research concerned the effect of punishment on learning, specifically, what effect different people have on each other as teacher and learner. A rigged drawing of slips of paper from a hat always resulted in the naive subject being the teacher and the accomplice being the learner or victim. After the drawing, the two actors and the real subject went to an adjacent room where the experimenter strapped the leaner into an apparatus that looked like an electric chair. The wires that were attached to the learner were said to be connected to a shock generator in the next room, and the experimenter said, "although the shocks can be painful, they cause no permanent tissue damage."

The false experimental task involved learning a list of pairs of words. After the list had been read, the initial word in the pair was presented and the learner/victim would indicate by throwing a switch, which one of four words was the correct response. The "teacher" was told that an incorrect response would be punished with a shock. The shock generator was a panel with a row of thirty switches. Each switch was labeled with a voltage designation that ranged from 15 to 450 volts in 15-volt increments. Groups of four switches from left to right had these verbal descriptions: slight shock, moderate shock, strong shock, very strong shock, intense shock, extreme intensity shock, danger—severe shock, and the last two switches were marked XXX. Various lights and labels added reality to this instrument, which generated no shock of any intensity to the learner. The 45-volt switch was used, however, to give a mild shock to the "teacher" to convince him that the machine really worked.

The experimenter instructed the teacher to punish incorrect responses from the learner beginning with the lowest level, but the critical instruction was to *increase* the shock by one step for each additional incorrect response. As the experiment proceeded, the learner gave about three wrong answers for every correct one, based on a predetermined schedule. No sound was heard from the learner until the 300-volt level was reached. At that point, when the "shock' was given, the learner pounded on the wall, but his answer did not appear on the response panel viewed by the teacher. The pounding occurred again at the 315-volt level, after which he was not heard from again, nor did his answers appear. The teacher was told that after ten seconds he should treat the absence of a response as an incorrect response and give another, higher shock.

At this point many teacher-subjects were unwilling to continue, but the experimenter urged them to do so using a series of "prods" or encouraging phrases: (1) "please continue," said the experimenter the first time a teacher refused to continue; (2) "the experiment requires that you continue," was the prod if a teacher refused again; (3) "it is absolutely essential that you continue," (4) "you have no other choice, you *must* go on," were the prods used when the teacher persisted. If the teacher refused to continue after all four prods, the experiment was ended. The measure of obedience was the level of the last shock given by the teacher. The major finding of the study was that, "of the 40 subjects, 26 obeyed the orders of the experimenter to the end, proceeding to punish the victim until they reached the most potent shock available on the shock generator" (p. 376), the one labeled XXX. Only five subjects stopped when the learner began pounding the wall at the 300-volt mark.

The results of the first experiment were surprising to Milgram and to others. At some other time, Milgram (1974) described his experiment to three groups of people: college students, middle-class adults, and psychiatrists. No one in any of these groups expected that any subject would go beyond the 300-volt level. This led Milgram to conclude that his results were important because not even sophisticated psychiatrists could predict what people would do. The students and other adults were people similar to those who took part in the actual research. The fact that they did not predict the results convinced Milgram that it would be impossible to study obedience without putting people into a realistic situation.

Milgram reported a second dramatic result. Extreme emotional tension was observed in some subjects. The following statement from his 1963 article is quoted frequently by critics of the ethics of this study:

> I observed a mature and initially poised businessman enter the laboratory smiling and confident. Within 20 minutes he was reduced to a twitching, stuttering wreck, who was rapidly approaching a point of nervous collapse. He constantly pulled on his earlobe, and twisted his hands. At one point he pushed his fist into his forehead and muttered: 'Oh God, let's stop it.' And yet he continued to respond to every word of the experimenter, and obeyed to the end. (p. 377)

Other subjects, however, "remained calm throughout the experiment, and displayed only minimal signs of tension from beginning to end" (p. 376). Milgram did not report how many subjects were observed to be calm or how many were extremely disturbed.

Milgram often pointed out that there would have been less criticism of the deceptions that he used if the results of the study had been less surprising.

However, he did not design this research to obtain unimpressive (and unpublishable) results. No one would attend to such extreme details (e.g., "the panel was engraved by precision industrial engravers" [p. 373]) to demonstrate the obvious. I am skeptical about Milgram's repeated claim to have been surprised by these 1963 results. In 1960 he had conducted "exploratory studies" (see footnote 1, p. 371, 1963). Presumably results from those studies would have been available before he conducted the study reported in 1963. Most researchers begin carefully designed research only after "pilot studies" convince them that the results will be interesting. He must have known, early in his research, that many, if not most, participants would obey and that some of them would be upset by the experience.

Some of Milgram's strongest critics, as well as his supporters, admire his creativity in designing this situation. It clearly had a strong impact on the participants. Whether the experiment could be generalized to other situations and whether the research should have been done at all were the issues that became matters of debate. A major advantage of the design was that it could be systematically varied to explore other important factors affecting the extent of obedience. This systematic investigation of specific variables is highly valued by experimental psychologists as being a characteristic of good science. Milgram was disappointed that, "in the popular press, these variations are virtually ignored, or assumed to be of only minor importance" (quoted in Miller, 1986, p. 255).

Revelation

Stanley Milgram was born August 15, 1933, in New York City. His interest in science emerged during his childhood, as did his flare for the dramatic. He and his friends enjoyed creating scientific experiments, one of which "involved lowering a large flask of sodium into the Bronx River. The 'sodium bomb' exploded, bringing fire engines and anxious mothers to the site" (Tavris, 1974a, p. 75). At Queens College, where he received his bachelor's degree in 1954, his interests shifted to political science, but he was not satisfied with philosophical approaches to human questions and was attracted to more objective behavioral science. He found this in Harvard's Department of Social Relations. Although rejected by Harvard on first application because of deficiencies in psychology, he persisted and was admitted as a special student (Tavris, 1974a).

Milgram identified two men who had an important influence on him in graduate school. One was Gordon Allport, who gave Milgram a "strong sense of [his] own potential" and was his "spiritual and emotional support" (Tavris, 1974b, p. 77). Although Allport did direct Milgram's doctoral thesis, it was a visiting professor at Harvard, Solomon Asch, who had the most important

intellectual influence on Milgram. Asch's studies of independence and
conformity fascinated Milgram who served as his teaching assistant at
Harvard and later worked for him at Princeton's Institute for Advanced
Study.

For his doctoral dissertation, Milgram (1961) used a modified form of
Asch's group pressure situation to study national characteristics related to
conformity in Norway and France. He pointed out that because psychological
research is not as common in Norway and France as in the United States,
"subjects are relatively unsophisticated about psychological deception" (1961,
p. 48). He quoted a student from Oslo: "It was a real trick and I was stupid to
have fallen into the trap. . . . It must be fun to study psychology" (p. 47).

The design of the obedience studies was a direct result of Milgram's
involvement in group pressure research and his contact with Asch. Asch,
however, may have been a reluctant mentor: "I did not propose his study of
obedience; that research was entirely his [Milgram's] own. Indeed, I was
unaware of his plans until we parted at the end of the year [at Princeton]."[3]
He thought that the obedience research was "a serious piece of work" but
made no published statements about it during the controversy that followed.
Asch's colleague, Henry Gleitman, said that "he [Asch] was never happy with
the Milgram experiments",[4] but was not sure why.

The obedience experiments grew out of Milgram's wish to modify the
Asch situation so that it would use a more significant task than merely
judging the length of lines. He wondered if group pressure could make a
person act with severity against another person.

> I envisioned a situation very much like Asch's experiment in which
> there would be a number of confederates and one naive subject, and
> instead of confronting the lines on a card, each one of them would
> have a shock generator. In other words, I transformed Asch's
> experiment into one in which the group would administer increas-
> ingly higher levels of shock to a person, and the question would be
> to what degree an individual would follow along with the group.
> (quoted in Evans, 1976, p. 347)

Milgram thought that before he could do that he would need to study a
control condition in which there was no group pressure. He thought the
experimenter could tell the person to give higher and higher shocks.
Milgram described this insight as a sudden revelation:

> Immediately I knew that was the problem I would investigate. It
> was a very excited moment for me, because I realized that although
> it was a very simple question, it would admit itself to measurement,

precise investigation. One could see the variable to be studied, with [the] dependent measure being how far a person would go in administering shocks. (quoted in Evans, 1976, pp. 347–348)

Milgram went to Yale University as an Assistant Professor and by 1964 had completed the entire series of obedience studies.

Variations on a Theme

His first studies of obedience brought a message about human nature that was frightening, in Milgram's view. In his variations he set out to find conditions in which people might be less willing to obey. Perhaps the extent of obedience was due to the location of the research in the "elegant interaction laboratory" at prestigious Yale University. Repeating the research in the seedy setting of an office building in a nearby industrial city moderately reduced the level of obedience; 48% of the subjects were completely obedient in Bridgeport compared to 65% at Yale. That was not as many, but still a surprisingly large proportion.

The closeness of the victim was varied in a series of experiments. In one condition, voice feedback (screaming from the victim) was added to the pounding on the wall. A second condition moved the victim into the same room with the teacher and experimenter. Closeness was greatest in a condition in which the teacher was ordered to use his own hand to force the victim's hand onto a shock plate. The results showed that obedience decreased as closeness to the victim increased. Yet even when the teacher was ordered to hold the victim's hand, 30% of 40 subjects were obedient to the highest shock level.

Closeness of the authority (the experimenter who gave the orders to the teacher) also was an important factor. Obedience was reduced when the experimenter gave instructions by telephone from another room and the teacher and learner also were in separate rooms. With the authority absent, 9 of 40 subjects (22.5%) were completely obedient. Some subjects (teachers) also cheated by giving lower shocks than required, and they lied by telling the experimenter over the telephone that they were increasing the shocks as ordered.

Each of the eighteen variations repeated the same basic deceptions and some added new twists. For Milgram, there was no way to investigate this topic without using deception, and for him the results justified the method and the psychological pain to the participants. The emotional reactions were no longer surprising after the first experiment. Milgram continued to deceive and disturb his participants in order to understand an important social issue in a scientific way, but Milgram did not think of his methods as deceptive.

He said, "It is true that technical illusions were used in the experiment. I would not call them deceptions because that already implies some base motivation. . . . I thought the illusion was used for a benign purpose" (quoted in Evans, 1976, p. 352). The title of this book, *Illusions of Reality*, reflects this view of the most famous of laboratory artists.

Eventually, many other investigators would conduct studies of obedience using a design similar to Milgram's situation. The 1963 study did not, however, immediately stimulate a significant amount of research in other laboratories. Keep in mind that I am referring only to published work, not to graduate student theses and other unpublished research. Arthur Miller (1986) conducted a complete review of related research and listed about forty laboratory studies in his bibliography. However, only four of these appeared before 1970. Two were done at Yale and Milgram was second author on one of them (Elms & Milgram, 1966). Miller described the impact of the 1963 article as being of "staggering proportions" (p. 3), but that is difficult to document. It did not stimulate much research by other investigators, and it did not receive much coverage in the popular press. Only one reference to anything about Milgram's work appeared in my search of *The New York Times Index* and *The Readers Guide to Periodical Literature* for the months following publication of the 1963 article.

My own experience, however, would support Miller's impression. As a graduate student in 1964 I can recall the discussions we had after the appearance of Diana Baumrind's (1964) stinging critique of the ethics of Milgram's research, and when I began teaching the introductory psychology course in 1966, Milgram's study was a featured example in the section on social psychology. The academic world knew that this was something important.

Arthur Miller's (1986) excellent book, *The Obedience Experiments*, provides detailed summaries of all the relevant research on obedience and the discussions of the ethics of that research. I will mention just a few studies to give the reader a sense of how the controversy was extended by research in other laboratories. Most of this research involved deception of the kind used by Milgram, although there are some interesting exceptions. The investigators who used this deception were, of course, aware of the stressful effects the situation was likely to have on research participants, but they must have believed that the stress was justified because their variations would add significantly to our knowledge of an important topic.

There are many good scientific reasons for conducting a variation on someone else's research: The investigator believes the topic has theoretical or practical importance and wants to study new variables, wants to test other explanations for the results, or challenges the validity of the method. Thus, some studies are extensions of the original (new variables) and others are critiques of the method and interpretation.

One of the alternative explanations for Milgram's results was that participants in obedience research might have been trying to figure out what to do in a bizarre situation. People want to meet the expectations of the experimenter and trust that they will not be asked to do anything wrong, like severely harming another person. Martin Orne and Charles Holland (1968/1972) published a critique based on this idea. They used data from Holland's doctoral dissertation to argue that participants in obedience research knew that there was something "fishy" about the situation, but behaved as they thought they were expected to behave in order to fulfill their contract. Even so, the reality of the deception made them extremely uncomfortable.

Some other investigators did not challenge the perceived reality of the situation but searched for variations that might decrease obedience. David Mantell (1971) thought this could be done by providing an example or model of disobedience. His experiment had three conditions: One repeated Milgram's basic 1963 situation; a second repeated one of Milgram's variations in which participants could choose, without direction from the experimenter, whether to give a shock and how much to give to the alleged victim; the third condition was called "modeling delegitimization." That meant that participants in that condition, before they participated, were shown an enactment of a situation in which the "teacher" refused to continue after giving the fourteenth shock, a clear example or model of disobedience.

The results surprised and discouraged Mantell because in the condition that was comparable to Milgram's original study, more subjects were obedient to the highest level in his study (85%) than in Milgram's study (65%). Self-selection of shocks did result in a relatively low level of obedience (7%). However, 52% of the people who had been shown how to disobey went ahead to the highest level anyway. Mantell was dismayed that people would follow orders under these conditions:

> It can only show how much pain one person will impose on another.
> ... It proves that the most banal and superficial of rationales is perhaps not even necessary, but surely is enough to produce destructive behavior in human beings. We thought we had learned this from our history books.... (p. 111)

The fact that Mantell's study was carried out in Germany gave added meaning to the results. It brought to mind images of Nazis and the holocaust, yet reminded us that similar results had been obtained in the United States.

Perhaps, as Orne and Holland thought, people do not believe that they would be asked to inflict harm as part of a psychology experiment. That idea was tested by giving real shocks to a real victim, although not to a person

(Sheridan & King, 1972). Students were deceived about the purpose of the experiment and ordered to administer painful shocks to a "cute, fluffy puppy;" 77% did so. Some students cheated by claiming that the dog actually had learned the problem and did not have to be given more shocks.

A variation that was particularly disturbing to me involved repeating Milgram's experiment with children (Shanab & Yahya, 1977). Ethical questions had been raised by the obedience studies, and this research should have added new dimensions to the debate. The new ethical issues related to this study concern first, the use of children in deceptive, stressful research and second, whether the moral values of our culture should be applied to research in another culture. The latter issue is of concern because this research was done in Jordan.

There were two conditions in this experiment. One was a slightly modified version of Milgram's 1963 situation; the other was the self-selection control condition in which teachers could decide whether to give a shock and how much to give. The median ages of three groups of children were 7.5, 10.5, and 14.5 years. Boys were ordered to shock male "learners" aged 11 or 15; girls had one 15 year old female as "learner." Across all groups, 73% of the children were obedient to the highest level in the obedience condition and 16% in the control condition. There were no significant differences related to age or gender. Symptoms of emotional tension were more common in girls and younger children.

It seems to me that subjecting children to this situation is unethical, even if one can justify the stress experienced by adults. I presented my ethical concerns to the psychologist who was the editor of the journal when this article was accepted for publication. Shanab, the first author of the article had told the editor that research procedures that might be unethical in the United States were considered acceptable in Jordan where the research was done. The editor accepted this reasoning and said that he had received no other letters expressing concern about using children as subjects in this situation (A. G. Greenwald, personal communication, April 7, 1984). Although the ethics of this study, using children, received little attention, the Milgram studies were quite controversial.

The Ethics of Obedience Research

In 1964 Diana Baumrind drew attention to some of the ethical issues related to Milgram's 1963 study. Milgram responded (1964) and a few other comments were published, but it would be several years before there was an extensive debate on research ethics in psychology (McGaha & Korn, 1995). I believe the major factor in stimulating that debate was not Milgram's research or any of the other ethically questionable studies that are discussed in this book, but rather pressure from the outside, particularly in the form of federal regulations protecting human research participants. Those regulations did not affect psychology in a major way until the 1970s. Milgram's research, especially after his book appeared in 1974, served as a clear, dramatic example of what psychologists might do with research subjects in their laboratories.

Just as philosophers have been unable to agree on a set of clear rules that can be used to resolve ethical dilemmas, so have psychologists who apply moral philosophy been unable to agree on the ethics of Milgram's obedience research or the use of deception in general. There are two issues that are critical in this discussion: first, the balance of harm and benefits to participants or others; second, the extent to which research participants must give informed consent. Baumrind's article is a significant document in the history of deception because she was one of the first psychologists to consider these two issues in judging the acceptability of psychological research.

Baumrind (1964) did not accept Milgram's assertion that research participants were not harmed. She quoted Milgram's descriptions of strong emotional reactions by individual subjects and wondered "what sort of procedures could dissipate the type of emotional disturbance just described" (1964, p. 422). Furthermore, she regarded "the emotional disturbance . . . as potentially harmful because it could easily effect an alteration in the subject's self-image or ability to trust adult authorities in the future" (p. 422). She doubted the effectiveness of Milgram's dehoaxing, questioned the representativeness of his sample, and denied the reasonableness of a parallel with obedience in Nazi death camps.

In this 1964 comment, Baumrind never directly mentioned deception as a problem, although she was critical of violations of trust that subjects have in the research relationship. She concluded, "I would not like to see experiments such as Milgram's proceed unless the subjects were fully informed of the dangers of serious aftereffects and his correctives were clearly shown to be effective in restoring their state of well being" (p. 423).

Milgram's (1964) reply to Baumrind focused on the latter issue of harm and benefits to participants, perhaps because it made no sense to discuss fully informed consent in a study where deception is essential. He provided data that he believed would show that subjects were not harmed, but did gain something important from their participation in his obedience research. Furthermore, Milgram argued, "momentary excitement is not the same as harm" (Milgram, 1964, p. 849).

Milgram presented two kinds of data in response to Baumrind's concern about long-term harm to research participants. First, some number of subjects (Milgram never said how many) completed a questionnaire in which only 1.3% said that they were sorry to have taken part in the experiment.

"Further, four-fifths of the subjects felt that more experiments of this sort should be carried out, and 74% indicated that they had learned something of personal importance as a result of being in the study" (p. 849).

Milgram promised that this follow-up data would "be presented more fully in a forthcoming monograph" (p. 849). That monograph (his book) would not come forth for another ten years and did not contain the additional data that was promised. A table that showed the percent of subjects who were "glad" or "sorry" to have been in the experiment was published in a *Hastings Center Report*, and reprinted in a collection of Milgram's work (Milgram, 1977/1992). The table shows only percentages, but not how many subjects, from which of the eighteen experiments the data had been taken, how many did not respond, or whether there were other items in the questionnaire.

The second source of data on long-term effects of participation came from "an impartial medical examiner, experienced in outpatient treatment, [who] interviewed 40 experimental subjects. The examining psychiatrist focused on those subjects he felt would be most likely to have suffered consequences from participation" (Milgram, 1964, p. 850). Milgram did not provide a reference to the psychiatrist's report and no complete report ever was published. A brief statement by the psychiatrist eventually appeared in a collection of documents about experiments with humans. He concluded that "no evidence was found of any traumatic reactions" (Errera, 1972, p. 400). The psychiatrist stated: "Not included in this report is a description of the selection process, a description of the population seen as compared to the overall sample, and an accounting of those who did not keep their return appointments" (p. 400). These are important details to omit from the one published source of this critical follow-up study. The unavailability of Milgram's follow-up data leads me to conclude that the absence of harmful effects was not proven.

Milgram concluded his reply to Baumrind with his version of what would become an essential part of the social psychologist's standard defense of deceptive research: "the laboratory psychologist senses his work will lead to human betterment, not only because enlightenment is more dignified than ignorance, but because new knowledge is pregnant with humane consequences" (Milgram, 1964, p. 852).

The debate on the ethics of Milgram's obedience research began in scholarly books and psychology journals. After Milgram's book was published in 1974, however, the debate was extended to publications read by the educated general public; for example, *Newsweek, Commentary,* and *The New York Times.* In this more public arena, the discussion again did not focus on deception per se, nor even so much on possible harm to participants. The dispute centered on whether the stress experienced by participants was justified by what, if anything, had been learned about human nature, particularly the extent to which we all share the potential for evil that was exhibited by the Nazi war criminals.[5] By 1974 incidents in Viet Nam had provided additional examples of the possible relevance of Milgram's research. Once again, I refer the reader to Miller's (1986) book for a summary of the various points of view.

Miller, however, overlooked one comment from an important psychologist. Lawrence Kohlberg was, and remains after his death, the premier psychologist of morality. He also was a friend and colleague of Milgram at Yale where, in the early 1960's, he found himself with an opportunity to get some unusual data related to his theory of moral development from participants in the obedience studies. But it is Kohlberg's (1974) observations about himself and Milgram that are of interest here. Kohlberg watched the experiment take place:

> [T]hrough the mentality of the one-way vision mirror. . . . I could more dispassionately observe the suffering of the subjects . . . just as the subjects could continue to shock their assumed victims when separated by a screen from them. In this sense, Milgram's belief in a social-science 'objectivity' operated as a false screen from the moral and personal understanding of the realities of the situation he created and allowed him to engage in a morally dubious experiment. He was himself a victim. . . . Serving the authority of science under the banner of 'objectivity,' he himself inflicted pain on others for the greater social welfare. (p. 42)

Kohlberg talked with some of the participants and asked what they had learned from their experience in the research. One subject said that "he acted just like Eichmann" and "enjoyed it." Another "learned a lot from the experiment that he could use in business. . . . [T]he susceptibility of man to authority and deception . . . and the notion that it is legitimate or scientific to play upon it." This is not the kind of learning that Milgram reported. The experiment would have been justified for Kohlberg, however, if it "had been used as a vehicle for moral dialogue and education for each individual subject."

Kohlberg recognized his own moral vulnerability:

> I was only an 'innocent' bystander watching this harm, but turning it to my own intellectual advantage by researching it. I too used a utilitarian logic to justify my action, blinded by the idols of scientific psychology. At that time I did not have what I now have, a conviction that I could have intervened, not by force but by moral

reason to aid my friend Milgram in clarifying and developing his
own moral reasoning about what he was doing. (p. 43)

Research as Theater: II

Milgram knew very well what he was doing and was clear about the
moral justification for his obedience research.

> The central moral justification for allowing a procedure of the sort
> used in my experiment is that it is judged acceptable by those who
> have taken part in it. Moreover, it was the salience of this fact
> throughout that constituted the chief moral warrant for the contin-
> uation of the experiments. (1974, p. 199; entire quotation in italics in
> original)

Milgram considered his research situations to be a form of theater with
himself as the director and the participants as actors who reveal deep truths
about human nature. He is the prototypical example of what social psychologists had become and would continue to be during the stage-production era
of research in the next twenty years. In a 1974 interview he said, "I am
interested in studying the behavior of people in real social circumstances,
and thus you must create that reality. You must be minutely concerned with
its detail. . . . [The obedience experiments] took a tremendous amount of
rehearsal. . . . Two full weeks with constant screaming on my part, constant"
(Tavris, 1974a, p. 75).

The 1963 study of obedience became a play within a play when it was
the setting for a stage production, *The Dogs of Pavlov*, which appeared in
London in 1971. The author of the play used the words "bullshit," "fraudu-
lent," and "cheat" to describe the experiment (Milgram, 1974, p. 198). In his
reply to this "excessively harsh" language, Milgram (1974) was clear about the
similarities he saw between plays and experiments.

> I will not say that you cheated, tricked, and defrauded your
> audience [in the play]. But I would hold the same claim for the
> experiment. Misinformation is employed in the experiment; illusion
> is used when necessary in order to set the stage for the revelation of
> certain difficult-to-get-at truths; and these procedures are justified
> for one reason only: they are, in the end, accepted and endorsed by
> those who are exposed to them. . . . (p. 198).

While some persons construe the experimenter to be acting in
terms of deceit, manipulation, and chicanery, it is . . . also possible to

see him as a dramatist who creates scenes of revelatory power, and who brings participants into them. So perhaps we are not so far apart in the kind of work we do. I do grant there is an important difference in that those exposed to your theatrical illusions expect to confront them, while my subjects are not forewarned. However, whether it is unethical to pursue truths through the use of my form of dramaturgical device cannot be answered in the abstract. It depends entirely on the response of those who have been exposed to such procedures. (p. 199)

Milgram was indeed a creative artist. He wrote stories and stage plays and used photography in some of his research. In the summer of 1960 he and some friends improvised street-theater scenes at restaurants along the Massachusetts Turnpike, enacting common human interactions and observing the reactions of others (Tavris, 1974b, p. 78). He also used the medium of television as a research setting, although unsuccessfully, when he wrote an antisocial act into a real TV program to see if it would influence viewers to commit that act.[6] But the effect was not demonstrated because "perhaps the antisocial act—breaking into charity boxes and stealing money—was not dramatic enough" (quoted in Tavris, 1974, p. 76).

Stanley Milgram died on December 20, 1984, at the age of 51. The author of an obituary compared him to Pablo Picasso, a comparison that also had been used for Leon Festinger.

Is it presumptuous to claim that the picture Milgram's experiments gives us of what we do to one another is as compelling as "Guernica?" Is there any picture of our nature that people have been as eager to reject as the one depicted in those experiments? What artist has done better at making us see who we really are? Which artist ought we miss more? (Sabini, 1986, p. 1379).

Milgram took social psychology to its limits in terms of creative research design, ethical standards, and the significance of his findings. He was an independent researcher, like Solomon Asch, working on problems that he saw as important, usually before other psychologists thought of studying them. He won prizes for his work, but not from the American Psychological Association, which had plenty of time to honor him before his death at the age of 51. Perhaps his research had become too controversial when the time came to bestow honors.

The use of deception in "impact experiments" already was on its rapid rise when Milgram conducted his obedience studies. Festinger's descendants were primarily responsible for maintaining the growth of deception in social psychology, and Milgram's role in this history was to confront the ethical limits of deception and bring dramatic psychological research to the attention of the general public. He was the creative artist who wrote and produced one great play that drew attention to what social psychologists were doing. After that stage productions became commonplace in the psychology laboratory.

—9—

The Stage Production Era

Deception had become a way of laboratory life for most social psychologists in the 1960s and 1970s. Many of the most dramatic forms of deception took place during this period, and the use of deception rose to its peak around 1972. We have seen how the use of dramatic deception was developed by a few of the leading figures in the history of social psychology. In this chapter I will try to provide a sense of the variety of creative research situations staged by social psychologists. I remind the reader that although the use of deception appeared to decline in the 1980s, It did not become an uncommon practice.

Growth and Change

Academic psychology grew rapidly after World War II and that growth accelerated in the 1960s. Among the factors contributing to this growth were increased undergraduate enrollments and new federal programs that provided grants for research and graduate education. Enrollments in psychology increased faster than in some other fields because students saw it as relevant to the issues of the time. That relevance did not come from the kind of rat psychology practiced in the field of animal learning, but from the kind of interesting real-world topics studied by clinical and social psychologists. The federal funding that supported researchers so they would not have to teach all these undergraduates,[1] allowed them to support graduate students who would do that teaching and run the actual laboratory studies for their professors. The increased enrollments also provided a large pool of subjects for the research.

As the size of the research enterprise grew, so did the range of topics that were studied by social psychologists. Some topics were not really new, but rather were elaborations on old themes; for example, person perception and social influence. Other topics, like bystander intervention in an emergency, appeared in the research literature for the first time. Deception was used in

the majority of studies in all these new areas; in the area of bystander intervention (helping behavior) it was the rare experiment that did not use
deception.

During the twenty-plus years from 1960 to the early 1980s, an important
change also occurred in the theories that dominated social psychology. Leon
Festinger's dissonance theory continued to have an important influence but
it was joined by a related theory that soon became the basis for an even larger
amount of research. Cognitive dissonance theory had been concerned primarily with motivation or the causes of behavior; thoughts that are inconsistent (dissonant) make people do something to reduce the dissonance.
Attribution theory, the new point of view, was concerned with how people
think about what causes the behavior of themselves and others. The focus
shifted from the motive to what people think is the motive.

The ideas of Fritz Heider (1958) laid the groundwork for later versions
of attribution theory (Jones, 1985). Heider was a theorist who did little
research himself, but in the middle 1960s, several psychologists developed
and tested variations of Heider's ideas (Jones & Davis, 1965; Kelley, 1967).
The details of these different versions of attribution theory are beyond the
scope of this book. This general approach has become the dominant
theoretical orientation in social psychology, and most of that research used
deception.

Directions for Deception

Many social psychologists during the 1970s were convinced that good
research required the use of situations that approximated real life as closely
as possible. Research was good if it was scientific, which meant manipulating
aspects of the situation and that required deception. Another criterion of
good research was that it could be generalized to other situations, so the more
realistic the experiment, the more it was like real life. Deception was used to
create the illusion of reality.

This view of research was made explicit in the 1968 edition of *The
Handbook of Social Psychology* (Lindzey & Aronson, 1968). The chapter on
experimentation (Aronson & Carlsmith, 1968) was presented as a guide that
would help graduate students and others learn how to conduct laboratory
research. The authors emphasized that the laboratory situation should be
realistic, but contrasted two kinds of realism. Experimental realism meant
that subjects became so involved in the situation that it would have a strong
impact on them, and they would be led to take it seriously. Mundane realism,
on the other hand, meant that the situation was like one that would occur in
the world outside the laboratory. Such a situation might be boring and have
little impact on the subject. The important thing was to involve the subject

in the research (experimental realism), whether or not the situation was similar to real life. The deception experiment was described as one important way of creating experimental realism. Many of the suggestions presented in this 1968 *Handbook* chapter had been made thirty-five years earlier by Saul Rosenszweig (1933), although his work was not cited. For example, one suggestion was to avoid the need for disguise "by using experimental organisms who are, by nature, unsuspicious" such as "four-year-old children" (Aronson & Carlsmith, 1968, p. 59).

The theater metaphor was an important feature of this guide to research design in social psychology, and Aronson and Carlsmith made experimentation sound exciting and creative. In a section headed, "setting the stage" (p. 37ff) they were explicit about the theatrical nature of experimental realism, which requires "a great deal of imagination and ingenuity" (p. 37) to create a believable cover story and write an involving scenario, and an "earnestness of demeanor" (p. 52) to sell the package effectively. "A good experiment never bores a subject unless boredom is the conceptual variable" (p. 53). Researchers were told that the success of deception was "an empirical question" (p. 39) that required checking to see if the story was believed.

Referring to social psychology as theater is more than a metaphor. Many of the studies that I described in previous chapters were staged productions with carefully chosen props, and actors who went through rehearsals. Stories have been told about the dramatics involved in staging famous experiments: Elliot Aronson told how difficult it was to train his friend, Merrill Carlsmith, to act naturally; Stanley Milgram remembered two weeks of constant screaming on his part as a director during rehearsals for his obedience studies; finding an experimenter-actor who could fake epileptic seizures was not easy for the designers of an early bystander intervention study. Researchers wrote scripts, memorized them, practiced their acting, and performed dress rehearsals before carrying out the study with actual participants. The experience of one research assistant provides an example:

> I was not allowed to read from a script. I was expected to act it out. I was to be judged, not just on the script, but on my performance of it. And it wouldn't do to woodenly greet subjects, sit them in a chair, and read them stiff lines. . . . [So] I rewrote the script to give myself additional casual lines. I practiced as if it were a Broadway debut. (Kozlowski, 1987, p. 191)

Many of the leaders in social psychology at that time encouraged the use of deception, usually by example but sometimes explicitly. Edward Jones, an important attribution theorist, was concerned with the reliability of what people said about their attitudes. Statements about other people may be biased one way or another because a person wants to look good or please the experimenter. To control these false reports, Jones and Harold Sigall (1971) proposed using a method called "the bogus pipeline." The method involved "the use of a device or machine that purportedly measures one's true feelings about a person or an issue, some means of validating the machine in the subject's eye, and finally the dependent variable itself: a prediction by the subject of the machine's telltale reading" (p. 349).

The bogus pipeline is similar to a lie detector and its effectiveness depends in part on the general belief that lie detectors work:[2] "if people can be made to believe that there are devices reflecting their true inner attitudes or feelings, the measurement possibilities are almost limitless" (Jones & Sigall, 1971, p. 354). In lie detection actual physiological responses are recorded, while the bogus pipeline procedure only pretended to do so. Research participants were told that the machine was recording their galvanic skin response (GSR) and that not only could this machine measure emotional arousal but it could distinguish between a person's likes and dislikes. These feelings were shown on a dial with a scale that ranged from −3000 to +3000.

A critical step in the procedure, as in lie detection, is convincing the subject that the machine works. Jones and his colleagues devised several ways of doing this. One involved showing a tape of another person being tested, with the bogus machine accurately revealing her responses. Another involved using responses from a questionnaire that had been given some time earlier in an apparently unrelated situation. Most subjects "expressed amazement at the accuracy of the meter" and "were characteristically quite surprised to learn after the experiment that the machine's properties were fictitious" (Jones & Sigall, 1971, p. 357).

After convincing the subject that the machine was accurate the experimenter would ask the subject certain questions concerning their impressions of another person. Instead of asking for a direct response, the subject was asked to predict the reading on the dial. If you were in such an experiment and were asked to say if you liked your partner in the experiment (actually an accomplice of the experimenter) you might hesitate to give a negative opinion. If, however, you believe that a machine is able to detect your true feelings, then your prediction of the machine's response should be less biased. Jones and Sigall reported several studies using this technique, one of which concerned an obnoxious confederate of the experimenter who was made to appear disabled by wearing large leg braces. The bogus pipeline technique has been used often since its introduction, and has been shown to be effective in reducing socially desirable responding (Roese & Jamieson, 1993).

Ubiquitous Watergate

One of the best examples of research in the stage production era was a study that combined experimental manipulation with contemporary relevance in an extremely realistic situation and used the new ideas of attribution theory to interpret the results (West, Gunn, & Chernicky, 1975). The study was conducted and published at a time when the Watergate burglary, which involved high level officials in the Nixon administration, had been a major news story. It was also a time in which social psychology was undergoing a "crisis of confidence" (Elms, 1975) because critics from within the field were doubting its methods, relevance, and ethics. The Watergate study is illustrative of each of these issues.

How could we explain the behavior of the Watergate burglars and government officials who covered up the crime? The answer to that question had both theoretical and real-world relevance. We could have attributed their behavior to the character of these men; they were immoral people or had undesirable personality characteristics. Social psychologists call this a dispositional explanation when causes of behavior are attributed to personal characteristics. According to attribution theory, however, there is a tendency for people who do something like committing a crime (actors) to give a different explanation for what they have done than the explanation given by other people (observers). The person who commits the act says that pressures in the situation caused the behavior, whereas people who observe what happened (e.g., when they read about it in the newspaper) say that the person who did it was bad (greedy, dishonest, etc.). The authors of the Watergate study thought it would be important to show how situational factors could have led to compliance in an illegal act and how actors and observers would give different explanations for what happened.

Stephen West, Steven Gunn, and Paul Chernicky (1975) designed two experiments to test these ideas. One was a field study, conducted in the community and disguised so as not to appear to be a psychology experiment. The other was conducted in university classrooms. It was the community study that raised ethical questions because some research participants (college students in criminology) were manipulated into committing an illegal act.

"Each subject was initially approached by the experimenter, who was known to most of the subjects as a local private investigator" (p. 57). The article does not indicate how the subjects knew that, or where the approach was made, but "every person approached did make an appointment to meet with the experimenter" at his home or in a restaurant, to discuss "a project you might be interested in" (p. 57). At that later meeting the experimenter/ private eye was accompanied by his assistant and "carried a briefcase that contained elaborate plans for the commission of a burglary of a local advertising firm" (p. 57). The confederate played the role of a member of the burglary team.

When the meeting began, the experimenter and his confederate revealed their intent to commit a burglary, gave the reasons for this, and presented the details of the plan. Some participants quickly objected to the idea of committing a crime and were asked to listen to the details before making a final decision. None of them left the meeting. This is the story they were told:

> [T]he burglary of an advertising firm located in a local office building had been carefully planned and . . . a four-person team was necessary to carry it out. This team was to consist of (a) the experimenter, who would monitor police calls in an office inside the building; (b) the confederate, who would serve as an outside lookout; (c) a lock-and-safe expert (not present in the experimental situation), who was described as having an extensive background in military intelligence; and (d) the subject, who was to serve as an inside lookout and who was also to microfilm the advertising agency records. The crime was presented to the subject in elaborate detail, including aerial photographs of the building and the surrounding area, lists of city and state patrol cars, their routes and times, and blueprints of the advertising office. The total effect of the situation was to create as great an impact as possible and to convince the subject that it was a well-planned, professional job with only a minimal chance of being caught. (pp. 57–58)

The experimental manipulation involved giving different reasons for committing the crime to different groups of subjects. Two groups of subjects were told that the Internal Revenue Service wanted the burglary team to microfilm

> an allegedly illegal set of accounting records maintained by the firm to defraud the United States Government out of 6.8 million tax dollars per year. It was further explained that the company was in reality a front for a Miami investment corporation and that a dual set of records was being kept. The microfilmed records were described as being necessary to get a search warrant and subpoena so that the original records could be seized. (p. 57)

Subjects in one of these two groups were told that, if they were caught, the government had promised them immunity from prosecution; in the second group, subjects were told there would be no guarantee of immunity if they were caught.

The reason for the burglary given to a third group of subjects was that a competing advertising firm had offered $8,000 for the information and $2,000 of this would go to each member of the burglary team, including the experimental subject. A fourth group served as a control to see how many subjects would agree to commit a crime when given a weak reason, "merely to determine whether the burglary plans designed by the experimenter would work" (p. 57). They also were told that nothing actually would be stolen.

After reasons for the burglary and details of the plot had been given, the experimenter asked the critical questions to find out if participants would agree to commit a crime by inviting them "to come to the final planning meeting, which would take place at the experimenter's office. If the subject refused, the experimenter emphasized that the plan was foolproof and asked the subject to reconsider his decision. If the subject refused a second time, the experiment was terminated" (p. 58). Simple acceptance or refusal, along with the reasons given for the decision, were the primary measures in the experiment. Finally, the experimenter explained in detail the true purpose of the experiment and reasons for using deception.

The second of the two experiments was conducted in classrooms, using students from introductory psychology classes. Each student received a booklet that described one of the four conditions used in the field study. They were asked to guess the proportion of people who would agree to take part in the burglary, why people would agree or refuse, and to describe the personalities of those people as well as that of the private investigator. The people in the classroom were the "observers" who read about the behavior of the subjects (actors) in the field study.

Of the participants in the field study who had faced a real decision (actors), 45% agreed to take part in the burglary they thought was sponsored by the IRS with immunity from prosecution, but only 5% agreed when immunity was not guaranteed. When the subjects thought they might get a $2,000 pay-off from a competing advertising firm, 20% agreed and 10% agreed when the reason was to help the experimenter test his plan. The authors thought that this rate of agreement was relatively low and explained this result in terms of the negative reputation of the agency (the IRS) chosen to sponsor the crime. Observers' estimates of probable agreement were 28% for IRS sponsorship with immunity, 14% for the IRS (no immunity condition), 12% for the $2,000 pay-off, and 16% for the control condition. The authors concluded that observers are poor predictors of actual behavior.

The reasons (attributions) given for agreeing or refusing were important for the theory being tested. As predicted, actors tended to explain their own behavior more in terms of the situation than the observers did. For the authors of this study, one implication of this result is "that when outside observers, including the press, view an action, they tend to give too much weight to dispositional factors as the cause of behavior" (p. 62).

A major part of the "crisis" in social psychology that I previously referred to concerned ethical issues in the use of deception. Critics recognized that deception was used extensively and sometimes dramatically. West and his colleagues confronted this issue directly in the final section of their article:

> The field portion of [this] study involved elaborate deceptions in which some subjects indicated an implicit agreement to become involved in a potentially illegal and possibly immoral activity. During the experiment and following disclosure of the experimental deceptions, it is possible that some subjects may have experienced some temporary loss of self-esteem: They may have felt embarrassed, guilty, or anxious when confronted with the full meaning of their implied agreement to participate in the alleged break-in. (p. 63)

The authors listed four "procedural aspects of the field experiment" that reflected their "concern with ethical considerations" (p. 63). Being concerned is not, however, the same as providing adequate information and protection for research participants. For example, the authors argue that "the experimental manipulations were not forced on any of the subjects. Following an initial information contact by the experimenter, all of the subjects attended the experimental 'meeting' *by their own choice*" (p. 63, italics mine). But the experimenters certainly had tried to influence that choice. At an earlier point in their discussion they listed "several techniques that were used in the present experiment that have been shown in previous research to increase compliance rates" (p. 61). These techniques included getting subjects to agree to a small request to come to a meeting before asking them to agree to a major request to commit a crime. In social psychology, this is known as the "foot-in-the-door" technique (Freedman & Fraser, 1966).

A lawyer served as a consultant to the project and the State Attorney's Office reviewed the experiment. These consultants found the research to be acceptable legally, so the experimenters could reassure participants that they had not broken the law. But they had done something illegal when they agreed to take part in a conspiracy to commit a crime. The fact that the other members of the conspiracy (the experimenters) did not really intend to commit the crime kept them all out of jail, but that might not make someone feel better after realizing that he *might* have been involved in illegal activity.

The authors say that "none of the subjects appeared to suffer any form of psychological trauma as a result of their participation in the field experiment" and "many subjects spontaneously commented that they found the experiment to be an interesting and even enlightening experience" (p. 63). No follow-up studies were done, however, to discover possible problems that may have remained with the participants. These authors, like many others who conduct controversial research, seem willing to accept subjects' testimonials concerning the benefits of their participation, while not willing to accept such statements as part of the experiment proper. Perhaps this is a place where the "bogus pipeline" should be used.

The editors of the journal in which the Watergate study was published were concerned enough about the ethics of that study to publish a comment from Stuart Cook (1975). He stressed the importance of careful debriefing of participants and of the value of follow-up studies, but he also pointed out the possibility that there could be negative reactions from "legislators and other public figures" who found out that students had been encouraged to break the law, "and that such reactions could lead to reduced backing for behavioral science in general" (Cook, 1975, p. 67).

Cook had chaired the American Psychological Association (APA) Ad Hoc Committee on Ethical Standards in Psychological Research that had developed the ethical principles that served as guidelines for psychologists who conduct research with humans. He was well qualified to apply those principles to the Watergate study and he did so in the objective manner of the research establishment at that time, which recognized the dilemmas involved in weighing costs and benefits and the validity of different points of view concerning the ethics of deception. (See the next chapter.) Cook's conclusion was that "the resolution of this [ethical] issue is a collective problem. . . . That we have no consensus on a value conflict as important as that raised by 'Ubiquitous Watergate' presents a challenge of high priority for the immediate future" (Cook, 1975, p. 68).

Ubiquitous Deception

As I mentioned earlier, the 1960s saw the development of many new topics in social psychology and new versions of old topics, all of which made extensive use of deceptive methods, often in dramatic fashion. Pick up any general textbook of social psychology, and some topics in most chapters will contain descriptions of experiments from the stage production era. I will present some examples that are important because they are typical of a large body of research on a specific topic (e.g., aggression) or because they were ethically controversial when they were published. Some of these examples are considered to be "classics" in the literature of social psychology.

Chemical Deception

Stanley Schachter and his student, Jerome Singer, staged an experiment that was one of the most widely discussed of the 1960s (Schachter & Singer, 1962). Schachter was a student of Leon Festinger and worked with him on the research that led to the book, *When Prophecy Fails*, which was discussed in chapter 7. Schachter himself influenced many students who went on to become famous social psychologists (Grunberg, Nisbett, Rodin, & Singer, 1987).

Schachter and Singer were interested in cognitive, social, and physiological determinants of emotional state. Their research attempted to show that in different situations, given the same physiological symptoms, the emotion that a person experiences depends on what that person thinks is going on in the situation. The procedures used in their study were described in several pages of small print. Briefly, subjects were injected with either epinephrine (adrenalin) or a placebo and then placed into a situation designed to make them feel either happy or angry. The research design was more complex, but I want to focus on the deceptions that were used.

The experiment was presented to subjects as "a study of the effects of vitamin supplements on vision" (p. 382). When a subject arrived at the laboratory, he (all were male) was told that this was a study of the effect on vision of a vitamin compound with the made-up name, Suproxin. All but one of 185 subjects agreed to be injected with this alleged vitamin supplement. A physician then came to the room and gave a subcutaneous injection of either epinephrine or a placebo, although all subjects were told it was Suproxin. Among the actual effects of epinephrine are increases in heart rate, blood pressure, cerebral blood flow, blood sugar, and respiration; salivation and peripheral blood flow are decreased. According to Schachter and Singer, "as far as the subject is concerned the major subjective symptoms are palpitation, tremor, and sometimes a feeling of flushing and accelerated breathing" (p. 382).

Subjects who received epinephrine were divided into three groups. One group was told to expect the correct symptoms from their injection. A second group was told that "the injection was mild and harmless and would have no side effects" (p. 383). The third group was given incorrect information about the symptoms they would experience: "What will probably happen is that your feet will feel numb, you will have an itching sensation over parts of your body, and you may get a slight headache" (p. 383).

The second act of this production took place after "the physician left the room and the experimenter returned with a stooge whom he introduced as another subject" (p. 384) who supposedly also had been injected with Suproxin. They were told to wait twenty minutes while the vitamin was "absorbed into the bloodstream." During this waiting period the stooge acted to create a situation of either "euphoria" or anger, depending on the group to which the subject had been assigned. In the euphoria condition, the stooge played with various items that had been left in the room and generally acted silly. In the anger situation, the stooge pretended to be indignant about aspects of the experiment, including a questionnaire that he and the real subject were filling out, which contained items of a personal nature.

Observations and measures of the real subject's emotional state were taken. Although some of the results were weak, the authors concluded that people will label their emotional state in a way suggested by the situation if they have no other explanation for their physiological arousal. When they know that their symptoms have been produced by a drug, they will use that as the explanation for the way they feel.

Two kinds of deception are represented in this study. One is misinformation about the drug administered to subjects and the other concerns the performance of the stooge. The latter involved careful rehearsal of a script by research assistants to fool the subjects. The former deception, although some acting was involved, was based on a lie about a powerful drug. This kind of physiological deception was unusual, and Schachter was concerned about these drug effects, according to Ladd Wheeler, one of his students.

Wheeler (1987) reported that the results of the Schachter and Singer "study were not very convincing, despite Stan's persuasive writing style and some clever internal analyses" (p. 47). A later study conducted by Wheeler (Schachter & Wheeler, 1962) used chlorpromazine, which would suppress emotional arousal rather than increase it as epinephrine had done. But the experimenters were not sure what dose to use.

> We pretested the chlorpromazine dose at 50 mg on ourselves and other graduate students, and Stan [Schachter] had us make notes of our feelings. Chuck Hawkins wrote that he had decided he was definitely going to die, after he clocked his pulse at 32 and falling. Bibb Latane came out of the testing room and promptly fell on his head, knocking over the coffee pot. Stan consulted all sorts of experts and finally decided to halve the dosage in the face of totally overwhelming ignorance on the part of the experts. Mental hospital patients are given extreme dosages, but no one knew what it might do to an undergraduate. Even then, we had a cot available for the chlorpromazine subjects, and it was used with some frequency after the experimental session. We were very careful about the welfare of the subjects. They were all cleared through the University Health Service, and a physician gave the injections and was in attendance at all times. (Wheeler, 1987, p. 48)

Wheeler also remembers that Schachter gave him the assignment of doing a rat experiment, "but I simply could not handle injecting the rats in the belly when they know what I was going to do" (p. 49).

These comments indicate a far more casual attitude toward both drugs and human (not rat) research participants than we would expect today. Drugs like chlorpromazine were relatively new and psychologists were experimenting with drugs at this time with little restraint other than their own judgment. Timothy Leary and Richard Alpert, for example, had begun their studies of hallucinogenic drugs, which they were administering with minimal medical supervision. The pretesting reported by Wheeler was quite unsystematic, the precautions were minimal, and participants were misinformed about important information.

Within a few years the Schachter and Singer study of emotion had become a classic, which means that it was described in most general psychology textbooks as research that everyone should know about. However, several major criticisms of that study had been published, and in 1979 Gary Marshall and Philip Zimbardo published their attempt to repeat part of Schachter and Singer's 1962 study (Marshall & Zimbardo, 1979). Marshall and Zimbardo designed an experiment that modified some of the conditions of the earlier study and added additional groups that were intended to evaluate Schachter and Singer's conclusions about what determines the experience of emotion.

Not all the aspects of the Schachter and Singer (1962) study could be repeated, however. After 1966, federal law required that all universities have research review committees that were charged with insuring adequate protection for research participants.[3] Research could not be carried out unless approved by the review committee at the investigator's institution. The review committee at Stanford believed that it was "unethical to induce anger in unsuspecting subjects" (Marshall & Zimbardo, 1979, p. 971) and would only allow the "euphoric" condition.

The Stanford review committee also was concerned about "possible adverse reactions to epinephrine injections in normal young adult males . . . based on an unreferenced comment in a general pharmacology" (p. 971) textbook. For many years the major pharmacology textbook has been *The Pharmacological Basis of Therapeutics* (Goodman & Gilman, 1975), so that probably was the source used by the reviewers. This statement concerning epinephrine should have caused concern: "Epinephrine may cause disturbing reactions, such as *fear, anxiety, tenseness, restlessness, throbbing headache, tremor, weakness, dizziness, pallor, respiratory difficulty*, and *palpitation*. The effects rapidly subside with rest, quiet, recumbency, and reassurance, but the patient is often alarmed and should perhaps be forewarned" (Goodman & Gilman, 1975, p. 491, italics in original).

These are symptoms that I certainly would want to be warned about, but that was not done for the students at Stanford. The review committee allowed epinephrine to be used and did not prohibit the investigators from misinforming participants about the purpose of the study, the nature of the substance that would be injected, or the symptoms that would be experienced. However, the concern for adverse reactions to the drug led the investigators to take several precautions. Health records of potential participants were screened to eliminate those who were likely to have negative reactions. The epinephrine was administered by a cardiologist who was available during the experiment, heart rate was monitored continuously by radio telemetry, and subjects did not leave the experiment until heart rate and other signs of arousal had returned to normal.

In some ways the 1979 experiment was staged like the one in 1962 but with variations that turned out to be important. The study was presented to participants as concerning "the effects of a special vitamin on vision" (Marshall & Zimbardo, 1979, p. 971), although now the vitamin was called D-27 rather than Suproxin. A different set of symptoms was described to subjects who were misinformed about the effects of epinephrine: "Subjects were led to expect dryness of the throat, slight headache, and some slight coolness in toes and fingers" (p. 972). The rehearsed sequence acted out by the euphoric confederate (the word *stooge* was not used in 1979) was similar to that in the 1962 study.

Their results led Marshall and Zimbardo to conclusions that differed from those reached by Schachter and Singer in 1962. Most importantly, the emotional feelings created by "the social environment had minimal effect" on subjects who had been stimulated by drug injections, and "negative affective reactions occurred in a social context where a confederate was perceived to be happy" (Marshall & Zimbardo, 1979, p. 970).

All of this did not make Schachter and Singer happy. In their published reaction (Schachter & Singer, 1979) to Marshall and Zimbardo's study, they say they were "bemused and perplexed" (p. 990) by the modifications that were made in their original method. First, rather than completely deceiving subjects about the symptoms of epinephrine, Marshall and Zimbardo's variation included two real symptoms, dryness of the mouth and coolness of hands and feet. The investigators mistakenly told the truth, when intending to deceive.

The second variation concerned the dosage of epinephrine. A negative emotional experience was produced only in one group of subjects for whom the dosage of epinephrine was much larger than that used by Schachter and Singer in 1962. They referred to their own experience with epinephrine as evidence for the differential effects on emotion of large and small doses of this drug:

[W]e ourselves tried doses as heavy as, and heavier than, that used by Marshall and Zimbardo in their increased arousal condition. We would not do it again and can only assume that Marshall and Zimbardo never tried their increased dose on themselves or, if they did, that they are made of considerably stronger stuff than are we. At this [larger] dose, we did not have palpitations—our hearts pounded; we did not have tremors—we shook. We might have been convinced by someone that we were about to die, but no amount of social psychological tomfoolery could have convinced us that we were euphoric, or angry, or excited, or indeed anything but that something was very wrong and that we felt lousy. (Schachter & Singer, 1979, p. 991)

The participants in Marshall and Zimbardo's study must have been similarly upset by what they thought was a vitamin injection.

However, the effect of the smaller doses that Schachter and Singer say they gave to themselves was quite positive:

[T]he sensation was for us curious and exhilarating—a feeling of emotional deja vu. We had felt this way often in the past, but in this laboratory context it made no sense to feel this way—a pure arousal state uncluttered by passion or fear, affection or hatred. It was neither pleasant nor unpleasant; it was, though, absorbing enough so that at mild doses, we were delighted to serve as our own subjects again and again. (1979, p. 995)

They concluded by inviting readers to convince a physician to inject them with epinephrine so that "they can decide which of us is right" (p. 995).

Schachter and Singer (1979) also expressed a bit of nostalgia for the good old days of research, before federally legislated review boards. "In these days [1979] of ethical guidelines and human subjects committees, this may very well be the end of the matter, for it is unlikely that anyone will do experiments such as ours or Marshall and Zimbardo's for quite a while, if ever again" (p. 995). In between the lines of this sentiment is the opinion that psychologists were quite capable of deciding what was best for research subjects, even to the point of deceiving them about a powerful drug, and that society will lose the benefits of significant social psychological research because review committees will not approve forms of deception that were acceptable in the past.

Other research groups in the 1970s also were studying the interaction of thoughts and physiological arousal. Princeton psychologist Joel Cooper and his colleagues conducted a series of studies on the arousal properties of cognitive dissonance. One of these studies (Cooper, Zanna, & Taves, 1978) involved misinforming participants about the effects of a drug that was given in the form of a pill rather than by injection. The subjects in this experiment had agreed in advance to take any of three possible drugs, although they did not know which drug they would receive. Thus, they had some choice in what they might experience as research participants.

Some aspects of this study were similar to the Schachter and Singer situation. Participants were misinformed about the purpose of the experiment; they were told it was about the effect of drugs on memory. A drug was given and most subjects were misinformed about its effects; all subjects were told they would receive a placebo, when in fact one group was given amphetamine, which is a stimulant, and another group received phenobarbital, a depressant. During a twenty-minute waiting period, subjects wrote an essay in which they were asked to take a position opposite to that of their true beliefs, thus creating a state of dissonance. The investigators predicted that amphetamine would enhance physiological arousal and thus the degree of dissonance and that the tranquilizer would decrease the dissonance effect. Their predictions were confirmed. Cooper's research shows that theoretically interesting results can be obtained without uncomfortable injections and with consent on the part of the subjects.

Helping in False Emergencies

One night in March of 1964, Catherine Genovese was assaulted and killed outside her apartment building in Queens, New York. She screamed through one attack and her assailant left her unable to move. Later he returned and killed her. The incident received considerable coverage by journalists who discovered that, although the murder had been witnessed by many of the residents of nearby apartments, no one had come to the assistance of the victim. Social commentators had many explanations for why people did not help Ms. Genovese.

This actual event stimulated an area of research in social psychology that has continued for many years.[4] Bibb Latane was one of the social psychologists who was impressed with the attention given to this crime and who would develop a research program and a theory to explain incidents of this kind, where bystanders failed to intervene in an emergency. He described the origins of his research (Latane, 1987):

One evening after another downtown cocktail party, John Darley . . . came back with me to my 12th Street apartment for a drink. Our common complaint was the distressing tendency of acquaintances, on finding that we called ourselves social psychologists, to ask why

New Yorkers were so apathetic. While commiserating on their ignorance as to the true nature and higher calling of social psychologists, we came up with the insight that perhaps what made the Genovese case so fascinating was itself what made it happen— namely, that not just one or two, but thirty-eight people had watched and done nothing. We decided then and there to set up a laboratory study to see whether the mere knowledge that others were aware of an emergency would reduce one's likelihood of helping. (p. 78)

The next week Latane and Darley "recruited the more theatrically inclined of our graduate students" to meet at the 12th Street apartment to record the scenario they had planned. Variations on their simple research plan would be repeated in dozens of studies in many laboratories, as well as in field experiments. Subjects are placed in a situation where they think someone (a confederate) may need help and the experimenters measure how long it takes before someone comes to the aid of the "victim" or calls someone for help.

The false emergency used in Latane and Darley's first study was an epileptic seizure. Earlier they had discovered that one graduate student, "Dick Nisbett stood head and shoulders above the rest of us in his ability to sound as if he were in the throes of" (Latane, 1987, p. 78) a convulsion. Latane must have appreciated the importance of good acting, because he had been the stooge in the Schachter and Singer (1962) experiment on epinephrine and emotion.

Undergraduates participating in a two-, three-, or six-person discussion of the personal problems of urban university students, conducted over an intercom to reduce embarrassment, heard Dick, initially calmly but with increasing agitation and urgency, tell of his propensity, in times of stress like the present, to fall into uncontrollable fits. We timed how long it took individual bystanders to emerge from their separate cubicles and report the emergency. As we had suspected, those who alone heard Dick's distress were quickest to respond. (Latane, 1987, p. 78)

Latane and Darley repeated the same basic experiment using different emergency situations. In one variation, students were filling out questionnaires in a small room when smoke began to come into the room through a vent. Students who were alone quickly reported the problem, whereas when students were in a group they were less likely to take action but would "remain seated, coughing and waving away the smoke (Latane & Darley, 1968)" (Latane, 1987, p. 79). In another study a female experimenter pretended to fall off a chair in an adjoining room. The tendency to help more readily when alone than when with others was called, "social inhibition of bystander intervention," and was demonstrated in "over four dozen studies, involving a total of almost 100 experimental comparisons" (Latane, 1987, p. 79) using various staged emergencies.

Some of these emergencies were quite dramatic. In chapter 1 I described the study conducted on a subway train of the effect of blood on reactions to a victim (Piliavin & Piliavin, 1972). Another experiment that involved bleeding shows the precision with which some of these events were staged (Shotland & Heinold, 1985; note that stage productions continued into the 1980s). Following the standard research design, subjects were either alone or with a group of confederates. As they were filling out forms, a confederate playing the role of a worker arrived at the scene and changed into a pair of white painter's overalls.

> These trousers were . . . equipped with special devices for sim-
> ulating an arterially bleeding wound below the right knee. A
> realistic imitation wound, plastic tubing, a hand pump, and
> theatrical blood were used to create the pulsating bleeding ema-
> nating from his leg. The 'wound' was glued under a jagged tear in
> the right pants leg just below the knee. The tubing was strapped
> inside the trousers and ran from the wound to the hand pump,
> which the worker could operate to pulsate blood to the wound.
>
> The worker made a pool of "blood" approximately 6 in. in
> diameter in the location where his right knee was going to be and
> placed shards of broken glass around the puddle. After the 'stage'
> was set, the workman toppled the ladder, causing a loud crash as
> ladder and tools . . . hit the linoleum-tiled floor. . . . Lying motionless
> and turned on his left side, the 'victim' pumped between 1/2- and 1-
> in. streams of 'blood' at approximately 1-s intervals with his right
> hand, which was laid across his chest (pp. 350–351).

The investigators pointed out that, "[a]ll procedures were cleared through the University Behavioral Science Ethics Committee" (p. 351).

A study by Shalom Schwartz and Avi Gottlieb (1980),[5] may have come closest to simulating the violence of the Genovese assault that inspired the vast amount of research on bystander intervention.

> Sessions were conducted at night in an isolated wing of a social
> science building. Subjects completed a questionnaire on ESP
> [extra-sensory perception] and were paid. They were then led to

their room, passing the open door of a room through which they saw the back of a seated male confederate. When the experimenter then turned on the subjects' TV monitor, it showed a (videotaped) frontal view of the same male confederate, who was now seen to be completing a questionnaire. (p. 420)

Participants then were given a reason to continue watching the monitor, and during that time the confederate revealed that he had an expensive pocket calculator. After about 7.5 minutes, the emergency was acted out on the television screen.

[A]fter a sound of knocking, a large, roughly dressed stranger was seen to enter [the confederate's] room. Following a short conversation about the ESP experiment, the stranger surreptitiously took the pocket calculator and started to leave. After a short but violent argument, the stranger suddenly attacked [the confederate]. Throwing him against a wall, the attacker punched him several times in the stomach, knocked him to the floor, and left him doubled up and helpless after several kicks. The attacker then escaped with the calculator. . . .

During the emergency, subjects' reactions were monitored via concealed cameras. Those who tried to go directly to the victim found his door locked and were subsequently met in the hall by the experimenter. . . .

While the 'research director' ostensibly cared for the victim, the experimenter checked the subjects' perceptions of the emergency, their intentions when reacting, and possible suspicions. . . . (p. 420)

In this experiment, Schwartz and Gottlieb manipulated the nature of the emergency (violent attack or seizure), how clear it was that help was needed (relatively ambiguous vs. unequivocally clear), and whether or not other people knew of the bystander's (the real subject) presence (anonymous vs. known to be present). They concluded that, "once emergencies are clear, anonymity (through evaluation apprehension) influences the decision regarding one's own obligation to help" (p. 418).

The investigators were aware that their research might have ethical problems. For example, participants might become frightened, or they might become violent themselves in attempting to help the "victim." To obtain "continuing approval of the Human Subjects Committee to conduct these studies" (p. 420), a questionnaire on the ethics of the study was given to all participants after they were debriefed. Apparently, the investigators were required "continuously" to report the results of this questionnaire to the review committee to assure that "there were no ethical grounds for halting the research" (p. 420). On three of the questions (the data were not reported in full) 95% or more of the subjects reacted positively to their participation, "and only 2% 'were resentful about having been deceived'" (p. 420). These investigators also published one of the only experiments that evaluated the long-term effects of having participated in deceptive research on bystander intervention (Schwartz & Gottlieb, 1980).

Research on helping gave many social psychologists an opportunity to be creative in a good cause. The same simple design was repeated over and over again in a variety of more or less dramatic settings. This research had clear relevance to a real-world event (if psychology had saints, certainly one of them would be Catherine Genovese) and the results conceivably could be used to increase our willingness to help others. The helping situation also was used to study gender differences, race relations, and child development. The deception and disruption in people's lives was justified by the researchers in terms of psychological and practical relevance.

One of the things that puzzles me about this and some other research in social psychology is how such dramatic situations were kept secret from students who had not yet taken part in a study. Surely a substantial number of students must have told their friends about the exciting (or frightening or silly) research that was going on in the psychology department. I have been told about campuses where the research deception became widely known before the study was completed. Some students might want to put on their own stage production if they know that the smoke coming under the door is part of the research and not a sign of real trouble. No data is available on how often this happened or what the effect on the research results might have been.

Aggression and "Pleasuring"

About the same time that Stanley Milgram was developing his method for studying obedience, Arnold Buss (1961) was using a similar method to study aggression.[6] A false shock generator that Buss called the "aggression machine" had a series of ten buttons that would deliver what the research subject believed were increasingly strong levels of shock. The buttons simply were numbered from one to ten; they were not labeled with voltages or any other verbal indicator of strength. Buss also used a false learning situation in which the subject would give shocks when a learner, really a confederate, gave incorrect responses. An important contrast with the Milgram procedures is that subjects in Buss's studies could choose the shock level; the level that they chose was the measure of interest because the higher the level, the more aggression was shown. Buss thought that his apparatus was "a potentially fruitful solution to the ethical, practical, and measurement problems that are associated with studying aggression in the laboratory" (Buss, 1961, p. 51).

Buss's machine became a relatively common device in the study of aggression. The typical research design involved exposing the subject to the real experimental manipulation, for example, an insult from the confederate who later would serve as learner, then beginning the pseudo-learning experiment and measuring the level of shock administered by insulted subjects compared to those who had not been insulted. A study by Albert Bandura and his students (Bandura, Underwood, & Fromson, 1975) is representative of this procedure.

One of the few examples of research in which the use of deception did not make subjects uncomfortable comes from the research of Timothy Brock who figured out a way to modify Buss's apparatus to study behavior that is the opposite of aggression. It shows that it is possible to make people feel good in the laboratory.

> The Brock Pleasure Machine is essentially a modified aggression machine (Buss, 1961) by means of which subjects give a recipient short intensity-graded waves of pleasure. The subject believes that he is conveying physical pleasure, which ranges from barely perceptible (Button 1) to extraordinarily pleasurable and exciting (Button 10). The recipient sits on a specially constructed chair containing a Niagara wave generator . . . covered with attractive upholstery. The subject may actually vary the frequency of a sinusoidal wave, thus varying the intensity of vibratory waves the recipient receives via his buttocks and thighs. (Davis, Rainey, & Brock, 1976, p. 91)

The procedure used is similar to that used by Buss and Milgram. There is a false learning task, a confederate playing the role of the learner, and a research subject who is assigned the role of teacher. The subjects are allowed to feel the vibrations and apparently find this pleasurable. Then the false task begins, but instead of punishing wrong answers, correct responses are rewarded with pleasant stimulation, although the buttons do not actually activate the vibrator. As in the Buss procedure, the subject (teacher) can choose any level of stimulation and that is the measure of interest. Some results were that responsive and attractive recipients received higher pleasuring in same-sex pairs and that anticipation of future interaction increased pleasuring (Davis, et al., 1976). Research on pleasuring has not, however, found the same popularity as that on aggression.

Life with Bogus Strangers

In the late 1980s one of the favorite words of suburban youth was *bogus*, a pejorative term meaning artificial and of little value. Earlier in this chapter I described the bogus pipeline, a method for giving people false information about their physiological state. Another method became known as the "bogus stranger technique" (Sabini, 1992).

This technique was and still is used often in research on attitudes toward other people, particularly on why we are attracted to people with certain characteristics. Research participants are asked to fill out a questionnaire that asks for their opinions on various important issues such as religion and sex. Some time later they volunteer for a study that falsely is presented as concerning how well we can predict the opinions of other people. They are shown a completed questionnaire like the one they have filled out and are told it is from another subject in the study. In fact it was completed by the experimenter in a way to make the bogus stranger's responses similar to or different from the real subject's own responses. Sabini (1992) has summarized some research using this technique:

> [I]f subjects fill out a personality scale and are then given a scale filled out by a bogus other subject, they will like the bogus other who is similar to them in personality; if they fill out a scale indicating how much money they have to spend, and receive responses from a bogus stranger on that scale, they will like the person more if he has a similar economic position. (p. 531)

One controversial study using a similar method involved giving male students false results of a personality test, which indicated that they had homosexual tendencies (Bramel, 1962). This study was a test of cognitive dissonance theory, carried out at Stanford University, with the advice of Leon Festinger and Stanley Schachter.

Social psychologists also make interventions into the lives of people who are not aware that they are taking part in research. Perhaps the best known of these is the study that demonstrated the foot-in-the-door method.

> Housewives were called on the telephone and asked to provide information about products that they use in their home (small request). Later to see if they would comply with a larger request, they were again called and asked whether they would allow five or six men to come to their home 'to go through the cupboards and storage places.' They were not told that they would not really be visited. (summarized by Korn, 1987, p. 207)

Other researchers made bogus requests to use a copy machine ahead of someone who was already using it and had secretaries send meaningless memoranda (Langer, Blank, & Chanowitz, 1978). Bogus strangers even appeared at urinals in a men's rest room (Middlemist, Knowles, & Matter, 1976).

In an unusual example of deceptive self-presentation, a member of the world's oldest profession was enlisted. A group of psychologists arranged to have a prostitute serve as the experimenter in a study that tested the common notion that women who are hard to get are more desirable. The prostitute/experimenter worked in her natural setting.

> When the customer arrived, she mixed a drink for him; then she delivered the experimental manipulation. Half of the time, in the hard-to-get condition, she stated, 'Just because I see you this time it doesn't mean that you can have my phone number or see me again. I'm going to start school soon, so I won't have much time, so I'll only be able to see the people I like best.' Half of the time in the easy-to-get condition, she did not communicate this information. From this point on, the prostitute and the customer interacted in conventional ways. (Walster, Walster, Piliavin, & Schmidt, 1973, p. 116)

I assume the last sentence means they negotiated and carried out a sexual encounter. This was done in the state of Nevada where knowledge and support of prostitution was legal, so the investigators were not breaking the law.[7]

Into the Nineties

In the 1980s the theaters began to close. The use of deception declined and the situations in which it was used were generally much less dramatic. The 1980s produced no single example of dramatic research, like the Milgram obedience study, and no fashionable research topic, like bystander intervention, that required theatrical productions. Part of the reason for the decline was the involvement of institutional ethics review committees that placed restrictions on the use of deception, especially when it might cause discomfort to participants. Researchers began to rely on techniques that involved only mild forms of deception, and the "staging" often was done on a computer screen, which was quite fitting for the student-subjects of the Atari-Nintendo video game generation. As far as we know, social psychologists are learning as much, or as little, about their subject as they were when live performances were in vogue.

Deceptive research continued into the 1990s on most of the topics discussed in this chapter.[8] At the time that I wrote this chapter, some investigators of aggressive behavior still used the Buss aggression machine, research on helping still involved staged emergencies, and people occasionally were misinformed about drugs they agree to take. It will be interesting to see whether a new theory or topic emerges that will revive the theatrical tradition begun by Kurt Lewin and his students.

I have taken the history of deception for almost one hundred years from the beginning of experimental psychology in the United States through its peak in the 1970s. As I did so, I raised questions about the ethics of much of this research, most directly in relation to Milgram's obedience research and studies during the stage production era. Concern for research ethics is relatively recent in the history of psychology as it is in other areas of research that use human participants (Faden & Beauchamp, 1986). The next chapter will present this history for psychology in relation to the general issues raised in medical research.

Questions of Right and Wrong

When did psychologists begin to raise questions about the ethics of the use of deception in their research? It may have been the first time that a research participant appeared to be upset by an experimental procedure. Perhaps a child who became a scapegoat in an authoritarian group moved one of Lewin's students at Iowa to raise the issue with other students during their evening discussion some time during the 1930s. We know that Hartshorne and May were sensitive to ethical issues in their studies of deceit in children in the 1920s, but researchers did not publish their ethical concerns in discussions of their results until Solomon Asch did so in his 1956 monograph (Asch, 1956). Even if they did not write about it, most psychologists who used deceptive methods that in any way disturbed their subjects must have been concerned about what they were doing. The time came when psychologists, through their professional organization, realized the need for ethical guidelines to control the more questionable research practices.

Psychologists' Ethical Principles for Research

In 1938 the Council of Directors of the American Psychological Association (APA) created "a Committee on Scientific and Professional Ethics to consider the advisability of drafting an ethical code, the purpose of which would be to serve as a guide to Members and Associates" (Olson, 1938, p. 590). A distinguished experimental psychologist, Robert S. Woodworth, was appointed chairperson of the committee. Although the special committee felt that it would be premature to legislate a complete code of ethics, in 1939 it did recommend that "a standing committee be appointed to consider complaints of unethical conduct" in several areas, including "[r]elations of the psychological experimenter to his research subjects" (Golann, 1970, p. 399). The Directors appointed this new committee in 1940 and the members began "to resolve some complaints on an informal basis" (Crawford, 1992, pp. 180–181). The questions raised in the area of experimenter-subject relations "included investigation into socially sensitive areas without regard for possible harm to subjects, deception, and experiments on temptation to behave dishonestly without regard to postexperimental effects on subsequent dishonesty" (Golann, 1970, p. 399).

The APA began work on a formal code of ethics in 1947 when the Directors appointed another special committee, chaired by another distinguished experimentalist, Edward C. Tolman. One of its members, Nicholas Hobbs, described the approach taken by the Committee on Ethical Standards for Psychology (Hobbs, 1948). He made it clear that the origins of this committee had more to do with applied problems than with experimental research as he listed the variety of clinical and industrial consultation services that "take the psychologist into situations which frequently demand decisions of an ethical nature" (Hobbs, 1948, p. 80). Later in his report he noted that a code would be helpful to "individuals and groups working on the problems of certification and licensing of psychologists" and that a code would "provide real guidance to the psychologist who is making an honest effort to *practice* his profession in the best ethical tradition" (p. 81, italics mine).

At about this same time the Nuremberg war crimes trials were taking place. The testimony revealed that Nazi doctors had used prisoners in so-called research that involved severe pain and often led to the death of their subjects (Lifton, 1986). The trial and conviction of these doctors led to the 1948 Nuremberg Code of ethics on research with humans. The trial and resulting code had little immediate impact on psychologists' ethical deliberations because psychologists were more concerned with professional practice and their research did not begin to approach the inhumanity of the Nazi doctors. With its strong emphasis on informed consent, however, the Nuremberg Code did influence all later ethical codes related to research participation.

Anthropologists were the first social scientists to adopt a code of ethics for their organization (Ethics in Applied Anthropology, 1951). The code was published in 1948 and was directly concerned with standards for anthropologists who served as consultants to industrial and other organizations. An important statement in that code is relevant to the use of deception in research, although that occurs rarely in anthropology: "the specific means adopted will inevitably determine the ends attained, hence ends can never be used to justify means" (p. 4).

The APA committee that was asked to develop an ethics code for psychologists designed a method that was innovative and in keeping with the strongly empirical nature of American psychology. Rather than having a committee of experts confer and decide what such a code should contain, Nicholas Hobbs and his colleagues proposed doing research that "would involve the collection, from psychologists engaged in all of the various professional activities, of descriptions of actual situations which required ethical decisions" (Hobbs, 1948, p. 83). In 1948 a letter requesting descriptions "from firsthand knowledge" of situations having ethical implications was sent to the approximately 7,500 members of APA (Golann, 1970).

The more than 1000 reports that were received were classified into six areas, one of which concerned research. Based on these incidents, standards were developed for each area and were then submitted to careful review and revision by various groups of psychologists. The process took about two and a half years and involved 200 individual reports before a final draft was submitted in September of 1952 and published in 1953 (APA, 1953). This empirical approach of data collection followed by careful review and revision also characterized the later major revisions of the APA ethical principles that have occurred at about twenty year intervals.

There is a clear, logical structure to the 1953 standards. Several principles are stated under each of six sections. Each principle is introduced with the statement of a problem followed by several incidents. Then the principle is given, usually with two or more qualifying statements. Section 4, Ethical Standards in Research, had three parts: 4.1, the psychologist's responsibility for adequately planning and conducting his research;[1] 4.2, reporting research results; 4.3, the psychologist's relation to his research subjects. The section on Ethical Standards in Teaching included a subprinciple (3.15) on requiring student participation in research.

These are the principles from the 1953 APA standards that are most relevant to our study of deception in research:[2]

> Principle 3.15–1. A teacher should normally require of his students only activities which are designed to contribute to the development of the students in the area of instruction.

> Principle 4.31–1. Only when a problem is significant and can be investigated in no other way is the psychologist justified in exposing research subjects to emotional stress. He must seriously consider the possibility of possible harmful after-effects and should be prepared to remove them as soon as permitted by the design of the experiment. Where the danger of serious after-effects exists, research should be conducted only when the subjects or their responsible agents are fully informed of this possibility and volunteer nevertheless.

> Principle 4.31–2. The psychologist is justified in withholding information from or giving misinformation to research subjects only when in his judgment this is clearly required by his research

problem and when the provisions of the above principle regarding the protection of subjects are adhered to.

Principle 4.33–1. Psychologists who assume obligations to research subjects in return for the subject's cooperation in research studies are obliged to fulfill these obligations.

The first published code of ethics in psychology did not come from the APA, however, but from the Department of Child Development and Family Relationships at Cornell University (Cornell Studies in Social Growth, 1952). It was published "as an example of a set of ethical standards for research workers" (p. 452), but it had no official status within the APA. This code was more restrictive with respect to deception, although that word was not used in the code. People were viewed "as individuals, not subjects to be exploited" (p. 453). The free consent of any person involved in the research was to be obtained by giving participants "as direct and explicit an account as possible of research objectives and purposes" (p. 453). The statement most relevant to the use of deception was that "consent to an unknown experience is not regarded as true consent" (p. 453). In effect the use of confederates also was prohibited by the statement that data "given to the investigator on the assumption that he is a personal friend or counsellor, rather than a research worker" (p. 454) is not suitable.

Not long after publication of the 1953 principles, the APA committee concerned with ethics began to consider revision. "On the basis of accumulated experience, it became possible to distill from the 1953 code a set of more general principles" (Golann, 1970, p. 400). This distillation led to a set of 19 principles published in 1959 (APA, 1959). Principle 16, "Harmful Aftereffects," said that "giving misinformation to research subjects" was justified only when there was no other way to investigate a problem. However, in the next revision in 1963 (APA, 1963), Principle 16, "Research Precautions," made no mention of misinformation. Five years later the Ethical Standards were published again (APA, 1968), and again the section on research did not mention deception, although a paragraph was added concerning the use of experimental drugs. The disappearance of any reference to "misinformation" (i.e., deception) happened at a time when the use of deception had begun to increase and some of the most controversial studies had been carried out. The next version of the standards would be a major revision in which careful attention would be given to the issues of informed consent and deception.

In 1970 (McKeachie, 1971) the APA Board of Directors appointed an Ad Hoc Committee on Ethical Standards in Psychological Research. It is likely that the strongest reason for putting this committee to work was the new federal regulations that required review of research proposals by institutional boards composed largely of nonpsychologists. Compliance with the review process was necessary in order to keep federal funds for research, and psychologists, like medical researchers, needed that money to do their work. Having a carefully developed set of principles for research with humans would help convince review boards and the government that psychology had its research house in order.

The new APA committee used a method similar to that of the Hobbs committee in the early 1950s, a long process of data collection and review by a variety of interested groups and individuals. Examples or "incidents" of ethical issues in research were solicited from over 18,000 APA members (about 2/3 of all members) in two separate surveys. This produced about 5000 descriptions which the Committee thought was "an adequate base of raw material from which to proceed" (APA, 1973, p. 4). In addition, several groups of experts (e.g., journal editors, writers on research ethics) were asked for information. Although these methods were similar to those used to develop the 1953 code, the data and their review were much more extensive. This clearly was an important area of concern for the APA. The result of the process was a list of ten principles for the conduct of research with human participants (APA, 1973). The use of the word participants, rather than subjects, is one indication of the change in attitude towards research that the committee wanted to convey; people should take part in research, not be subjected to it.

The full version of the Ad Hoc Committee's report was published as a book by APA (1973), as had been done in 1953. The format of the report had sections beginning with commentary on an area of ethical concern, followed by a few incidents, then one or two relevant principles, followed by discussion of those principles. The discussions were quite lengthy and presented different points of view on controversial issues, usually concluding that it was ultimately the responsibility of the individual researcher, usually after consultation with others, to decide what should be done. The third and fourth principles were related most directly to the use of deception and indicate the ambiguity in these guides to conduct:

> 3. Ethical practice requires the investigator to inform the participant of all features of the research that reasonably might be expected to influence willingness to participate and to explain all other aspects of the research about which the participant inquires. Failure to make full disclosure gives added emphasis to the investigator's responsibility to protect the welfare and dignity of the research participant.

4. Openness and honesty are essential characteristics of the relationship between investigator and research participant. When the methodological requirements of a study necessitate concealment or deception, the investigator is required to ensure the participant's understanding of the reasons for this action and to restore the quality of the relationship with the investigator. (p. 1)

These principles required full disclosure and said that openness and honesty were essential, but then allowed the investigator to make exceptions. The discussion of each principle explained how various considerations must be balanced and weighed by the investigator, who always should be aware of and respect the dignity of the individual participant. In every case, however, it is the investigator who makes the final decision concerning what happens to people in research. These principles presented investigators with a special set of dilemmas because conducting well-designed research was said to be "an obligation," and as scientists, that was the psychologist's "distinctive way to contribute to human welfare" (p. 8). But that would create problems.

> The obligation to advance the understanding of significant aspects of human experience and behavior is especially likely to impinge upon well-recognized human rights. Significant research is likely to deal with variables and methods that touch upon sensitive human concerns. And if ambiguity in causal inference is to be reduced to a minimum—an essential of good science—research must be designed in ways that, on occasion, may make the relationship between the psychologist and the human research participant fall short of commonly held ideals for human relationships. (p. 8)

The high value placed on a scientific method based on statistical concepts was a continuation and codification of the version of experimentation that had dominated American psychology for several decades. Controlled research was thought to be so important that it could outweigh "commonly held ideals for human relationships."

The discussion of the principle concerning deception did provide some criteria to help the researcher (APA, 1973, p. 37): First, deception may be used when "the research problem is of great importance," "the research objectives cannot be realized without deception," and participants "may be expected to find it reasonable." Second, participants should be "allowed to withdraw from the study at any time," and, if deception is used, they are told about the reasons for using it and are free to withdraw their data. Third, the investigator was to be responsible "for detecting and removing stressful aftereffects," as well as for judging the importance of the research, trying to find alternate nondeceptive methods, and creating conditions in which participants could exercise their rights to withdraw from the study or withhold their data.

Both in psychology and more generally, concern for the ethics of research with humans grew during the 1970s. More articles and books than ever before were being published that were critical of or defended research practices, including the use of deception. *Psychological Abstracts* is a publication of the APA that gives brief summaries of almost all articles on psychology published each year in scientific and professional journals. One indicator of the growth of interest in the topic of the ethics of research with human subjects is the number of articles on that topic published each year from 1927, the first year the *Abstracts* were published, through 1991 (McGaha & Korn, 1995).

From 1927 to 1950 only two articles on research ethics were listed (both were in German), even though some research was being done during that period that might have raised ethical questions.[3] There were six articles listed from 1951 to 1960, 16 articles from 1961 to 1970, 130 articles from 1971 to 1980, and 200 articles from 1981 to 1991.[4] Relatively few publications on ethics were stimulated by the research of Asch, Festinger, and Milgram during the 1950s and 1960s, or by the APA principles of 1953, but many articles appeared after the development of federal regulations in the 1970s and the publication of the 1973 version of the APA ethical principles.

In 1978 APA responded to this growing interest in and concern for research ethics by establishing a standing Committee on the Protection of Human Participants in Psychological Research that was charged with reviewing and recommending policies in this area, but not with considering possible violations of the Principles.[5] There was a separate committee for that. The Protection Committee reviewed the 1973 document and found that not much change was needed. Some of the changes they recommended were editorial (e.g., examples of incidents were deleted from the text), but "other sections were elaborated extensively, including those dealing with deception research" (APA, 1982, p. 13) and informed consent. The changes were approved and published in 1982.

It is difficult to find any extensive elaboration of the sections on informed consent and deception. The removal of examples of incidents actually made the more recent version shorter than the 1973 document. The one important addition in 1982 was a section on "disguised field experimentation in public situations" (p. 38) that concerned research that "not only records the behavior of unsuspecting individuals but also manipulates their experiences." Although it sometimes may be possible to obtain consent to participate in such research, "offenses to human dignity and other risks to participants are readily imaginable in this sort of experimentation," and if many studies of this kind are carried out, "their cumulative effect may undermine confidence in human relationships." This section seems to describe most of the research on bystander intervention, and many studies of that kind were carried out both before and after these guidelines were published.

One way in which the application of ethical principles could have been controlled would have been through the publication system. The APA controls the editorial policy of a family of journals that are recognized as among the best in most areas of psychology. That policy, which is stated in the association's publication manual, might have required evidence of care in implementing informed consent and debriefing procedures, but instead simply told authors, "When you submit your article, indicate to the journal editor that the treatment of participants (human or animal) was in accordance with the ethical standards of the APA. . . ." (APA, 1974, p. 17). The next edition of the publication manual included the same statement (APA, 1983, p. 26).[6]

The editor of the *Journal of Personality and Social Psychology* in his 1976 policy statement (Greenwald, 1976, p. 5) simply assumed that authors had followed the APA Ethical Principles and stated that ethical questions were not the responsibility of editors. Stuart Cook, who had published a comment on the ethics of the "ubiquitous Watergate" study, said that in the 1970s "it was hoped that editors might promote ethical research behavior in this way" (by publishing comments on controversial studies), but "nothing much came of the idea" (Cook, personal communication, April 13, 1984). Relatively few published journal articles contain even a short statement concerning consent and debriefing in the section on methods (Adair, Dushenko, & Lindsay, 1985; Korn & Bram, 1988), whereas all empirical articles must include detailed descriptions of research design and statistical analysis. This is another indication of the priority given to a particular methodology in this empirical field.

In the preceding chapters I presented many examples of studies using dramatic deception that many reasonable people might consider to be ethically questionable. Yet the APA Ethics Committee that reviews cases in which psychologists are accused of violating the ethical principles has rarely considered cases based on failure to obtain informed consent. A 1975 communication from that committee (McNamara & Woods, 1977) stated "that not one formal charge of ethical impropriety in the conduct of human research had been dealt with by the committee in the last three years" (p. 707). The communication was dated June 19, 1975, so the three-year period would be 1971 to 1974, when the use of deception was highest. The authors of the article in which this communication was reported interpreted it as evidence of "ethical indolence among psychologists affiliated with the APA."

Ten years later psychologists apparently were more willing to "blow the whistle" on ethically questionable research, although there still were not many cases of this. In 1981 the Ethics Committee began to publish data on the types of cases it considered. During the five-year period from 1981 through 1985, 44 of 710 (6.2%) cases involved research issues (Ethics Committee, 1986). The largest number (17) concerned authorship controversies; for example, disputes about who should have been listed as the first author of an article. The category, "improper and unsafe use of research techniques," had 16 cases. This is the category that would include issues of consent and deception, but the committee cannot provide details of the cases because it must protect the confidentiality of those involved. However, none of the sixteen cases resulted in finding someone guilty of violating the APA ethical principles, and only two led to other committee action, such as an "educative" letter (D. H. Mills, personal communication, June 6, 1986).

Informed Consent in Medicine and Law

While psychologists were developing their realistic research methods and addressing the ethical issues raised by these developments, medical doctors were forced to confront their relationships with patients and research subjects. This confrontation often took place in the courtroom, usually as the result of a medical malpractice suit, but also from charges of extreme cases of abuses in biomedical research. Informed consent was the major issue in these cases and included both insufficient information and misinformation to patients. Psychologists apparently gave little attention to these developments in medicine until the federal government lumped behavioral and biomedical research together in legislation proposed to protect research participants.

I want to look closely at the concept of informed consent because it is clear that if that concept is put into practice, deception is not possible. What to tell patients about their treatment or research subjects about an experiment has been an issue at least since the nineteenth century, according to Ruth Faden and Tom Beauchamp who published an extensive review of the history of informed consent (Faden & Beauchamp, 1986).[7] However, it was not until 1957 that informed consent was first used as a legal term and concept. The 1950s can be viewed as a transition period between two views of how to justify what people are told by professionals about the procedures to be used. Faden and Beauchamp call these views the beneficence model and the autonomy model (p. 59).

The beneficence model presents the researcher's responsibility as that of providing benefits while avoiding harm to subjects. The autonomy model is governed by the principle of autonomy or respect for persons, which states that "persons should be free to choose and act without controlling constraints imposed by others" (p. 8). Before the 1950s the beneficence model was dominant in medicine (the doctor knows what is best for the patient); after that time the autonomy model came to control what patients are told (patients have rights). Conflict between these two views has always been present and continues today. That conflict is very clear in all versions of the APA ethical principles, which make frequent statements about respect for the rights of individual subjects followed by qualifiers which state that it is the researcher who has the ultimate responsibility for weighing the benefits of the research against the risks to participants.

There are several elements to informed consent: "(1) a patient or subject must *agree* to an intervention based on an *understanding* of (usually disclosed) relevant information, (2) consent must *not be controlled* by influences that would engineer the outcome, and (3) the consent must involve the intentional giving of *permission* for an intervention" (p. 54, italics in original). Thus, more than simple agreement is necessary. The procedures must be explained in terms the person can understand, not in technical jargon. People do not have to be told everything but they do need relevant information that any reasonable person would want to know. For example, subjects do not need to know the details of the theory being tested but any reasonable person would want to know the effects of a drug they will be given. Finally, true consent is not manipulated by the use of psychological techniques, course requirements, or other coercive incentives.

The most important event in the history of informed consent was the trial of the Nazi doctors that led to the Nuremberg Code in 1948, "the first major curb on research in any nation" (p. 153). The first principle of this code "states, without qualification, that the primary consideration in research is the subject's voluntary consent, which is 'absolutely essential.'" That consent "must be voluntary, competent, informed, and comprehending" (p. 155).

In spite of the shock produced by the revelation of the cruel, pseudo-experiments conducted by the Nazis and the clear message on ethics from Nuremberg, medical researchers in the United States were doing experiments that violated reasonable standards of conduct. In 1963, "three doctors [at] the Jewish Chronic Disease Hospital in Brooklyn, New York, injected 'live cancer cells' subcutaneously into twenty-two chronically ill and debilitated patients. The doctors did not inform the patients that live cancer cells were being used or that the experiment was designed to measure the patients' ability to reject foreign cells—a test unrelated to their normal therapeutic program" (Katz, 1972, p. 9).[8]

Research in psychology is not, of course, even close to medical research in terms of either risks or benefits. Injecting college students with epinephrine but telling them it is a vitamin may be unethical, but it is on a different moral plane from misinforming debilitated patients about the injection of live cancer cells. Researchers in psychology were surely aware of the abuses of the Nazi doctors and may have known about other ethically questionable medical research, and probably viewed these examples as unrelated to the ethical issues in their experiments. But that was not the view of government officials who during the 1960s began to be concerned with research using human subjects.

The examples of extreme violations of human rights in medical research stimulated the action of the federal government, but the power behind the action that made it effective was the millions of dollars being spent to support research. Although most of the funds went to biomedical research, there had also been a significant increase in grants for behavioral research. The agencies that provided those funds began to set policies about how human subjects should be treated in the research supported by the government, and those policies later became laws that applied to all federally funded research.

In February of 1966 the Surgeon General issued a policy statement "that would become a landmark in the history of informed consent in the United States" (p. 208). The policy required that all institutions receiving research support from the Public Health Service should have that research reviewed by a committee that would consider the rights and welfare of subjects, the methods used to obtain informed consent, and the balance of risks and benefits (p. 208).

At first, "social and behavioral scientists offered mild opposition to these developments" (p. 210), but "by 1969 complaints began to mount that a *biomedical* model was engulfing the social and behavioral sciences in irrelevant and meaningless criteria [that] . . . might seriously impair research in fields such as social psychology" (p. 211). An institutional guide published by the government in 1971 specifically included behavioral research but stated that consent "could be obtained *after* research participation if a complete and prompt debriefing were provided" (p. 212). It was this guide that influenced the APA in its 1973 version of ethical principles for research with humans. Later developments in federal regulation liberalized the policies even more by exempting some forms of behavioral research and allowing "expedited" review of low-risk research. Nothing in the regulations prohibited the use of deception.

These developments in federal regulation had a strong influence on research practices in psychology, leading to a decrease in the use of deception in psychological research. The decrease took place gradually as Institutional Review Boards became more powerful and careful in their reviews from the 1970s into the 1980s. It was this review process that caused some leading social psychologists to abandon the use of dramatic situations involving elaborate deception. These performances still take place but they no longer hold center stage.

The Deception Debate

Edgar Vinacke (1954) published the first comment by a psychologist that dealt with the ethics of deception in research. He raised the question of the "proper balance between the interests of science and the thoughtful treatment of" research subjects, and he saw a general lack of concern for this issue among psychologists: "In fact, one can note an element of facetiousness. It has reached the point where a man who reads a paper at the APA convention is almost embarrassed when he adds, with a laugh, that the subjects were given the 'usual' postsession explanations" (p. 155). Apparently this comment prompted Arthur MacKinney to conduct an experiment in a few classes at the University of Minnesota (MacKinney, 1955). He found little evidence that students were bothered by a mild deception, but recognized the limited generality of his results.

It would be ten years before the next comments were published. Then, in 1964, Stanley Milgram's research became the occasion for the beginning of the debate concerning ethical issues in psychological research. His exchange of views with Diana Baumrind was summarized in chapter 8. It is interesting that these comments were published at about the same time that specific mention of deception was removed from the APA ethical principles.

Although published comments on research ethics were infrequent before 1974 (McGaha & Korn, 1995), there were several notable contributions to the ethics debate. Herbert Kelman wrote two articles that provided strong criticisms of deception and other research practices. His first article was titled, "human use of human subjects" (Kelman, 1967), and discussed both ethical and methodological issues in the use of deception, as well as implications for the future of the discipline of psychology. He concluded that deception could be used when clearly justified, but hoped that new techniques could be developed that would eliminate the need for deceiving subjects.

Kelman's second article was an analysis of power and legitimacy in the research situation (Kelman, 1972). He pointed out that research subjects have relatively little power when confronted with the legitimate authority of the scientist, and this relationship supports the use of deception. Kelman's statements about deception generally were negative, but reflected the ambivalence that many psychologists felt about its use. He said, "Deception violates the respect to which all fellow humans are entitled and the trust that is basic to all interpersonal relationships." But earlier on the same page he said, "Only if a study is very important and no alternative methods are available can anything more than the mildest form of deception be justified" (Kelman, 1972, p. 997).

Preliminary versions of the 1973 APA ethical principles had been published and circulated for comments before its final approval. The differing views of psychologists at that time about the limits placed on research, were reflected in two articles published in the *American Psychologist*. Diana Baumrind (1971) was critical of the draft principles because, "The risk/benefit approach that the Committee has adopted may have the effect of justifying . . . violations by offering to the investigator appealing rationalizations for risking the subjects' welfare based upon the anticipated 'benefits' to society of the proposed research" (p. 887). She admits to being "severe" in her criticism: "most of the investigators who conduct research that I regard as ethically reprehensible do so because they are interested in socially significant problems and are committed to well-controlled methodology.[9]

Whereas Baumrind wanted stronger restrictions, Kenneth Gergen (1973) doubted that we needed a code of ethics. He cited two studies that showed that research subjects are generally unconcerned about being deceived and are not harmed. He argued that there is no philosophical basis for a particular set of ethical principles, and that important research will not be done under the limits stated in the proposed APA principles.[10]

After Stanley Milgram had moved from his studies of obedience to other research, indeed for the remainder of his life, he was called upon to justify the research that made him famous. He published one article (Milgram, 1977/1992) devoted to justifying the use of technical illusions (his preferred word for deception) in research, in which he presented three major reasons. Most importantly, he said that his own data showed that subjects recovered from any distress they may have had and they gave positive evaluations of their research experience. He also argued that laboratory deception was no worse than deception in everyday life.

Milgram added a third reason that I have not read elsewhere. He said that, "virtually every profession [has] some exemption from general moral practice which permits the profession to function" (p. 182). For example, lawyers need not report their knowledge of a client's crime because that is a privileged communication, and gynecologists may examine the genitals of strange women. If the use of deception is necessary for social psychologists to do their work, with its consequent benefits to society, Milgram thought they too should have a comparable exemption.

The debate continued in the 1980s, and once again Diana Baumrind's views were featured (Baumrind, 1985). She argued that the APA ethical guidelines that she had criticized in 1971 had not led to a decrease in the incidence or extremity of deception in psychological research. Her strongest argument was "that the scientific and social benefits of deception research cannot be established with sufficient certitude to tip the scale in favor of procedures that wrong subjects" (p. 170).

Most critics of deception and some defenders have based their positions primarily on philosophical arguments. Larry Christensen (1988), however, presented a clear case supporting the use of deception in research that was based on empirical evidence showing "that subjects who have participated in deception experiments versus nondeception experiments enjoyed the experience more, received more educational benefit from it, and did not mind being deceived or having their privacy invaded" (p. 664). He recognized that there should be greater ethical concern for the use of deception when there is a risk of harming participants or revealing private behavior. However, given "the fact that research participants do not mind being deceived, and that it can also be viewed as immoral not to conduct research on important problems," Christensen concluded that, "the scale seems to be tipped in favor of continuing the use of deception in psychological research" (p. 664).

My summary of this debate has not adequately presented the depth of analysis or strength of opinion on the ethics of research in psychology,[11] but this section does show that the use of deception, at least after the Baumrind-Milgram exchange in 1964, was done with awareness of the ethical issues. Most researchers in psychology considered these issues carefully, but some did not welcome criticism or federal regulation. In her discussion of the Lewin tradition, Shelly Patnoe (1988) described "the frustration expressed by experimental social psychologists when the ethics of their enterprise came into question. They reacted as painters would if deprived of the nude for study, simply on the grounds of moral outrage" (p. 271).

Vulnerable Experimenters

One research participant who rarely is considered in this debate is the experimenter, often a graduate student assistant, who conducts the experiment and performs the illusions. Deception can have negative effects not only on subjects, but on the assistants who carry out the research. Adam Oliansky (1991) helped design and played the role of a confederate in an experiment in which students were told that the research concerned the effectiveness of trained versus untrained student counselors. All subjects were told that they were in a control (untrained) group that would attempt to help another student (the confederate) with his or her problem. The study really was about how feelings were affected by one's perceptions of success in helping another person in emotional distress. In the primary experimental manipulation,

[T]he confederates proceeded to act in one of two randomly determined fashions. In the 'no-improvement' condition, the confederate listened to advice offered by the subject but rejected it, continuing to act in a depressed manner throughout the 15-min interchange (one of the confederates was so convincing that he was asked if he had contemplated suicide). In the 'improvement' condition, however, the confederate first rejected the subject's advice and then gradually became more receptive to suggestions, ending the session on an optimistic note. (Oliansky, 1991, p. 255)

Oliansky reported that some subjects became quite angry when informed of the deception, feeling that they had been set up to fail (no-improvement condition) or were depressed because what they thought were successes were really tricks. But "the most offended group [were] those subjects (in both conditions) who had attempted to aid confederates by bringing up similar problems of their own" (p. 256). They had been tricked into revealing sensitive private information about themselves. The negative reactions were so extensive that the investigator "felt obliged to terminate the experiment because of complaints from subjects" (p. 255). These reactions occurred in spite of the fact that the investigator apparently followed the required procedures for obtaining informed consent, and even told all subjects that deception might be involved in the research. Of course, informed consent is problematic when a person can not know what feelings and thoughts will be evoked by the experimental situation.

There also were negative effects on the research assistants. "Everyone who was involved in the experiment was, and continues to be, doubtful and guilty about their part in the study. . . . (p. 256). The assistants were embarrassed when some subjects did not believe the deception. Others felt awkward when subjects offered their telephone numbers so they could continue to provide help after the experiment. The discomfort extended to chance meetings between confederates and subjects in their every day roles as students outside the laboratory.

Oliansky's disclosure is unusual. I know of no studies that examine the effects of deception on those who misinform subjects or play confederate roles. I would expect that the results would be similar to those for research subjects; most assistants probably find the experience to be interesting and are not upset. This one case, however, should make us aware that when there are negative reactions, they may be present on both sides of the deception.

Did Psychologists Break the Law?

In both laboratory and field studies, deception has been used to get people to do things they might not ordinarily do and in ways that upset people to differing degrees. Some of these acts could have been considered as fraud, harassment, or illegal in other respects, and might have led to court cases against psychologists, but that rarely has occurred. One example of illegal activity being part of an experiment was presented in the previous chapter. The "ubiquitous Watergate" study involved manipulating college students into agreeing to commit a burglary. This conspiracy would have been a crime if the experimenters had intended to carry out an actual burglary.

Irwin Silverman (1975) selected ten examples of field studies published between 1966 and 1972 and asked two attorneys to give their opinion concerning whether a law had been broken and, if so, what a court was likely to determine. All ten studies used "nonreactive methods," which means that people were not aware that they were part of an experiment. The deception involved roles played by experimenters who faked accidents or made false requests.

The two lawyers gave quite different opinions. One believed that no criminal laws were involved and that only one case might have grounds in civil law. In that latter case the damages probably would have been so small that a court would not have bothered with it. The other lawyer thought the cases were serious offenses involving harassment, disorderly conduct, and "infliction of mental suffering." Silverman noted that the different opinions likely were related to the specialties of the two lawyers, the former being a defense attorney and the latter a specialist in the rights of medical patients. Although they disagreed, both attorneys had legal grounds for their opinions, which might have led to a reasonably competitive situation if any of these experiments had led to a law suit.

I know of only two examples of psychological research leading to legal action. One involved charges of violations of federal and state regulations concerning institutional review of research. The other concerned a research participant who charged that she had suffered mental harm because of experimenter negligence. Both cases illustrate how disruptive and stressful legal action can be for the researchers regardless of the legitimacy of the charges.

The Albany Shock Experiments

In October of 1977, as reported in *Science* magazine (Smith, 1977), attorneys for the State University of New York at Albany "admitted that nonfederally funded research in the school's psychology department had not been submitted for review to the university's Human Subject Research Committee[,] . . . that proper consents were not obtained from participants in three experiments, and that the participants were not given a fair explanation of risks. One of the experiments involved 45 women who were subjected to electric shocks with a machine that the health department said was malfunctioning and could have administered a lethal shock" (Smith, 1977, p. 383).

That study was testing the hypothesis that suffering to reach a goal leads to that goal becoming more attractive. Some subjects were given small shocks that lasted 20 seconds "as an 'initiation ritual' to join a fictitious sensitivity group" (Smith, 1977, p. 383).

A graduate student research assistant, who had been dismissed from the university for poor academic work, brought the charges that led to the state action. In addition to charging violations of the ethics review procedure, the graduate student "charged that introductory psychology students had been coerced into participation in the shock experiment and other experiments" (p. 383), and that other research had been conducted with grade school children without their parents' permission. He also took the electrical generator used in the shock experiment to an electrical engineer who "said the machine was unsafe for use" and "could have administered a fatal shock." Subsequently, the state health department ordered the university to stop doing research on human subjects and set a date for public hearings.

In a response to this news article (Tedeschi & Gallup, 1977), the investigator in charge of the shock study and his department head argued that students had not been coerced because they had other options, that subjects were informed about the use of uncomfortable electric shock and were free to withdraw from participation, and that noncompliance with the review procedure was unintentional because of the ambiguity of the law at that time. They also pointed out that the engineer had examined the shock machine some time after the completion of the experiment and after it had been modified by students intending to use the machine in a different study.

Apparently the Albany research psychologists were following reasonable procedures to review ethical practice, although not the procedures specified by the law, and were doing so with good intentions for protecting participants. It is quite possible that the dismissed graduate student had motives for filing charges other than concern for Albany undergraduates and school children. Regardless of those motives, officials of the state of New York took the charges seriously and disrupted research with humans on several campuses in the state. The psychologists involved spent many hours preparing and delivering testimony concerning their research.

The Pittsburgh Victims

Social psychologists have used deception to create situations that most people believe are real. That is, people accept the cover story as true and trust the statements and actions of researchers and their confederates. Even with careful postexperiment debriefing, however, it is difficult to determine how many people were not fooled, how many resented the deception, and how many were emotionally upset. Not every research participant accepts the role of good sport in the service of behavioral science but formal complaints are rare perhaps because offended participants believe it is not worth the trouble or may fear some form of retribution if they challenge authority.

In one case, however, the resentment of a disturbed research subject led to a law suit. Martin Greenberg and his colleagues at the University of Pittsburgh were conducting research on the conditions under which victims of crime will report an offense (Greenberg, Wilson, & Mills, 1982). They had set up a fictitious research organization in a suite of offices in a Pittsburgh business district. Subjects were recruited with an advertisement in the Pittsburgh newspapers that asked for volunteers for research on work efficiency and offered $10 for 1 1/2 hours of clerical work. Those who responded by telephone were told they would have an opportunity to earn more money.

When subjects arrived at the office for the research another participant already was there. He was a confederate "programmed to play the role of thief" (p. 81). The real subject and the confederate were presented with the clerical task, which was to transcribe numbers from a card to a work sheet and place the completed work in a box. Each of them received an additional $20, but was told that the one who completed the fewest work sheets would have to pay the other participant. The situation was arranged to make it appear later that the confederate had stolen completed work sheets from the real subject and had taken money he did not deserve.

After the clerical work had been completed subjects went to the secretary's office, where they were made aware of the theft. The secretary, also a confederate, made certain that the evidence of a theft was clear to the subject and then suggested that the subject should call the police. The major measure of interest in the research was how much encouragement it took before the subjects agreed to make the call, if they agreed at all. This was the basic research situation, but a variety of manipulations were used in a series of studies on victim decision making (Greenberg & Ruback, 1992).

One of these studies involved another confederate in the secretary's office who apparently was a bystander when the subject learned of the theft. The bystander had been instructed to say that the theft made her angry and to advise the subject to call the police. At this point, however, one participant, a 52-year-old housewife, decided that something was wrong and that she should leave the building. Her hasty exit surprised the confederates. The secretary quickly called a research supervisor, who hurried to try to catch up to the woman who had gone down a hallway. The woman refused to listen to the supervisor or to another staff member who tried to help (Greenberg & Ruback, 1992, p. 246).

Martin Greenberg and other members of the research staff were contacted immediately. About a half an hour after the woman had left she returned with her husband and two police officers. The officers wrote a report that described the event as a "miscellaneous incident" and concluded: "Both parties satisfied. No action to be taken . . . (p. 247). The husband, however, "was quite irate and stated that if the police had not been there, he would have beaten the supervisor with a tire iron" (p. 247).

The participant and her husband changed their minds and on March 14, 1979, they filed a civil suit one year, eleven months, and one day after the incident, which also was less than a month before the Pennsylvania statute of limitations would have prevented legal action. The suit charged the University of Pittsburgh and the researchers with negligence and the infliction of emotional distress. The charge of negligence included allegations that the defendants had failed to follow accepted psychological research techniques, employed scare tactics in the research, and failed to obtain any type of consent. Damages of $10,000 were claimed because the participant said she suffered a variety of injuries including insomnia, traumatic neurosis, paranoid ideas, digestive disturbances, and a permanent change in personality. The husband claimed to have lost the "care, comfort, and society" of his wife.

The case came to trial before a judge three and one-half years later, in September 1982. After five witnesses for the plaintiff (the research participant) were heard, the defense attorney moved for a directed verdict against the plaintiff, which if accepted would mean that there was not enough evidence to establish that the defendants caused the problem. "The judge said he had no choice but to dismiss the lawsuit" (p. 258). Although Greenberg did not have an opportunity to present his side in court, he published a description of how his defense would have been presented (Greenberg & Ruback, 1992). According to this statement, he did use careful, accepted procedures designed to minimize risk to research subjects and his research did not lead to the alleged problems of the plaintiff and her husband. Greenberg also revealed how the case affected his personal life. His relationships with colleagues changed and he, like the Albany psychologists, was forced to spend a large amount of time preparing for his defense. He and his associates also were victims.

The reactions of local newspaper reporters to this case are instructive because they show how journalists can represent deceptive research to the public. Several newspaper articles and one editorial were published in March of 1979 around the time the law suit was filed, but nothing was published in 1982 when the case was dismissed. One article (Pierce, 1979) included an interview with Greenberg that presented some preliminary results of his research and discussed ethical issues. The last few paragraphs of the article gave the impression that Greenberg did not want to discuss negative opinions of participants about his research and that institutional review was casual.

The most dramatic article was written by an editorial clerk at the newspaper, who had been a subject in one of Greenberg's studies (Patton, 1979). The headline was, "'I felt like a fool,' woman who took the test says." She wrote this "more than a year" after she took part in the research. "I got into a crowded bus after the test and felt as if everyone knew I had been duped. I was paranoid and tried to conceal my embarrassment by smiling so the other passengers wouldn't know how I felt."

She then described the basic experimental procedure including learning of the theft and being urged by the secretary to call the police. She said she was less bothered by the "feeling of being ripped off" than by having "been set up." She concluded, however, that she "also felt that the research this group was doing was valuable," that her "contribution would help a real victim and it was okay to have my head on the block just this once. But never again."

With only two actual cases and the speculation of two attorneys, it is difficult to reach a reliable conclusion about the legality of all types of deception. However, it does seem reasonable to conclude that with proper precautions and institutional approval there is nothing illegal about deceiving participants. A greater risk may be drawing public attention to deceptive research because, from the perspective of the journalist, social psychologists who use deception make better villains than heros.

Research Ethics in 1993

American psychologists have devoted a large amount of time to developing ethical principles for research with human participants, with major versions published in 1951, 1973, and 1992. In the intervening years committees of the APA reviewed the principles and considered policies and issues related to research ethics. Ethical treatment of research participants has become a topic in many textbooks and chapters on research methodology, and now is part of the training of most graduate students in psychology. I believe that social (and other) psychologists consider these issues carefully but, I am not convinced that they would have begun to do so were it not for the federal regulations that required institutional review.

From 1950 to 1990 the United States was involved in major changes regarding human rights. The civil rights movement had a tremendous impact. Women, the elderly, disabled persons, and other groups gained political influence, as did organizations to protect consumers and the environment. Human research participants also were among the groups whose rights were strengthened and who gained increased power in the law.

The major revision of the APA ethics code that was approved in 1992 (APA, 1992) placed new restrictions on the use of deception. Deception still is permitted if the researcher thinks it is justified by the "prospective scientific, educational, or applied value" of the study and if non-deceptive procedures "are not feasible." However, "[p]sychologists never deceive research participants about significant aspects that would affect their willingness to participate, such as physical risks, discomfort, or unpleasant emotional experiences." The word *never* does not allow options for the researcher. This new standard would have prohibited many of the studies that were conducted in the past and are reviewed in this book.

This limit on the use of deception may simply codify what already has been imposed by institutional review committees. It is highly unlikely that review committees in the 1990s would allow psychologists to deceive subjects about drug effects, potentially lethal electric shock, or criminal activity. Some social psychologists may yearn for the good old days, but the impact experiment is out of style, having mostly been replaced with paper-and-pencil or keyboard-and-monitor manipulations involving minor deception. Now the major risk to subjects is boredom.

—11—

Deception in Psychology and American Culture

In 1973, when the use of deception was at its peak, *The Sting* won the Academy Award for best motion picture. It told the story of a "big con," in which an elaborate, illegal betting parlor was set up to trick a powerful gangster into believing that he actually was placing bets on horse races. A company of con-artists was created to be confederates who would help lead the gangster into making a large wager that he would lose in the final "sting." The staging and acting of the sting were perfect so the victim had no idea that he had been conned.

By the 1970s many social psychologists had become con men and women of sorts who spent considerable time and energy trying to convince research subjects of the false reality of their laboratory situations. These illusions were used to produce the data that are the basis for many of the knowledge claims of this field. Now, I want to put this research in perspective by considering the cultural context in which it evolved.

In this book I have focused on deception as one identifiable element of the relationship that developed between psychologists seeking to understand people and the people who served as subjects in their research. Social psychologists were not the only psychologists who used deception, but they did so with much greater frequency than did their colleagues in other areas of psychology. In chapter 3 we saw that to become part of mainstream psychology, social psychologists in the 1930s and 1940s had to adopt the scientific approaches of manipulation and quantification. The stimuli of social psychology were people and situations. These stimuli could not be manipulated and quantified as easily as the lights and sounds used in the study of perception or the artificial nonsense words that were used to study human learning.

It seems unlikely, however, that the use of deception could have become commonplace if it had been in conflict with dominant cultural values. Our culture does not, for example, tolerate the intentional production of extreme physical suffering (although there are important exceptions). However, our values do support the kinds of deception used in social psychological research.

Con Men and Sitcoms

Arrest of the Confidence Man—For the last few months a man has been travelling about the city, known as the "Confidence Man," that is, he would go up to a perfect stranger in the street, and being a man of genteel appearance, would easily command an interview. Upon this interview he would say, after some little conversation, "have you confidence in me to trust me with your watch until to-morrow;" the stranger, at this novel request, supposing him to be some old acquaintance, allows him to take the watch, thus placing "confidence" in the honesty of the stranger, who walks off laughing. (*New York Herald*, 8 July, 1849)

This is the epigraph to William Lenz's (1985) study of the confidence man as a character in literature. Psychologists who use deception share many of the characteristics of this American tradition. The confidence man is a familiar character in American literature and history dating back at least to the early nineteenth century. He appears in the work of Melville, Twain, and many lesser authors as one "who seeks and wins confidence by deliberate deceit and then abuses that confidence for personal advantage" (Lenz, p. 64).

Americans seem to enjoy being fooled; we love magic, illusion, flying saucers, and cowboy presidents. The career of P. T. Barnum, the most famous American con man, is instructive as an example of the social functions of deception. Lenz quoted from a study of that showman's life suggesting that

Barnum's exaggerations and confessions, his humbugs and deceits, were the dreams of many Americans who could not try them. His audacity in donning the mantle of morality appealed to Americans convinced that the older boundaries of human behavior were no longer valid, but who dared not overstep these limits themselves. (p. 24)

In discussing Barnum's success, Lenz adds that this reveals "the American admiration of expertise, technique, and success without moral reflection. In fact, nineteenth-century Americans seemed to enjoy successful cons; they enjoyed the direct challenge to their intellect and sensibilities, the chance to debunk and unmask fraud, the lively controversy aroused, the ingenuity of hoaxes and harmless tricks, and perhaps most important and most particularly American, they enjoyed that which was new" (p. 25). Barnum himself delighted in creating "humorous stratagems and skillful manipulations" (p. 24). He would have appreciated social psychology in the mid-twentieth century.

Appreciation of clever deceit is not limited to nineteenth-century literature, although Lenz concluded that the Civil War destroyed the character of the con man as a literary convention. Confidence games continued to be practiced and reported (Nash, 1976). *Caveat emptor*, let the buyer beware, expresses the self-reliant attitude of Americans toward the victims; the person who was duped should have known better. Deception became a common theme in films and television where comedy provided the justification. Lucy regularly used disguise and deceit to fool Ricky. One popular program, The Phil Silvers Show, used fraud and deception as the major theme, even representing it in the name of the main character, Sergeant Bilko. Situation comedies gained in popularity with the growth of television in the 1950s and continue to attract large viewing audiences. Although the situations have changed (e.g., from traditional families in the fifties to single-parent families today), deception is still a common theme.

Candid Camera was the television show that had the most obvious relationship with deceptive research. It was a form of confidence game in that the success of its deceptions was based on participants' trust. The show was quite popular, and segments from it have been used as classroom demonstrations by psychology teachers. In 1985 *Psychology Today* published an interview (Zimbardo, 1985) with Allen Funt, the creator and producer of Candid Camera. That interview was conducted by social psychologist Philip Zimbardo. What Funt had to say shows how closely popular entertainment is related to social psychology and provides additional insight into the reasons that deception is widely accepted.

In his introduction to the interview, Zimbardo compared Funt to his "most creative colleagues" (including Leon Festinger) because of Funt's "ability to design and manipulate social situations" (p. 44). Funt revealed that he had attended Cornell University where, in his senior year, he worked as a research assistant to Kurt Lewin. His experience observing children through a one-way mirror was influential in his development of Candid Camera. While in the Army he learned about audio recording devices that could be concealed, and decided that he would enjoy using this technology as a way to make a living. This led to the 1947 radio program, *Candid Microphone*. Soon he began to use a motion picture camera, and during the 1950s *Candid Camera* became one of the highest-rated television shows in America. Funt estimated that he recorded about 1,250,000 people.

Most of the situations are funny and often are instructive examples of human behavior. One of Funt's purposes, however, was to "expose basic human weaknesses" (p. 46) and that could be embarrassing. In responding to a question about the ethics of these situations, Funt said: "We appeal to wha is universal in human nature . . . [and] are essentially laughing at ourselves and our weaknesses. . . . *Candid Camera* also works because it is part of the American tradition to be 'a good sport,' to accept a limited amount of hazing, to go along with a joke." Being a good sport may be uncomfortable, but people "almost never" became angry and Funt gave them a hug and a medal for their participation. The medals were inscribed, "I was on *Candid Camera* and I was big enough to let other people share the experience with me." Funt did "worry about what happens when the same type of deception or exposé of human frailty is used by the wrong people" (p. 47). Although he is "a good person, benign and caring about those I work with," others may be con men or spies, and some TV programs may even "encourage people to make fools of themselves for money." Funt said that before the production of the popular "funniest home video" programs.

Funt's comments on how people have changed since he began his program are instructive for social psychologists who use deception: "It's also harder to deceive people now [in 1985]. They are more knowledgeable about technology, more sophisticated about their rights, more cynical and assertive, and, of course, sensitized to the *Candid Camera* type of experience" (p. 47).

Popular Philosophy

We enjoy deception when it doesn't hurt, but some confidence games are not fun. One of the oldest is "the pigeon drop" that continues to take money from the poor and elderly. In this con game, a person who supposedly has found some money offers to share it with you if you put up some of your own money "to show good faith." You put your money in an envelope, and when you are distracted by an arranged diversion, the envelope containing your money is switched with one containing only paper. We also have fake medical cures that play on the sick and dying, financial swindlers who play on our greed, and television preachers presenting false morality. All these types of deception have a long history.

Why are some deceptions acceptable, while others are thought to be wrong? That depends, in part, on another characteristic of American culture, our pragmatic, utilitarian popular philosophy. Pragmatism, an idea developed by William James, says that truth is tested by the practical consequences of belief. We know what is true by taking some action and then examining the evidence produced by the consequences. In its popularized version (which is not the same as James's idea) something is true if it works.

Another widely accepted idea is the utilitarian view that what is right depends on the usefulness of the consequences judged in terms of the balance of benefits over costs. In popular terms this philosophy says that we should seek the greatest good for the greatest number, even if a minority have to sacrifice or suffer. Social psychologists are being pragmatic when they use their research results to justify deception, and they are utilitarian when they decide that the general value of their results outweighs the discomfort to some research participants.

Perhaps the strongest value in our culture is that of individualism (Bellah, Madsen, Sullivan, Swidler, & Tipton, 1985). We go to great lengths to protect the rights of individuals, we value independence over conformity to the group, and we respect the rights of individuals to make their own decisions. When individualism is added to the use of consequences as the test of what is true and right, this creates a situation that has produced many of our American heros. Dirty Harry (Clint Eastwood's movie detective) or real-life characters like Oliver North decided, as individuals, that it was all right to break the law because, as individuals, they concluded that their action would produce more benefit than harm (utilitarian) and believed that others later would agree that what they did was right because it was successful (pragmatic). This reasoning is similar to that used to support the practice of deception in social psychological research.

I will assume that most of our heroes, as well as most social psychologists, are decent people who care for their fellow humans and want to help rather than harm them. This beneficence is another tradition in our culture. We believe that it is wrong to harm our neighbor, that if someone is in trouble we should help, and, at the highest level, that we should help even if we are not asked. These are ideals that we state, although sometimes we may not act on them. Nevertheless, in American culture we have the frequent themes of riding to the rescue and helping those in need, which we are told is why the United States sent troops to Kuwait in 1991, Somalia in 1993, and Bosnia in 1995. Much of the research in social psychology is based on this cultural value because the major justification for doing the research and for deceiving subjects is that it will benefit society.

Society never requested those benefits, however, and the subjects who were deceived may have preferred to avoid the situation, but the experimenters decided to do the research anyway to provide the alleged benefits. Paternalism is the view that sometimes people should be helped even when they don't ask for it because what they are made to do is for their own good and is something they later will appreciate. Paternalism also has a long tradition in American culture, particularly in the form of twentieth century social laws in areas such as child labor, food and drug regulations, and environmental safety. These controls generally are accepted as providing important benefits and protection. Whenever deception occurs in research, one also finds the use of the power of authority to control and manipulate other persons in order to produce alleged benefits. It is a paternalistic relationship when the experimenter decides what is good for the subject.

Social psychologists were, and are, part of an American culture that is practical (pragmatic and utilitarian), individualistic, beneficent, and paternalistic. These cultural values provided a large part of the context in which deception became a major research practice in social psychology. The illusions created in the laboratory were a kind of confidence game, justified by the consequences, especially in terms of benefits to society. Although there was an academic debate about the use of deception (see chapter 10), this was a problem for a relatively small number of psychologists. The research subjects also are part of this culture. Most of the data indicates that the students who took part in dramatic impact experiments enjoyed the experience; they were good sports who could go along with a clever trick.

The context of American culture clearly influenced social psychologists' choice of topics, as well as their use of deception. Kurt Lewin's study of democratic and autocratic groups in the 1930s, clearly was an analog of the clash between the idealized view of our democratic society and the autocratic fascists in Germany. The work of the OSS Assessment Staff during World War II (see chapter 5) was particularly important in showing new ways to make research realistic by using actors in contrived situations. Solomon Asch expressed American values when he was disturbed by the extent of conformity and pleased when he saw independent individuals. The research on bystander intervention was significant because it helped us to understand why people did not help others, behavior which went against the value we place on beneficence. Numerous individual studies have been based on conventional ideas from our culture, like the foot-in-the-door technique (Freedman & Fraser, 1966) and playing hard to get in romantic relationships (Walster, Walster, Piliavin, & Schmidt, 1973).

Social Psychology and Academic Life

Experimental realism, including deception, fit our cultural values, but it could not have become so widespread without the influence of significant individuals in the history of social psychology: Kurt Lewin, Leon Festinger, Solomon Asch, and Stanley Milgram. Asch and Milgram were relatively independent, and were influential as creators of powerful situations, rather than as leaders of extended groups of students. Lewin and Festinger, however, were part of a large academic family that can be traced through generations from the 1930s into the 1990s (Patnoe, 1988). Lewin's role in this history was to bring real life into the laboratory and stimulate others to create their own illusions. He then became more concerned with applications of psychology outside the laboratory, before his death at an early age. Leon Festinger continued the Lewin tradition in the laboratory, and in the context of a changed academic world.

After World War II, the number of college students increased dramatically, and required more faculty to teach them. Government support for basic research also increased and had a major impact on what faculty did. Those who wanted to become famous did not teach undergraduates, but spent their time in graduate seminars, in which their own research was the major topic for discussion. Psychology grew more than most fields as a popular subject in spite of faculty attempts to enhance the image of a hard science, but it was that image that gained large amounts of federal funds for research. In social psychology, as in the rest of psychology, more faculty had more money to do research with more student subjects.

Faculty also were influenced by the characteristics of the academic marketplace of the 1950s (Caplow & McGee, 1958), which have not changed much since that time. Publication was the currency of the market; its idealized products were the creation of new knowledge and the betterment of humanity, but the driving force was the acquisition of prestige. The managers of this system controlled who published what and where they published it (i.e., they controlled the most prestigious journals). They also controlled who entered the system (i.e., who was admitted into the most prestigious departments) and who the system glorified with prestigious awards. These same leaders consulted with foundations and served on the panels of the agencies that provided the research funds that made it easier to publish by providing money for equipment, travel, and support for the graduate students who did the work. Regardless of whether one is cynical about this system or supports it, the fact remains that there is a pattern of influence and selection. Publication is the measure of success and acceptance is neither random or entirely based on merit (Campbell, 1988; Strickland, Aboud, & Gergen, 1976).

The power structures of academic disciplines are informal and implicit. There is no organizational chart with a leader sitting atop a hierarchy of subordinates. There are informal networks, however, in which some people communicate with each other more than with others, and some of these networks involve the people who control access to the means of gaining prestige.[1] This system exerts powerful control on all its members, especially those who are lower in the hierarchy and want to achieve the prestige given to those at the top. Graduate students, young faculty and those at less prestigious institutions know that to be successful one must do what is acceptable, and that means choosing the correct topics and theories, and conducting their research using the right methods. It is the established leaders who set the standards for what is correct and right. Leon Festinger was a leader in one of these networks, and his students carried on his ideas and methods even after he moved on to interests outside of social psychology.

Standards for acceptability of ideas and practices in psychology are set by cultural values, by the dominant values of the academic community, and most directly by the values of the leaders of academic specialties, such as social psychology.[2] Leon Festinger gained his position of great influence within a particular system of cultural and academic values. He became a dominant figure because he met the need for a theory in social psychology that would be comparable to the major theories of learning, which at that time were influential in experimental psychology. He did not gain his influence through calculated political manipulation in formal organizations, but through the network of his students who followed his example.

Two of these Festinger students published a widely accepted guide to doing research in social psychology, a guide that promoted staged situations with the necessity of deception. Elliot Aronson and J. Merrill Carlsmith (1968) aimed their instruction at social psychology graduate students, and their directions for carrying out laboratory experiments were published in the second edition of *The Handbook of Social Psychology* (Lindzey & Aronson, 1968), which was a standard reference work in social psychology. Given the prestige and wide circulation of this source, the directions were bound to have a major influence.

The chapter promoted the scientific superiority of the "true" experiment in which people are randomly assigned to two or more groups, thus continuing and confirming the establishment view of research methodology that I discussed in chapter 3. The most important emphasis in this handbook chapter, however, was the importance of psychological involvement of the subject in the research. Experimental realism forces subjects to take the situation seriously; it has an impact on them, which led to the use of the phrase, "impact experiments." Mundane realism that simulated the world outside the laboratory was less important because it might not involve subjects and consequently would have little impact.

The use of deception was presented as "one way of attaining experimental realism" (p. 26). The authors cautioned readers to be aware of potential ethical problems in using deception and to avoid its use whenever possible, although they said that "many questions in social psychology can be answered only by designing experiments which cause subjects some psychological discomfort" (p. 28). Aronson and Carlsmith devoted almost eight pages to their discussion of ethical problems. They made it quite clear that "deception, even when innocuous, presents an ethical problem because a lie has been told," that when not innocuous it may result "in some anguish, upset, or discomfort on the part of the subject," and that "experimenters have no special right to expose people to unpleasant facts about themselves in the name of education" (p. 30). They also emphasized the importance of the debriefing process to reduce subjects' discomfort and convince them that they have made an important contribution. There was a firm conclusion to this discussion of ethics and deception:

The experimenter should always keep the welfare of his subjects in mind, even if it involves compromising the impact of his experimental procedures. Most important, the experimenter, as he goes about his business, should never lose sight of the obligation he owes to his subjects, and should be constantly on the alert for alternative techniques. (p. 36)

The remainder of this lengthy chapter described how to plan, conduct, and evaluate experiments, including a section headed, "setting the stage" (p. 37ff) in which the authors discussed the theatrical nature of experimental realism. Students and others who read this Handbook chapter must have been quite excited by the prospect of being involved in this kind of creative research, and it was something most of them were required to do in order to get their academic degrees, get jobs and be promoted.

Although they drew attention to ethical problems, Aronson and Carlsmith gave prospective researchers another justification for using deception:

[T]he fact remains that he [the experimenter] has deceived the subject, and no amount of restoration can erase the fact that he *has* behaved dishonestly. *Most experimental social psychologists are willing to assume this ethical burden*, feeling that, if using deception experiments is the only feasible way to uncover an interesting fact, then the truths so uncovered are worth the lies told in the process so long as no harm befalls the subject. The experimenter can also take some comfort in the knowledge that in most cases, although the subject was not aware of the true purpose of the experiment, he at least knew he was in an experiment. As such, he is aware of the fact that his relationship to the experimenter is that of a subject. Indeed, the two principles are, in effect, parties to an experimenter-subject contract. The occasional use of deception can be considered one of the implicit clauses in this contract. (Aronson & Carlsmith, 1968, p. 35, italics mine)

Here the idea of *caveat emptor* is brought to the psychology laboratory.

The next (third) edition of *The Handbook of Social Psychology* (Aronson, Brewer, & Carlsmith, 1985) included a revision of the chapter on experimentation. During the intervening 17 years the use of deception had declined, particularly in impact experiments. The authors of this new chapter attributed this change in part to the political events of the era.

[I]n the late 1960s and early 1970s, most of us were strongly affected by the cynical, self-serving duplicity employed by our national

leaders during the Vietnam War and during the Watergate investigation. In this atmosphere, many social psychologists grew alarmed
lest we as a profession might lose the confidence of the public by
behaving in a way that bore any resemblance to that exposed in
Watergate investigations—no matter how superficial that resemblance might be. The rapid growth in government regulations on
the protection of human subjects also reflected the same concerns.
(Aronson, et al., 1985, p. 442)

The last sentence on the impact of federal regulation seems to be an after-
thought, when this really was a major factor in the declining use of deception.
In fact, deception continued at high levels after Viet Nam and Watergate,
and the Watergate hearings became the basis for a deceptive study (West,
Gunn, & Chernicky, 1975) that raised ethical questions (see chapter 9).
Although "most" social psychologists may have been concerned about it,
many continued to deceive research participants.

However, there may have been some need to be concerned about losing
the "confidence of the public." Although Stanley Milgram's book on his
obedience experiments had appeared in 1974, more publicity in the popular
press was given to the "Golden Fleece Awards" presented, somewhat sarcas-
tically, by Senator William Proxmire of Wisconsin during the 1970s and
1980s. The awards were given, in press releases, to projects that Proxmire
and his staff thought were a waste of government money. A minority of these
went to research projects and a few of those were in social psychology. The
March 1975 Award was presented to the National Science Foundation, "For
squandering $84,000 to try to find out why people fall in love" (Fleece,
1982), research that was conducted by social psychologists Ellen Berscheid
and Elaine Walster.

This is not the kind of public recognition that psychologists seek, and
one (Shaffer, 1977) saw the presentation of the Golden Fleece Award to
Berscheid and Walster to be an example of anti-intellectualism. He said that,
after that award, "newspapers and magazines quickly followed up on the
press releases and parlayed the participants' interviews into a 2-month series
of letters, editorials, and articles" (p. 814). However, no data were presented
concerning how many newspapers and magazines did that, other than those
in New York, Washington, and the home states of the investigators. One
headline read, "Prox Plays for Snickers" (Shaffer p. 818), which probably is
all the general public did before ignoring the research. There certainly was
no public outcry against the use of deception; not even Senator Proxmire
cared about it.

American culture has had a great influence on research in social psychology, including providing the context for the creation of illusions of reality

in the laboratory, but there is little evidence that the public paid much attention to specific research studies or to the methods used in psychological research. The kinds of deception used by social psychologists are not that impressive, even in staged impact experiments, compared to the intricate intrigues of modern mystery films or the political scandals unearthed by journalists. Occasionally, creative experiments will get attention in the science or features sections of the newspaper, but never as front-page news across the country.[3] In a society in which deception is everywhere, what social psychologists did hardly caused a ripple.

— 12 —

The Power of Positive Illusions

I began this history in chapter 2 with descriptions of the mild forms of deception that were used in psychological research early in the twentieth century. Margaret Washburn (1909), for example, told her subjects that there would be different distances between two points of touch, when the distance was always the same. Hulsey Cason (1925) told students that some words would produce more vivid images than other words, when he previously had determined that they were similar in evoking images. Even these simple forms of deception were not common at the time.

Then two significant things happened in the early years of social psychology; the field became experimental and it began to simulate real life in the laboratory. These two developments led to the need to manipulate experimental conditions in controlled situations in ways that would be believable to subjects. These illusions of reality later came to be called impact experiments. Kurt Lewin and Saul Rosenzweig were the first to describe how this could be done, and after the 1930s, the use of deception gradually increased until it was a common practice in social psychological research.

In the 1950s and 1960s a new generation created even more dramatic research situations that are among the most interesting and widely cited experiments in all of psychology. By example and in written statements this approach to research was encouraged, and was supported by the characteristics of American culture and the structure of academic life. Although the general public expressed relatively little concern regarding the use of deception, psychologists themselves have continued to debate the ethics of this practice.

I have tried to emphasize the historical development of a distinctive approach to behavioral research, and to include comments on ethical questions or methodological issues where they fit into the story. In several places, however, I was critical of some things that psychologists did when it seemed they were not sufficiently concerned with the feelings of the research participants. Negative examples of the abuse of deception are common enough to warrant concern, but many studies have shown that subjects generally give positive evaluations to their experience in deception experiments (e.g., Smith & Richardson, 1983; Soliday & Stanton, 1995). I will conclude this history with an evaluation of the use of deception in research, and the benefits that have resulted from the use of this approach.

Acceptable Deception and Effective Illusions

Stanley Milgram (1977/1992) thought that using the word "deception" imposed a negative bias on discussions of research. He preferred to use "morally neutral terms such as . . . 'technical illusions' in describing such techniques" (p. 181). His idea is reflected in the title of this book, *Illusions of Reality*, but it seems to me that the same issues exist whether we speak of illusion or deception.

When is deception acceptable? The most restrictive position is that its use in justified only in emergencies, when there is no truthful alternative. Sissela Bok (1979) has taken this position in her popular book on lying in public and private life, and Diana Baumrind (1985) has done so for research in psychology. Others see deception as a normal and necessary part of daily life. It is "an essential component of our ability to organize and shape the world, to resolve problems of coordination among individuals who differ, to cope with uncertainly and pain, to be civil and to achieve privacy as needed, to survive as a species and to flourish as persons" (Nyberg, 1993, p. 219).

In daily life there are social norms that we use as guides that tell us what forms of deception are acceptable to reasonable people. We take into account the intent of the deceiver, and possible effects on the person deceived; "be untruthful to others as you would have others be untruthful to you" (Nyberg, 1993, p. 137). Using this guideline, judgments of the acceptability of deception in research would be made by individuals, and those individuals who are potential participants in research would decide what is reasonable. A large proportion of all the research in social psychology would pass this test, and this would have been true even in the stage production era.

Deceptive research, of course, can be effective only if the subjects are not aware that they are being deceived, which makes it difficult to ask potential subjects to evaluate the research, that is, to give informed consent for their participation. It is interesting that two suggestions for resolving this problem came from Stanley Milgram (1977/1992), whose research on obedience provoked so much controversy. First, he suggested "presumptive consent." This procedure would solicit the opinions of an experimental procedure from a large number of people, and this group would decide whether it is acceptable. Milgram did not say how large a majority he thought would be needed to allow a researcher to proceed with an experiment.

A better solution according to Milgram would be

> to obtain *prior general consent* from subjects in advance of their actual participation. This . . . would be based on subjects' knowing the general types of procedures used in psychological investigations, but without their knowing what specific manipulations would be employed in the particular experiment in which they would take part. . . ." [People] could exclude themselves from any study using deception or involving stress *if they so wished.* (Milgram, 1977/1992, p. 189, italics in original)

Finally, he suggested giving subjects "monitoring cards" that would be submitted to a review committee after taking part in the experiment. The experiment would be stopped if a sufficient number of subjects had objections. Another form of monitoring would involve observation of the experiment while it is taking place by someone who is not part of the research team (Zimbardo, 1973), and who is trained to detect signs of distress.

In the 1990s very few experiments are being done that would require this kind of monitoring or the kinds of preliminary screening of potential subjects suggested by Milgram. A different and continuing problem concerns the psychology of the experimental situation, a situation that is quite different in the 1990s from the one that Rosenzweig analyzed in 1933. Research subjects, most of whom are college students, are wise to the use of deception and have been for a long time. Typically, these students are enrolled in psychology courses in which they read about dramatic deception experiments., so it may be the researcher who is experiencing the illusion that subjects are being deceived. Most subjects approach laboratory studies as a game of trying to figure out what really is taking place, while they follow the experimenter's instructions.

It is unrealistic to try to outwit research subjects with even more elaborate forms of deception, and it would be unfortunate to give up the option of conducting interesting experiments that involve subjects. It seems to me that honesty is the best policy, that is, honesty with respect to the fact that the experiment is a creation that may involve various forms of deception, and that the subject probably knows this. The phrase, honest deception, may sound incongruous, but I think it describes a realistic and ethical approach. It is not difficult to think of ways to implement both of Milgram's suggestions, and to develop criteria for the acceptability of deception based on the judgments of potential subjects. Mild forms of deception would easily be approved and those likely to cause discomfort would be denied. Where there was doubt about a procedure it would be implemented gradually, with observation. More consideration also should be given to "prebriefing" (Wiener & Erker, 1986),

because under some conditions alerting subjects to the possibility of deception has little effect on the results. The objectives of this approach are to make
the research experience educational for the subject and the results valid for
the researcher by involving the subject in the research, that is, by maintaining
experimental realism.

Over the years there have been suggestions for procedures that are alternatives to the use of deception (e.g., Geller, 1982), including naturalistic
observation, role playing and computer simulation. There are methodological
problems with all of these techniques, as well as some ethical concerns. Role
playing, for example, can be produce strong emotional reactions (Haney,
Banks, & Zimbardo, 1973). Experimenters should at least be aware of their
options.

The creation of illusions of reality through the use of deception is a
powerful technique for the study of human experience. That approach should
not be eliminated, but rather should be examined carefully for the benefits it
can yield. It must be used, however, with maximum concern for the feelings
of research participants (experimenters, as well as subjects), and with the
knowledge that subjects have their own ideas about the experimental
situation. Involving people does not always require that they be fooled.

Social Psychology as a Positive Force

Social psychologists justify their use of deception partly in terms of the
benefits to society that will result from the research. One of these benefits is
that we now have a better understanding of human nature because of
research in social psychology. Solomon Asch (chapter 6) showed us that most
people will reject the unreasonable judgments of a unanimous majority,
although there are a few who will always conform. Stanley Milgram (chapter
8) helped us to see that we might follow the directions of an unreasonable
authority. Psychologists who study attribution have described our tendency
to explain our own behavior in terms of our circumstances, but to explain
what others do in terms of their character. These findings go beyond everyday, common-sense psychology, and for that reason they are examples of
important contributions to knowledge.

Many social psychologists are sensitive to their role in the larger society
and go beyond the illusions of their research. In the 1930s, Kurt Lewin was
one of the founders of the Society for the Psychological Study of Social
Issues (SPSSI). Every issue of the quarterly journal of this organization, *The
Journal of Social Issues*, provides examples of the application of research to
improving human welfare. Recent topics included environmental hazards,
conflict management, and human values.

The movement toward equality for women is a major area in which
individual social psychologists have had a significant impact through their

research and political activity. There is a large amount of published research on gender roles, discrimination, and sexual harassment which has advanced our understanding and in doing so may have helped to change our attitudes. Beyond that, some of this research has been used to inform legal decisions concerning sex discrimination (Fiske, Bersoff, Borgida, Deaux, & Heilman, 1991).

Research in social psychology *has* produced benefits for society; we have a better understanding of human nature and that knowledge has been used to promote human welfare. Some of the research that produced these benefits involved the use of deception. It is impossible to say whether similar benefits would have resulted if deception had not been used, and if alternatives to deceptive impact experiments had been developed. Social psychology is a fascinating subject and I encourage readers to make their own judgments of the value of research in this area by reading a good textbook (e.g., Aronson, 1995; Myers, 1990; Sabini, 1992).

Much of the research in social psychology today (the 1990s) is theoretically complex and uses sophisticated techniques of statistical analysis (Reiss & Stiller, 1992). It often is not very interesting to read, and probably was not as much fun to do as the stage productions of the 1960s. The social psychology knowledge industry continues to produce results, and some of these results may turn out to be important. As our culture continues to change, psychology will change with it. New methods may evolve and enter the main stream of psychological research. Whatever these methods turn out to be, whether they are more or less dramatic and deceptive, my hope is that psychologists will transform subjects into true *participants*, in an honest attempt to understand human nature.

Notes

Chapter 1

1. My sources here were two sociologist colleagues at Saint Louis University, James F. Gilsinan and Buford E. Farris.

Chapter 2

1. Almost all of my examples come from articles published in United States journals. This example is taken from a book and refers to an event that took place in Germany. I include it because it is a precedent for a well-known demonstration in psychology and for the use of confederates, and was presented by an important figure in early American psychology.

2. The number and percent (in parentheses) of empirical articles reporting the use of deception in the *Journal of Abnormal and Social Psychology* from 1933 to 1947 are: 1933—1 (3.6); 1934—1 (2.9); 1935—2 (6.0); 1936—3 (9.1); 1937—1 (4.5); 1938—1 (4.2); 1939—2 (6.1); 1940—3 (12.0); 1941—4 (13.3); 1942—2 (7.1); 1943—0; 1944—4 (12.9); 1945—1 (3.2); 1946—4 (12.5); 1947—2 (5.7).

3. Two articles (McNamara & Woods, 1977; Seeman, 1969) contained no definition. Stricker's (1967) definition was general: ".studies in which subjects were intentionally misled about some aspect of the investigation, either explicitly or implicitly" (p. 13). Deception was broadly defined by Menges (1973) as inaccurate (misleading or erroneous) or incomplete (partial or no) information. Levenson, Gray, and Ingram (1976) were a little more specific: "when subjects were purposely given or led to believe inaccurate information" (p. 160). Gross and Fleming (1982) used seven categories of deception including both misinforming subjects and subjects being unaware that they were in a study. A clear definition was provided by Adair, Dushenko, and Lindsay (1985): "the provision of information that actively misled subjects regarding some aspect of the study . . ., either about the study's purpose or task, or provided false information about others or about their own or others' behaviors" (pp. 62–63).

4. Sandra Nicks and I conducted this search assisted by several students, including Tina Mainieri, Andrew Pomerantz, and James Sweeney. She reported our preliminary findings at the 1990 meeting of the American Psychological Association (Nicks, 1990).

5. Vitelli (1988) sampled four journals in social psychology and found a significant decrease in the use of deception. Sieber, Iannuzzo, and Rodriguez (1995) reported a decrease from 1978 to 1986 but an increase in 1992. In both these studies the number of years sampled is not sufficient to confirm trends one way or the other. Sandra Nicks surveyed all articles in the 1994 volumes of JPSP and found that 31.3% reported the use of deception, a percentage that is not much larger than the 29.9% that we found in 1989.

Chapter 3

1. An important alternative to the treatment group design in psychology is the single subject (N of 1) approach developed by B. F. Skinner as behavior analysis. In this approach, one individual is studied in a controlled environment (e.g., a rat in a "Skinner box") while stimulus conditions are varied systematically. This method more closely approximates that used in the physical sciences.

2. A Likert scale is a paper-and-pencil measure that asks subjects to provide a quantitative rating of an attitude that reflects their agreement or liking. Most often this is a five-point scale ranging from, for example, 1 = strongly disagree, to 5 = strongly agree.

3. Rosenzweig reported that when he was designing one of his experiments he was working in the Harvard Psychological Clinic. His research space included a closet, and he built a one-way mirror into the wall of the closet so he could observe subjects in the next room. He learned how to construct the mirror-window by visiting local gambling clubs. Using this device, Rosenzweig made motion pictures of some of his subjects without their knowledge (Rosenzweig, 1986, p. 84).

4. It is difficult to understand why these and other writers on research methodology continued to overlook Rosenzweig's paper after 1960. Perhaps Orne, Rosenthal, and others simply were careless when reviewing the literature, or it may be that recognition of this earlier contribution would have made their "discoveries" in the 1960s less impressive. Rosenthal recognized his oversight in a 1971 letter to Rosenzweig (personal communication from Rosenthal to Rosenzweig, August 13, 1971). Other authors writing on the psychology of human subjects (Rosnow, 1981; Silverman, 1977) did recognize the importance of Rosenzweig's early paper.

Chapter 4

1. Rosenzweig (personal communication, December 27, 1995) said that at the time he was writing his 1933 paper he had been collecting all of Lewin's publications, including the 1929 monograph, written in German, that was quoted by MacKinnon and Dukes (1962). The comments on the experimental situation were incidental to the major thesis that Lewin was presenting, and Rosenzweig did not recall reading or being influenced by those comments.

Chapter 5

1. A *New York Times* review of Winks' book was titled "Yale - A Great Nursery of Spooks."

2. Staff members included child psychologist Urie Bronfenbrenner, social psychologists Robert Chin and Theodore M. Newcomb, and animal learning psychologists David Krech, O. H. Mowrer, and Edward C. Tolman.

3. An exception is the research reported by Campbell, Sanderson, and Laverty (1964) in which respiratory paralysis, caused by a drug injection, was used to establish a conditioned response in male alcoholic patients. They all "said that they thought they were dying" (p. 631).

Chapter 6

1. Asch's quote is from an unpublished interview with Howard Gruber, and reported in Ceraso, Gruber, & Rock, 1990.

2. Interview with Solomon Asch at his home in Princeton, New Jersey, July 14, 1989.

3. Interview with Henry Gleitman at his office at the University of Pennsylvania, November 3, 1989. As a young assistant professor at Swarthmore College, he was Asch's colleague in the early 1950s, and worked with Asch on this research. Asch (1956, p. 1) credits Gleitman with "help in the designing of many experiments" and "statistical analysis of the data." Gleitman also conducted some of the experiments.

4. Gleitman recognized that it is possible that he may have overdramatized the emotion 42 or 43 years after it happened.

5. Gleitman interview.

6. Gleitman interview.

7. Asch interview.

8. There continues to be some confusion over whether subjects in Asch's experiments conformed or were independent. The November 1992 newsletter of the Society for the Psychological Study of Social Issues contains reports of remarks made during a tribute to Solomon Asch on August 17, 1992 at the American Psychological Association convention in Washington, DC. Howard Gruber said that "most subjects resisted"; Alice Ginott said, "most of the subjects went along with the group"; and Beatrice Wright said that it depended on which experiments you look at. As Ronald Friend and Dana Bramel point out in this newsletter, most of the subjects gave independent responses on most of the critical trials. That is, although most people may have gone along with the majority once or a few times, very few did so on all the tests they were given.

9. Gleitman interview.

10. Asch interview.

11. Gleitman interview.

12. Gleitman interview.

13. Gleitman interview.

14. Asch interview.

Chapter 7

1. Solomon Asch also published an article with Hertzman (Asch, Block, & Hertzman, 1938).

2. This is the procedure that Festinger used in his undergraduate research, which became his first publication with Max Hertzman, and his Iowa studies of level of aspiration.

3. Actually, all subjects were male in this study.

4. This anecdote told by Festinger perhaps is an indication of the researchers attempts to be clever:
On the first visit that all three of us made to the group an event occurred that was to make a difficult study much more so. Stanley, with his own characteristic style of humor, introduced himself as Leon Festinger and there I was left to be Stanley Schachter. Once done it could not be undone but had to be maintained throughout—I've wondered if they even noticed the small lapses that occurred (Festinger, 1987, p. 5).

5. Brewster Smith (1983) recognized the importance of dissonance theory, but disagreed with the notion that this was a valuable contribution to social psychology. "It was the side effects of the torrent of dissonance research that especially dismayed me. A normative pattern of deceptive, manipulative laboratory experimentation was established that seemed to me bad for the field, both ethically and intellectually" (p. 175).

Chapter 8

1. Arthur Miller (1986, p. 262) cites a June 1984 personal communication from Milgram stating that the first submission of this article was rejected by the editor of the *Journal of Abnormal and Social Psychology*, but that "several months later, the editor . . . recalled the rejected paper and published it. Sabini and Silver (1992) also say the first version was rejected. However, M. Brewster Smith, editor of *JASP* before 1962, said that he is *"quite certain* I never dealt with the Milgram research editorially" (personal communication, June 30, 1992, italics in original). Daniel Katz

who succeeded Smith as editor in 1962 did accept the 1963 paper, but does "not recall an earlier rejection" (personal communication, June 29, 1992). I had written to these former editors to try to find the reasons that Milgram's article might have been rejected.

2. All quotations in this section are from Milgram's 1963 article unless otherwise indicated.

3. Interview with Solomon Asch, July 14, 1989.

4. Interview with Henry Gleitman, November 3, 1989.

5. Neil Lutsky (1995) reviewed research in contemporary history that "presents a more complex and problematic view of the Holocaust than that implied by social psychology's application of obedience to authority" (p. 55). Other forms of social influence also operated to induce soldiers and ordinary citizens to participate in the atrocities. In this same article, Lutsky also shows that the obligation to obey an authority is not a sufficient explanation for the behavior of subjects in the Milgram experiments.

6. This study is reprinted in an edited volume of Milgram's work (Milgram, 1977/1992). See chapter 21, "Television and antisocial behavior: field experiments."

Chapter 9

1. Philip Zimbardo said that "when I arrived at Stanford University in 1968 [I] was told by my idol, Leon Festinger, who had heard that I enjoyed teaching, that: 'Every hour in the classroom is an hour away from the laboratory, and since it's only research that gives meaning to one's career as a psychologist, cut down on the teaching" (Zimbardo, 1995, p. 13).

2. The use of the polygraph as a method to detect lying is itself a form of deception. The validity of lie detection has been challenged by psychologists (e.g., Kleinmuntz & Szucko, 1984) who have documented the high error rates that result in the misclassification of truthful individuals. These errors may be the basis for decisions that have significant harmful effects for those who submitted to the test. Kleinmuntz and Szucko (1984) have shown, however, that one can learn to fake honest responses to a polygraph test, thereby deceiving the deceiver.

3. In 1971, social and behavioral scientists specifically were included in the law.

4. Stanley Milgram says that he and his students thought of doing research on this topic three years before the Genovese incident (Tavris, 1974b, p. 78).

5. Although the investigators in this study were sociologists, the study uses the general approach used by psychologists and was published in the major journal of social psychology.

6. In a footnote to his 1963 study of obedience, Milgram said that he learned of Buss's method after developing his own. In his 1974 book (p. 167), Milgram says that his method is more effective.

7. The details of the procedure for this study were given in an unpublished paper dated 1971, but which is no longer available (Elaine (Walster) Hatfield, personal communication, Nov. 18, 1992).

8. For a description of a staged experiment reminiscent of those of the 1970s, see Richard Nisbett's (1993, p. 446) report of a study of violent responses to insults.

Chapter 10

1. The masculine pronoun was used throughout the 1953 code. The APA began to encourage the use of nonsexist language in 1974.

2. Some principles that concern research are not quoted here. They cover the quality of research design, reporting research, participant confidentiality, and the use of animals in research.

3. The remaining data in this paragraph include only articles published in English language journals. Very few articles on research ethics from foreign-language journals were listed in the *Abstracts* after 1950.

4. See McGaha & Korn (1995) for yearly numbers of articles on research ethics from *Psychological Abstracts*, and for data separated by whether the articles were essays or empirical studies, and articles that were from psychology versus non-psychology journals.

5. In 1990 the name of this committee was changed to the Committee on Standards in Research. Then, in 1993, the APA Board of Scientific Affairs, to which this committee reported, recommended that it be discontinued.

6. The latest edition of the *Publication Manual* (APA, 1994) requires authors to "certify" (rather than "indicate") that they have followed the ethical standards. This may be done in a cover letter sent with the manuscript, in the text of the article, or by signing a form. As in earlier editions of the manual, there is no requirement to submit evidence of compliance, such as a copy of the informed consent statement, the text of a debriefing statement, or data on participants' reactions to the experiment.

7. Unless otherwise noted, all page references in this section will be to Faden and Beauchamp (1986).

8. See Beecher (1966) for examples of twenty-two other unethical medical experiments.

9. In this article, Baumrind included a statement from her secretary describing her negative reaction to being deceived in an experiment when she was a college sophomore (Baumrind, 1971, pp. 888–889). It is unusual to find such anecdotes in

print. Although they are not representative of most students' experiences, they form part of the basis for the concerns that many psychologists have about research practices.

10. See Diener and Crandall (1978) for a balanced view of the pros and cons of the use of deception, as well as of other ethical issues in psychology, and for the research that had been done before 1978 to support those positions.

11. See Beauchamp, Faden, Wallace, and Walters (1982) for an excellent collection of chapters by various authors concerning the philosophical issues in behavioral and social research.

Chapter 11

1. Kenneth Gergen made this explicit during a discussion printed in Strickland, Aboud, and Gergen (1976, p. 315): "I think it's very clear what constitutes power. In fact, there's a certain interlocking directorate in social psychology in the United States which controls the journal space, who gets into school, whether you publish or not, whether you get money for research, and you'll find the same people on committees in Washington giving away the money, on the journals, at the heads of social psychology programs. . . ." In a following comment Robert Zajonc said "I would support what he says."

2. There even is a pecking order among specialties. In her review of the "increase in the status and centrality of social psychology within psychology, Ellen Berscheid said that "back in 1965, and for many years after, social psychologists were the lowest of the low. . . . The reigning prima dons were the 'experimentalists' in learning psychology, [who were] searching for universal laws of behavior that would span millions of years of evolutionary time. . . . [T]he experimental psychologists, one must admit, were doing a fine job of imitating their acknowledged betters in the 'hard' sciences. . . ." (Berscheid, 1992, p. 528).

3. Social psychology did make it into one of the most popular cartoon features of the 1990s. A 1993 "Far Side" cartoon by Gary Larson showed a person in a military uniform seated behind a large desk. A man and woman in white laboratory coats stood in from of him. The man said, "Sorry your highness, but you're really not the dictator of Ithuvania, a small European republic. In fact, there is no Ithuvania. The hordes of admirers, the military parades, this office—We faked it all as an experiment in human psychology. In fact your highness, your real name is Edward Belcher, you're from Long Island, New York, and it's time to go home, Eddie."

References

Adair, J. G., Dushenko, T. W., & Lindsay, R. C. L. (1985). Ethical regulations and their impact on research practice. *American Psychologist, 40*, 59–72.

Allport, F. H. (1924). *Social psychology*. Boston: Houghton Mifflin Company.

Allport, F. H., & Allport, G. W. (1921). Personality traits: Their classification and Measurement. *Journal of Abnormal and Social Psychology, 16*, 6–40.

Allport, G. W. (1937). *Personality: A psychological interpretation*. New York: Holt.

American Psychological Association. (1953). *Ethical standards of psychologists*. Washington, DC: Author.

American Psychological Association. (1959). Ethical standards of psychologists. *American Psychologist, 14*, 279–282.

American Psychological Association. (1963). Ethical standards of psychologists. *American Psychologist, 18*, 56–60.

American Psychological Association. (1968). Ethical standards of psychologists. *American Psychologist, 23*, 357–361.

American Psychological Association. (1973). *Ethical principles in the conduct of research with human participants*. Washington, DC: Author.

American Psychological Association. (1974). *Publication manual of the American Psychological Association (2nd ed.)*. Washington, DC: Author.

American Psychological Association. (1982). *Ethical principles in the conduct of research with human participants*. Washington, DC: Author.

American Psychological Association. (1983). *Publication manual of the American Psychological Association (3rd ed.)*. Washington, DC: Author.

American Psychological Association. (1992). Ethical principles of psychologists and code of conduct. *American Psychologist, 47*, 1597–1611.

American Psychological Association. (1994). *Publication manual of the American Psychological Association (4th ed.)*. Washington, DC: Author.

Aronson, E. (1991). Leon Festinger and the art of audacity. *Psychological Science, 2*, 213–217.

Aronson, E. (1995). *The social animal* (7th Ed.). New York: W. H. Freeman and Company.

Aronson, E., Brewer, M., & Carlsmith, J. M. (1985). Experimentation in social psychology. In G. Lindzey & E. Aronson (Eds). *Handbook of social psychology*, Third edition, Vol. 1. New York: Random House.

Aronson, E., & Carlsmith, J. M. (1968). Experimentation in social psychology. In G. Lindsay & E. Aronson (Eds.), *The handbook of social psychology* (2nd ed.). Vol.2. Reading, MA: Addison–Wesley.

Asch, S. E. (1940). Studies in the principles of judgments and attitudes: Determination of judgments by group and by ego standards. *Journal of Social Psychology*, 12, 433–465.

Asch, S. E. (1952/1987). *Social psychology*. New York: Oxford University Press.

Asch, S. E. (1955). Opinions and social pressure. *Scientific American, 193*, No. 5, p. 31–35. (Offprint No. 450, 7 pp.).

Asch, S. E. (1956). Studies of independence and conformity: I. A minority of one against a unanimous majority. *Psychological Monographs: General and Applied, 70*, 9 (Whole No. 416), 70 pp.

Asch, S. E. (1958). Cacophonophobia. Review of *A theory of cognitive dissonance* by Leon Festinger. *Contemporary Psychology, 3*, 194–195.

Asch, S. E., Block, H., & Hertzman, M. (1938). Studies in the principles of judgments and attitudes: I. Two basic principles of judgment. *Journal of Psychology*, 5, 219–251.

Ash, M. G. (1992). Cultural contexts and scientific change in psychology: Kurt Lewin in Iowa. *American Psychologist, 47*, 198–207.

Bandura, A., Underwood, B., & Fromson, M. E. (1975). Disinhibition of aggression through diffusion of responsibility and dehumanization of victims. *Journal of Research in Personality, 9*, 253–269.

Baumrind, D. (1964). Some thoughts on ethics of research: After reading Milgram's "behavioral study of obedience." *American Psychologist, 19*, 421–423.

Baumrind, D. (1971). Principles of ethical conduct in the treatment of subjects: Reaction to the draft report of the Committee on Ethical Standards in Psychological Research. *American Psychologist, 26*, 887–896.

Baumrind, D. (1985). Research using intentional deception: Ethical issues revisited. *American Psychologist, 40*, 165–174.

Beauchamp, T. L., Faden, R. R., Wallace, R. J., Jr., & Walters, L. (1982). *Ethical issues in social science research*. Baltimore, MD: The Johns Hopkins University Press.

Beecher, H. E. (1966). Ethics and clinical research. *The New England Journal of Medicine, 274*, 1354–1360.

Bellah, R. N., Madsen, R., Sullivan, W. M., Swidler, A., & Tipton, S. M. (1985). *Habits of the heart: Individualism and commitment in American life.* Berkeley, CA: University of California Press.

Berkun, M. M., Bialek, H. M., Kern, R. P., & Yagi, K. (1962). Experimental studies of psychological stress in man. *Psychological Monographs: General and Applied, 76,* (15, whole no. 534), 1–39.

Bok, S. (1978). *Lying: Moral choice in public and private life.* New York: Vintage Books.

Boring, E. G. (1957). *A history of experimental psychology.* New York: Appleton-Century-Crofts.

Bramel, D. (1962). A dissonance theory approach to defensive projection. *Journal of Abnormal and Social Psychology, 64,* 121–129.

Brown, J. F. (1929). The methods of Kurt Lewin in the psychology of action and affection. *Psychological Review, 36,* 200–221.

Brown, R. (1986). *Social psychology, the second edition.* New York: The Free Press.

Buss, A. H. (1961). *The psychology of aggression.* New York: Wiley.

Campbell, D., Sanderson, R. E., & Laverty, S. G. (1964). Characteristics of a conditioned response in human subjects during extinction trials following a single traumatic conditioning trial. *Journal of Abnormal and Social Psychology, 68,* 627–639.

Campbell, D. T. (1988). A tribal model of the social system vehicle carrying scientific knowledge. In D. T. Campbell. *Methodology and epistemology for social science: Selected papers.* Chicago: University of Chicago Press.

Campbell, D. T. (1990). Asch's moral epistemology for socially shared knowledge. In Rock, I. (Ed.). *The legacy of Solomon Asch: Essays in cognition and social psychology.* Hillsdale, NJ: Lawrence Erlbaum Associates.

Campbell, D. T., & Stanley, J. C. (1963). Experimental and quasi–experimental designs for research on teaching. In Gage, N. J. (Ed.). *Handbook of research on teaching.* Chicago: Rand-McNally and Co.

Caplow, T., & McGee, R. J. (1958). *The Academic Marketplace.* New York: Basic Books.

Cartwright, D. (1948). Social psychology in the United States during the second world war. *Human Relations, 1,* 333–352.

Cartwright, D., & Festinger, L. (1943). A quantitative theory of decision. *Psychological Review, 50,* 595–621.

Cason, H. (1925). Influence of suggestion on imagery in a group situation. *Journal of Abnormal and Social Psychology, 20,* 294–299.

Ceraso, J., Gruber, H., and Rock, I. (1990). On Solomon Asch. In Rock, I. (Ed). *The legacy of Solomon Asch: Essays in cognition and social psychology.* Hillsdale, NJ: Erlbaum.

Christensen, L. (1988). Deception in psychological research: When is its use justified? *Personality and Social Psychology Bulletin, 14,* 664–675.

Coach quits after faking shooting at team rally. (1993, November 25). *St. Louis Post-Dispatch,* p. D1.

Cook, S. W. (1975). A comment on the ethical issues involved in West, Gunn, and Chernicky's "ubiquitous" Watergate: An attributional analysis. *Journal of Personality and Social Psychology, 32,* 66–68.

Cooper, J., Zanna, M. P., & Taves, P. A. (1978). Arousal as a necessary condition for attitude change following induced compliance. *Journal of Personality and Social Psychology, 36,* 1101–1106.

Cornell Studies in Social Growth. (1952). Principles of professional ethics. *American Psychologist, 7,* 452–455.

Craik, K. H. (1986). Personality research methods: An historical perspective. *Journal of Personality, 54,* 18–51.

Crawford, M. P. (1992). Rapid growth and change at the American Psychological Association: 1945 to 1970. In R. B. Evans, V. S. Sexton, & T. C. Cadwallader (Eds.), *The American Psychological Association: A historical perspective.* Washington, DC: American Psychological Association.

Danziger, K. (1985). The origins of the psychological experiment as a social institution. *American Psychologist, 40,* 133–140.

Danziger, K. (1990). *Constructing the subject: Historical origins of psychological research.* Cambridge: Cambridge University Press.

Danziger, K. (1993). The project of an experimental social psychology: Historical perspectives. Unpublished manuscript.

Dashiell, J. F. (1935). Experimental studies of the influence of social situations on the behavior of individual human adults. In C. Murchison (Ed.). *A handbook of social psychology.* Worcester, MA: Clark University Press.

Davis, D., Rainey, H. G., & Brock, T. C. (1976). Interpersonal physical pleasuring: Effects of sex combinations, recipient attributes, and anticipated future interaction. *Journal of Personality and Social Psychology, 33,* 89–106.

Diener, E., & Crandall, R. (1978). *Ethics in social and behavioral research.* Chicago: University of Chicago Press.

Douglas, J. D. (1976). *Investigative Social Research: Individual and Team Field Research.* Beverly Hills, CA: Sage Publications.

Edwards, A. L. (1944). The signs of incipient fascism. *Journal of Abnormal and Social Psychology, 39,* 301–316.

Elms, A. C. (1975). The crisis of confidence in social psychology. *American Psychologist, 30,* 967–976.

Elms, A. C., & Milgram, S. (1966). Personality characteristics associated with obedience and defiance toward authoritative command. *Journal of Experimental Research in Personality, 1,* 282–289.

Errera, P. (1972). Statement based on interviews with forty "worst cases" in the Milgram obedience experiments. In Katz, J. (Ed.). *Experimentation with Human Beings.* New York: Russell Sage Foundation.

Ethics Committee of the American Psychological Association. (1986). Report of the ethics committee: 1985. *American Psychologist, 41,* 694–697.

Ethics in Applied Anthropology. (1951). *Human Organization, 10,* 4.

Evans, R. I. (1976). *The making of psychology.* New York: Knopf.

Faden, R. R., & Beauchamp, T. L. (1986). *A history and theory of informed consent.* New York: Oxford University Press.

Festinger, L. (1942). Wish, expectation, and group standards as factors influencing level of aspiration. *Journal of Abnormal and Social Psychology, 37,* 184–200.

Festinger, L. (1947). The role of group belongingness in a voting situation. *Human Relations, 1,* 154–180.

Festinger, L. (1953). Laboratory experiments. In L. Festinger & D. Katz (Eds.), *Research methods in the behavioral sciences* (pp. 136–172). New York: Holt, Rinehart, and Winston.

Festinger, L. (1954). A theory of social comparison processes. *Human Relations, 7,* 117–140.

Festinger, L. (1957). *A theory of cognitive dissonance.* Evanston, IL: Row, Peterson and Company.

Festinger, L. (1987). A personal memory. In Grunberg, N. E., Nisbett, R. E., Rodin, J., & Singer, J. E. (Eds.). A distinctive approach to psychological research: The influence of Stanley Schachter. Hillsdale, NJ: Lawrence Erlbaum Associates.

Festinger, L. (1989). Looking backward. In Schachter & Gazzaniga (Eds.). *Extending psychological frontiers: Selected works of Leon Festinger.* New York: Russell Sage Foundation.

Festinger, L., & Carlsmith, J. M. (1959). Cognitive consequences of forced compliance. *Journal of Abnormal and Social Psychology, 58*, 203–211.

Festinger, L., Riecken, H. W., & Schachter, S. (1956). *When prophecy fails*. New York: Harper & Row.

Fillenbaum, S. (1966). Prior deception and subsequent experimental performance: The "faithful" subject. *Journal of Personality and Social Psychology, 4*, 532–537.

Fiske, S. T., Bersoff, D. N. Borgida, E., Deaux, K., & Heilman, M. E. (1991). Social science research on trial: Use of sex stereotyping research in *Price Waterhouse v. Hopkins. American Psychologist, 46*, 1049–1060.

Freedman, J. L., & Fraser, S. C. (1966). Compliance without pressure: The foot-in-the-door technique. *Journal of Personality and Social Psychology, 4*, 195–202.

French, J. R. P. (1941). The disruption and cohesion of groups. *Journal of Abnormal and Social Psychology, 36*, 361–377.

French, J. R. P. (1944). Organized and unorganized groups under fear and frustration. In Lewin, K., Meyers, C. E., Kalhorn, J., Farber, M. L., & French, J. R. P. *Authority and Frustration. Studies in Topological and Vector Psychology III*. Iowa City, IA: University of Iowa Press.

Friend, R., Rafferty, Y., and Bramel, D. (1990). A puzzling misinterpretation of the Asch 'conformity' study. *European Journal of Social Psychology, 20*, 29–44.

Geller, D. M. (1982). Alternatives to deception: Why, what, and how? In J. E. Sieber (Ed.). *The ethics of social research, Vol. 1: Surveys and experiments*. New York: Springer-Verlag.

Gergen, K. J. (1973). The codification of research ethics: Views of a doubting Thomas. *American Psychologist, 28*, 907–912.

Golann, S. E. (1970). Ethical standards for psychology: Development and revision, 1938–1968. *Annals of the New York Academy of Sciences, 169*, 398–405.

Goodman, L. S., & Gilman, A. (1975). *The pharmacological basis of therapeutics*. (4th ed.). New York: The Macmillan Company.

Greenberg, M. S., & Ruback, R. B. (1992). *After the crime: Victim decision making*. New York: Plenum Press.

Greenberg, M. S., Wilson, C. E., & Mills, M. K. (1982). Victim decision-making: An experimental approach. (pp. 73–94) In Konecni, V. J. & Ebbesen, E. B. (Eds.). *The Criminal Justice System: A Social-Psychological Analysis*. San Francisco: W. H. Freeman and Co.

Greenwald, A. G. (1976). An editorial. *Journal of Personality and Social Psychology, 33*, 1–7.

Gross, A. E., & Fleming, I. (1982). Twenty years of deception in social psychology. *Personality and Social Psychology Bulletin, 8*, 402–408.

Grunberg, N. E., Nisbett, R. E., Rodin, J., & Singer, J. E. (Eds.). (1987). A distinctive approach to psychological research: The influence of Stanley Schachter. Hillsdale, NJ: Lawrence Erlbaum Associates.

Haines, H., & Vaughan, G. M. (1979). Was 1898 a "great date" in the history of experimental social psychology? *Journal of the History of the Behavioral Sciences, 15*, 323–332.

Haney, C., Banks, W. C., & Zimbardo, P. G. (1973). Interpersonal dynamics in a simulated prison. *International Journal of Criminology and Penology, 1*, 69–97.

Hardyck, J. A., & Braden, M. (1962). Prophecy fails again: A report of a failure to replicate. *Journal of Abnormal and Social Psychology, 65*, 136–141.

Hartshorne, H., & May, M. A. (1928). Studies in deceit, Book One, General Methods and results. In *Character Education Inquiry, Studies in the Nature of Character*. New York: The Macmillan Company.

Heider, F. (1958). *The psychology of interpersonal relations*. New York: Wiley.

Heider, F. (1983). *The life of a psychologist: An autobiography*. Lawrence, KS: University Press of Kansas.

Hertzman, M., & Festinger, L. (1940). Shifts in explicit goals in a level of aspiration experiment. *Journal of Experimental Psychology, 27*, 439–452.

Hobbs, N. (1948). The development of a code of ethical standards for psychology. *American Psychologist, 3*, 80–84.

Howells, T. H. (1933). An experimental study of persistence. *Journal of Abnormal and Social Psychology, 28*, 14–29.

Humphreys, L. (1970). *Tearoom trade*. Chicago: Aldine.

Jones, E. E. (1985). History of social psychology. In Kimble, G. A. and Schlesinger, K. (Eds.) *Topics in the History of Psychology*. Vol. 2. Hillsdale, NJ: Erlbaum, 1985.

Jones, E. E., & Davis, K. E. (1965). From acts to dispositions: The attribution process in person perception. In L. Berkowitz (Ed.), *Advances in Experimental social psychology* (Vol. 2). New York: Academic Press.

Jones, E. E., & Sigall, H. (1971). The bogus pipeline: A new paradigm for measuring affect and attitude. *Psychological Bulletin, 76*, 349–364.

Jones, J. H. (1981). *Bad blood: The Tuskegee syphilis experiment*. New York: The Free Press.

Katz, J. (1972). *Experimentation with human beings*. New York: Russell Sage Foundation, 1972.

Kelley, H. H. (1967). Attribution theory in social psychology. In D. Levine (Ed.), *Nebraska symposium on motivation*. Lincoln, NE: University of Nebraska Press.

Kelman, H. (1967). Human use of human subjects: The problem of deception in social psychology. *Psychological Bulletin, 67*, 1–11.

Kelman, H. (1972). The rights of the subject in social research: An analysis in terms of relative power and legitimacy. *American Psychologist, 27*, 989–1016.

Ketchum, R. M. (1991). *The borrowed years 1938–1941: America on the way to war*. New York: Doubleday (Anchor).

Kleinmuntz, B., & Szucko, J. J. (1984). Lie detection in ancient and modern times: A call for contemporary scientific study. *American Psychologist, 39*, 766–776.

Kohlberg, L. (1974). More Authority. *The New York Times Book Review*, March 24, 42–43.

Koocher, G. P. (1977). Bathroom behavior and human dignity. *Journal of personality and social psychology, 35*, 120–121.

Korn, J. H. (1987). Judgments of acceptability of deception in psychological research. *Journal of General Psychology, 114*, 205–216.

Korn, J. H., & Bram, D. R. (1988). What is missing in the method section of APA journal articles? *American Psychologist, 43*, 1091–1092.

Korn, J. H., & Hogan, K. (1992). Effect of incentives and aversiveness of treatment on willingness to participate in research. *Teaching of Psychology, 19*, 21–24.

Kozlowski, L. T. (1987). Observations, demonstrations, and applications: Research on cigarettes, coffee, walking, and sense of direction. In N. E. Grunberg, R. E. Nisbett, J. Rodin, & J. E. Singer (Eds.). *A distinctive approach to psychological research: The influence of Stanley Schachter*. Hillsdale, NJ: Lawrence Erlbaum Associates.

Langer, E., Blank, A., & Chanowitz, B. (1978). The mindlessness of ostensibly thoughtful action: The role of "placebic" information in interpersonal interaction. *Journal of Personality and Social Psychology, 36*, 635–642.

Latane, B. (1987). From student to colleague: Retracing a decade. In Grunberg, et al. (Eds.). *A distinctive approach to psychological research: The influence of Stanley Schachter*. Hillsdale, NJ: Lawrence Erlbaum Associates.

Leahey, T. H. (1981). The mistaken mirror: On Wundt's and Titchencer's psychologies. *Journal of the History of the Behavioral Sciences, 17*, 273–282.

Lenz, W. E. (1985). *Fast talk and flush times: The confidence man as literary convention*. Columbia, MO: University of Missouri Press.

Levenson, H. Gray, M. J., & Ingram, A. (1976). Research methods in personality five years after Carlson's survey. *Personality and Social Psychology Bulletin, 2*, 158–161.

Lewin papers, Box M946. Commission on Community Interrelations, Oct. 25, 1966, p. 13. Archives of the History of American Psychology, University of Akron.

Lifton, R. J. (1986). *The Nazi doctors: Medical killing and the psychology of genocide.* New York: Basic Books.

Lindzey, G., & Aronson, E. (Eds.) (1968). *The handbook of social psychology*, 2nd ed. Reading, MA: Addison–Wesley.

Lowenthal, M. M. (1978). *The Central Intelligence Agency organizational history.* Congressional Research Service, Library of Congress, Publication No. 78–168.

Lutsky, N. (1995). When is "obedience" obedience? Conceptual and historical commentary. *Journal of Social Issues, 51*, 55–65.

Mabee, C. (1987). Margaret Mead and behavioral scientists in World War II: Problems in responsibility, truth, and effectiveness. *Journal of the History of the Behavioral Sciences, 23*, 3–13.

MacCoun, R. J., & Kerr, N. L. (1987). Suspicion in the psychological laboratory: Kelman's prophecy revisited. *American Psychologist, 42*, 199.

MacKinney, A. C. (1955). Deceiving experimental subjects. *American Psychologist, 10*, 133.

MacKinnon, D. W., & Dukes, W. F. (1962). Repression. In Postman, L. (Ed.). *Psychology in the making: Histories of selected research problems.* New York: Knopf.

Mandler, J. M., & Mandler, G. (1969). The diaspora of experimental psychology: The Gestaltists and others. In D. Fleming and B. Bailyn (Eds.). *The intellectual migration: Europe and America*, (pp. 371–419). Cambridge, MA: Harvard University Press.

Mantell, D. M. (1971). The potential for violence in Germany. *Journal of Social Issues, 27*, 101–112.

Marcus, S. (1974). Obedience to Authority. *The New York Times Book Review*, Jan. 13, pp. 1–3.

Marrow, A. J. (1969). *The practical theorist: The life and work of Kurt Lewin.* New York: Basic Books.

Marshall, G. D., & Zimbardo, P. G. (1979). Affective consequences of inadequately explained physiological arousal. *Journal of Personality and Social Psychology, 37*, 970–988.

McDougall, W. (1908). *Introduction to social psychology.* London: Methuen.

McGaha, A. C., & Korn, J. H. (1995). The emergence of interest in the ethics of psychological research with human participants. *Ethics and Behavior, 5*, 147–159.

McKeachie, W. J. (1971). Proceedings of the American Psychological Association, Incorporated, for the year 1970: Minutes of the annual meeting of the Council of Representatives. *American Psychologist, 26,* 22–49.

McNamara, J. R., & Woods, K. M. (1977). Ethical considerations in psychological research. *Behavior Therapy, 8,* 703–708.

Menges, R. J. (1973). Openness and honesty versus coercion and deception in psychological research. *American Psychologist, 28,* 1030–1034.

Middlemist, R. D., Knowles, E. S. & Matter, C. F. (1976). Personal space invasions in the lavatory: Suggestive evidence for arousal. *Journal of Personality and Social Psychology, 33,* 541–546.

Milgram, S. (1961). Nationality and conformity. *Scientific American, 205 (6),* 45–51.

Milgram, S. (1963). Behavioral study of obedience. *Journal of Abnormal and Social Psychology, 67,* 371–378.

Milgram, S. (1964). Issues in the study of obedience: A reply to Baumrind. *American Psychologist, 19,* 848–852.

Milgram, S. (1965). Some conditions of obedience and disobedience to Authority. *Human Relations, 18,* 57–76.

Milgram, S. (1974). *Obedience to Authority: An experimental view.* New York: Harper & Row.

Milgram, S. (1977/1992). *The individual in a social world: Essays and experiments.* (2nd ed., edited by J. Sabini & M. Silver). New York: McGraw–Hill.

Miller, A. G. (1986). *The obedience experiments: A case study of controversy in social science.* New York: Praeger.

Miller, A. G., Collins, B. E., & Brief, D. E. (1995). Perspectives on obedience to authority: The legacy of the Milgram experiments. *Journal of Social Issues, 51,* 1–19.

Münsterberg, H. (1908). *On the witness stand.* Garden City, NY: Doubleday, Page & Company.

Murchison, C. (Ed.) (1935). *A Handbook of Social Psychology.* Worcester, MA: Clark University Press.

Murphy, G., & Murphy, L. B. (1931). *Experimental Social Psychology.* New York: Harper and Brothers.

Murphy, G., Murphy, L. B., & Newcomb, T. M. (1937). *Experimental Social Psychology,* (Revised Edition). New York: Harper and Brothers.

Murray, H. A. (1938). *Explorations in Personality.* New York: Oxford University Press.

Myers, D. G. (1990). *Social Psychology* (3rd Ed.). New York: McGraw–Hill.

Napoli, D. S. (1981). *Architects of adjustment*. Port Washington, NY: Kennikat Press.

Nash, J. R. (1976). *Hustlers and con men: An anecdotal history of the confidence man and his games*. New York: M. Evans and Company.

Nicks, S. D., Korn, J. H., & Mainieri, T. R. (1996). *The rise and fall of deception in social psychology and personality research, 1921 to 1989*. Manuscript submitted for publication.

Nisbett, R. E. (1993). Violence and U. S. regional culture. *American Psychologist, 48,* 441–449.

Nyberg, D. (1993). *The varnished truth: Truth telling and deceiving in ordinary life*. Chicago: University of Chicago Press.

Oliansky, A. (1991). A confederate's perspective on deception. *Ethics and Behavior, 1,* 253–258.

Olson, W. C. (1938). Proceedings of the forty–sixth annual meeting of the American Psychological Association, Incorporated, Columbus, Ohio, September 7, 8, 9, 10, 1938. *Psychological Bulletin, 35,* 579–592.

Orne, M. T. (1962). On the social psychology of the psychological experiment: With particular reference to demand characteristics and their implications. *American Psychologist, 17,* 776–783.

Orne, M. T., & Holland, C. H. (1968/1972). On the ecological validity of laboratory deceptions. In Miller, A. G. (Ed.). *The social psychology of psychological research*. New York: The Free Press.

OSS Assessment Staff. (1948). *Assessment of men: Selection of personnel for the Office of Strategic Services*. New York: Rinehart and Company.

Patnoe, S. (1988). *A narrative history of experimental social psychology: The Lewin tradition*. New York: Springer–Verlag.

Patton, C. (1979). 'I felt like a fool,' woman who took test says. *Pittsburgh Post-Gazette,* March 21, p. 5.

Pearce, H. J. (1902). Experimental observations upon normal motor suggestibility. *Psychological Review, 9,* 329–356.

Pierce, H. W. (1979). Is lying justified in psychological research? *Pittsburgh Post-Gazette,* March 21, pp. 1, 6.

Piliavin, J. A., & Piliavin, I. M. (1972). Effect of blood on reaction to a victim. *Journal of Personality and Social Psychology, 23,* 353–361.

Reiss, H. T., & Stiller, J. (1992). Publication trends in *JPSP*: a Three–decade review. *Personality and Social Psychology Bulletin, 18,* 465–472.

Robinson, F. G. (1992). *Love's story told: A life of Henry A. Murray.* Cambridge, MA: Harvard University Press.

Rock, I. (Ed.) (1990). *The legacy of Solomon Asch: Essays in cognition and social psychology.* Hillsdale, NJ: Erlbaum.

Roese, N. J., & Jamieson, D. W. (1993). Twenty years of bogus pipeline research: A critical review and meta-analysis. *Psychological Bulletin, 114,* 363–375.

Rosenthal, R. (1964). Experimental outcome–orientation and the results of the psychological experiment. *Psychological Bulletin, 61,* 405–412.

Rosenzweig, S. (1933). The experimental situation as a psychological problem. *Psychological Review, 40,* 337–354.

Rosenzweig, S. (1986). Background to idiodynamics. *The Clinical Psychologist, 39,* 83–89.

Rosnow, R. L. (1981). *Paradigms in transition: The methodology of social inquiry.* New York: Oxford University Press.

Rothman, D. J. (1987). Ethics and human experimentation: Henry Beecher revisited. *The New England Journal of Medicine, 317,* 1195–1199.

Rucci, A. J., & Tweney, R. D. (1980). Analysis of variance and the "second discipline" of scientific psychology: A historical account. *Psychological Bulletin, 87,* 166–184.

Sabini, J. (1986). Stanley Milgram (1933–1984). *American Psychologist, 41,* 1378–1379.

Sabini, J. (1992). *Social psychology.* New York: W. W. Norton.

Scarborough, E., & Furumoto, L. (1987). *Untold lives: The first generation of American women psychologists.* New York: Columbia University Press.

Schachter, S., & Gazzaniga, M. (Eds.). (1989). *Extending psychological frontiers: Selected works of Leon Festinger.* New York: Russell Sage Foundation.

Schachter, S., & Singer, J. E. (1962). Cognitive, social, and physiological determinants of emotional state. *Psychological Review, 69,* 379–399.

Schachter, S., & Singer, J. E. (1979). Comments on the Maslach and Marshall-Zimbardo experiments. *Journal of Personality and Social Psychology, 37,* 989–995.

Schachter, S., & Wheeler, L. (1962). Epinephrine, chlorpromazine, and amusement. *Journal of Abnormal and Social Psychology, 65,* 121–128.

Schneidman, E. S. (Ed.). *Endeavors in Psychology: Selections from the Personology of Henry A. Murray.* New York: Harper & Row, 1981.

Schwartz, S. H., & Gottlieb, A. (1980). Bystander anonymity and reactions to emergencies. *Journal of Personality and Social Psychology, 39,* 418–430.

Seeman, J. (1969). Deception in psychological research. *American Psychologist, 24,* 1025–1028.

Shaffer, L. S. (1977). The golden fleece: Anti–intellectualism and social science. *American Psychologist, 32,* 814–823.

Shanab, M. E., & Yahya, K. A. (1977). A behavioral study of obedience in children. *Journal of Personality and Social Psychology, 35,* 530–536.

Sheldon, H. D. (1898). The institutional activities of American children. *The American Journal of Psychology, 9,* 425–448.

Sheridan, C. L., & King, R. G. (1972). Obedience to Authority with an authentic victim. *Proceedings of the American Psychological Association, 7,* 165–166.

Sherif, M. (1935). An experimental study of stereotypes. *Journal of Abnormal and Social Psychology, 29,* 371–375.

Sherif, M. (1936/1966). *The psychology of social norms.* New York: Harper and Row.

Shotland, R. L., & Heinold, W. D. (1985). Bystander response to arterial bleeding: Helping skills, the decision-making process, and differentiating the helping response. *Journal of Personality and Social Psychology, 49,* 347–356.

Shulman, A. D., & Silverman, I. (1972). Profile of social psychology: A preliminary application of "reference analysis." *Journal of the History of the Behavioral Sciences, 8,* 232–236.

Sieber, J. E. (1982). Deception in social research I: Kinds of deception and the wrongs they may involve. *IRB, 4* (9), 1–5.

Sieber, J. E. (1983). Deception in social research II: Evaluating the potential for harm or wrong. *IRB, 5* (1), 1–6.

Sieber, J. E., Iannuzzo, R., & Rodriguez, B. (1995). Deception methods in psychology: Have they changes in 23 years? *Ethics and Behavior, 5,* 67–85.

Silverman, I. (1975). Nonreactive methods and the law. *American Psychologist, 30,* 764–769.

Silverman, I. (1977). *The Human Subject in the Psychological Laboratory.* New York: Pergamon Press.

Silverman, I., & Shulman, A. D. (1970). A conceptual model of artifact in attitude change studies. *Sociometry, 33,* 97–107.

Simon, H. A. (1991). *Models of my life.* New York: Basic Books.

Slosson, E. E. (1899). A lecture experiment in hallucination. *Psychological Review, 6,* 407–408.

Smith, C. E. (1936). A study of automatic excitation resulting from the interaction of individual opinion and group opinion. *Journal of Abnormal and Social Psychology, 31*, 138–164.

Smith, M. B. (1957). Of prophecy and privacy. *Comtemporary Psychology, 2*, 89–92.

Smith, M. B. (1983). The shaping of American social psychology: A personal perspective from the periphery. *Personality and Social Psychology Bulletin, 9*, 165–180.

Smith, R. J. (1977). Electroshock experiment at Albany violates ethical guidelines. *Science, 198*, 383–386.

Smith, S. S., & Richardson, D. (1983). Amerlioration of deception and harm in psychological research: The important role of debriefing. *Journal of Personality and Social Psychology, 44*, 1075–1082.

Soliday, E., & Stanton, A. L. (1995). Deceived versus nondeceived particpants' perceptions of scientific and applied psychology. *Ethics and Behavior, 5*, 87–104.

Solomons, L. H. (1897). Discrimination in cutaneous sensations. *Psychological Review, 4*, 246–250.

Stagner, R. (1937). *Psychology of personality.* New York: McGraw-Hill.

Stein, G. (1898). Cultivated motor automatism: A study of character and its relation to attention. *Psychological Review, 5*, 295–306.

Stricker, L. J. (1967). The true deceiver. *Psychological Bulletin, 68*, 13–20.

Strickland, L. H., Aboud, F. E., & Gergen, K. J. (Eds.) (1976). *Social psychology in transition.* New York: Plenum.

Suls, J. M., & Rosnow, R. L. (1988). Concerns about artifacts in psychological experiments. In J. G. Morawski (Ed.) *The rise of experimentation in American psychology.* New Haven, CN: Yale University Press.

Tavris, C. (1974a). A man of 1,000 ideas. *Psychology Today, 8*, 74–75.

Tavris, C. (1974b). The frozen world of the familiar stranger. *Psychology Today, 8*, 71–73, 76–78, 80.

Tedeschi, J. T., & Gallup, G. G., Jr. (1977). Human subjects research. *Science, 198*, 1099–1100.

The Editors. (1921). Editorial announcement. *The Journal of Abnormal and Social Psychology, 16*, 1–5.

Triplett, N. (1898). The dyamogenic factors in pacemaking and competition. *American Journal of Psychology, 9*, 507–533.

Triplett, N. (1900). The psychology of conjuring deceptions. *The American Journal of Psychology, II*, 439–510.

Vinacke, W. E. (1954). Deceiving experimental subjects. *American Psychologist, 9*, 155.

Vitelli, R. (1988). The crisis issue assessed: An empirical analysis. *Basic and Applied Social Psychology, 9*, 301–309.

Walster, E., Walster, G. W., Piliavin, J., & Schmidt, L. (1973). "Playing hard to get": Understanding an elusive phenomenon. *Journal of Personality and Social Psychology, 26*, 113–121.

Washburn, M. F. (1909). An instance of the effect of verbal suggestion on tactual space perception. *American Journal of Psychology, 20*, 447–448.

Watson, P. (1978). *War on the mind: The military uses and abuses of psychology.* New York: Basic Books.

Wiener, R. L., & Erker, P. V. (1986). The effects of prebriefing misinformed research participants on their attributions of responsibility. *The Journal of Psychology, 120*, 397–410.

West, S. G., Gunn, S. P., & Chernicky, P. (1975). Ubiquitous Watergate: An attributional analysis. *Journal of Personality and Social Psychology, 32*, 55–65.

Wheeler, L. (1987). Social comparison, behavioral contagion, and the naturalistic study of social interaction. In Grunberg, N. E., et al (Eds). (1987). *A distinctive approach to psychological research: The influence of Stanley Schachter.* Hillsdale, NJ: Lawrence Erlbaum Associates.

White, R. K. & Lippitt, R. (1960/1972). *Autocracy and Democracy: An Experimental Inquiry.* Westport, CT: Greenwood Press.

Winks, R. W. (1987). *Cloak & gown: Scholars in the secret war, 1939–1961.* New York: William Morrow & Co.

Zajonc, R. B. (1990). Leon Festinger (1919–1989). *American Psychologist, 45*, 661–662.

Zimbardo, P. G. (1973). On the ethics of intervention in human psychological research: With special reference to the Stanford prison experiment. *Cognition, 2*, 243–256.

Zimbardo, P. G. (1985). Laugh where we must, be candid where we can. *Psychology Today, 18*, (June) 43–47.

Zimbardo, P. G. (1995). On the synergy between teaching and research: A personal account of academic "cheating." *Psi Chi Newsletter, 21(1)*, p. 1, 13–20.

Zimbardo, P. G., Andersen, S. M., & Kabat, L. G. (1981). Induced hearing deficit generates experimental paranoia. *Science, 212*, 1529–1531.

Zukier, H. (1989). Introduction. In Schachter & Gazzaniga (Eds.). *Extending psychological frontiers: Selected works of Leon Festinger.* New York: Russell Sage Foundation.

Index

CPSIA information can be obtained at www.ICGtesting.com
Printed in the USA
BVOW011959090812

297512BV00001B/47/A